The Educational Consultant

Helping Professionals, Parents, and Mainstreamed Students

Timothy E. Heron
The Ohio State University

Kathleen C. Harris
California State University, Los Angeles

Allyn and Bacon, Inc.

BOSTON · LONDON · SYDNEY · TORONTO

Library of Congress Cataloging in Publication Data
Heron, Timothy E.
    The educational consultant.

    Bibliography: p.
    Includes index.
    1. Handicapped children—Education—Handbooks, manuals, etc.
2. Mainstreaming in education—Handbooks, manuals, etc.
I. Harris, Kathleen C.   II. Title.
LC4019.H47   371.9   81-14986

ISBN 0-205-07726-9   AACR2

Printed in the United States of America.
10 9 8 7 6 5 4 3 2 1   86 85 84 83 82

TO OUR PARENTS

Raymond, Bernice, Roland, and Mary

*Who always have been and
always will remain—our consultants.*

Contents

Preface

Since the enactment of Public Law 94–142 ("the right to education act" of 1975), an increasing number of handicapped students have been integrated into the regular classroom. Some handicapped students have been integrated for part of the school day, and daily instruction is shared in some proportion by the regular and special education teachers. Some handicapped students, because of a lesser degree of handicap, have been integrated for almost the whole day. These students may only receive supplemental services from a tutor once per week. Nevertheless, the influx of these students into the regular classroom at any point along the continuum has presented several challenges to professionals, parents, and the students themselves.

One challenge which has surfaced has been how to help the regular education teacher devise, implement, and evaluate functional programs that meet the unique learning needs of the students. Another challenge is, of course, how the parents can become involved in this so-called mainstreaming process.

This text is designed to provide field-based consultants (for example, supervisors, resource teachers, coordinators, counselors, principals, and even parents) in special and regular education settings with consultation skills to facilitate the integration of handicapped students in least restrictive programs. It offers up-to-date knowledge and research on teaching students within least restrictive environments, and it presents specific techniques for use in applied settings. Additionally, each chapter has a series of questions and discussion points or exercises so that readers will have the opportunity to practice the skills, strategies, or techniques described in the text in their own settings.

The ideas, strategies, and suggestions have been derived from two primary sources: our experience in consultation and supervision and research that has been conducted in the field. We made every attempt to integrate these two sources because it is our belief that advances in the educational process come about when individuals blend what has been empirically demonstrated to be effective with their personal consulting, teaching, or parenting style.

The text is divided into eleven chapters. The first two chapters present information on the consultation process and strategies that consultants can use to provide direct and indirect service to students, teachers, and administrators. The next three chapters provide the consultant with techniques for working with 1) teachers in mainstreamed settings; 2) teachers in self-contained classrooms; and 3) parents. Chapters 6 and 7 discuss strategies for individualizing instruction at the elementary and junior and senior high levels respectively. Chapter 8 focuses on the consultant's role as an observer. Eight representative techniques are presented in the chapter which can be used in applied settings. Chapter 9 provides the consultant with a strategy to select and implement behavior management approaches with handicapped and nonhandicapped students. Individual as well as group contingencies are presented. Chapter 10 addresses the issue of career education, a new focus for consultants, especially those who work with teachers and students at intermediate and secondary levels. The last chapter emphasizes litigation and legislation, and why and how it affects consultation services.

The completion of this text could not have been accomplished without the support of our colleagues, students, friends, and families. We would like to acknowledge their assistance.

Our thanks go to Dr. David S. Hill for his contribution·of Chapter 10. It is one of the few resources for consultants on the topic of career education for elementary and secondary-level handicapped students in least restrictive programs.

Also, we would like to acknowledge Dr. William L. Heward's careful review of earlier drafts of the manuscript. His incisive comments on the content and organization of the book and his contribution of the behavioral contract, Figure 9–1, are most appreciated.

We would like to express our gratitude to Dr. Richard Iano for his encouragement and thought-provoking discussions which, in great measure, stimulated the completion of the text.

Our colleagues, Drs. John O. Cooper, Thomas M. Stephens, Donald Hammill, Steve Larsen, Saul Axelrod, and Robyn Redinger deserve our thanks for their comments on earlier drafts of the text and their continued support of our professional development.

We would like to thank all the graduate students who provided us with feedback on several concepts and features of the text. The senior author would especially like to thank Nancy L. Cooke for her support, and her contributions to the peer-tutoring sections of this text.

The staff at Allyn and Bacon, especially Gene McCann, Steve Mathews, Susanne Canavan, Susan Weber, and Cynthia Hartnett, and the reviewers who provided us with constructive criticism and direction deserve a special thank-you.

Our heartfelt thanks also go to Evelyn Johnson and Cheryl Estep for typing preliminary chapters of the text, in spite of the senior author's illegible handwriting, and to Beverly Shoemaker who masterfully prepared the final draft.

Last, and most important, we would like to thank Edward, Elizabeth, Kathleen, Christine, and our spouses, Marge and Blaine, for their understanding and patience during this arduous undertaking. Without their unfailing and unwavering support, the first word of this text would never have been written.

1

The Consultation Process

The consultation process involves the interaction between two or more professionals for the purpose of mutually preventing or solving problems. The consultation process can be initiated by a consultant (for example, the principal, supervisor, or resource room teacher), who might observe that a school-related problem needs attention, or by a consultee (regular class teacher, parent, or student), who might seek additional assistance with solving a problem. Regardless of whether the consultant or consultee initiates the process, it is generally accepted that both parties share the responsibility for solving it.

The purpose of this chapter is to define the nature of school consultation and to present three models that have been used to conceptualize and apply the school consultation process. Applied examples will be provided to illustrate how the model has or might be used.

Objectives

After reading this chapter, the reader should be able to:

1. define the term *school consultation*.

2. distinguish between developmental consultation and problem-centered consultation.

3. identify three models for school consultation and be able to describe the major components of each.

4. identify individuals who can serve in consultant roles and indicate what their roles are.

Key Terms

The consultation process

Developmental consultation

Problem-centered consultation

Triadic model

Mediator

Target

Systems model

Vermont Consulting Teacher Program

THE CONSULTATION PROCESS

According to Meyers, Martin, and Hyman (1977) *the consultation pro-*
cess always includes at least three persons—the consultant, the consultee,
and the client. Tharp (1975) states that consultation services are provided through an intermediary, the consultee, with the expectation that
behavior change will be observed not only with the consultee directly,
but also with the client. Success with the consultation process is determined by noting improvement with both of these agents. Wiederholt,
Hammill, and Brown (1978) indicate that consultation with teachers is
best described in terms of its three primary components—advising, instructing, and follow-up.

Several authors have distinguished between types of consultation that
can be provided. Caplan (1970), for example, referred to the practice
of mental health consultation, while Bergan (1977) described a behavioral consultation approach. To classify consultation approaches, the
focus of the consultation and the relationship between the consultant
and the consultee must be determined (Brown, Wyne, Blackburn, &
Powell, 1979). This relationship is usually considered collaborative insofar as both the consultant and consultee work jointly to solve a mutually
recognized problem. Mutual cooperation, however, does not always occur
spontaneously, and consultants should be prepared to handle resistance
to the consultation effort.

Meyers (1974) indicated that consultee unwillingness to work col-
laboratively might be overcome when consultants share the responsibility for problem solving, view the teacher as an expert in dealing with
the student's problems, de-emphasize their contribution in the consultative process, and communicate to teachers that they are free to accept
or reject any suggestions or recommendations made by the consultant.
Nelson and Stevens (1980) state that to overcome personal as well as
institutional resistance, consultants must be capable of changing a variety of behaviors and, more important, have a formal role in the school.
That is, their role with respect to the rest of the school staff must be
clear. Morse (1980) suggests that consultants who help teachers make
their work more meaningful and productive are more likely to gain acceptance in the school and to obtain favorable changes in behavior.

Bergan and Tombari (1976) state that the consultation process serves
as a link between knowledge producers, the researchers, and knowledge
consumers, the teachers. Since teachers may not have access to educa-
tionally relevant research, the consultant can help bridge the gap by
informing them of new materials, methods, or technology.

Sandoval, Lambert, and Davis (1977) indicate that the consultation
process is interactive. They suggest that the consultee learn to use the

services of a consultant more efficiently. They feel that consultees who learn the tasks that consultants are able to perform with them, and who are able to state their problems and evaluation strategies more succinctly, will find the consultation process more rewarding.

Definitions of Consultation

Brown et al. (1979) define consultation as "a process based upon an equal relationship characterized by mutual trust and open communication, joint approaches to problem identification, the pooling of personal resources to identify and select strategies that will have some probability of solving the problem that has been identified, and shared responsibility in the implementation and evaluation of the program or strategy that has been initiated." (p. 8). Parker (1975) indicates that consultation is a process whereby teachers receive assistance with solving the social, learning, and emotional problems of students. Bergan (1977), on the other hand, indicates that two forms of consultation exist—*developmental consultation* and *problem-centered consultation.*

Developmental consultation. This form of consultation focuses on long range goals for a student. It usually involves the accomplishment of several sequenced subordinate objectives. For example, a student who has extreme social adjustment problems might be a candidate for developmental consultation. A subordinate objective might involve teaching the behaviorally disordered student to relax during academic work periods using systematic desensitization—a procedure whereby the student might be conditioned to work without fidgeting as other students are gradually assimilated into the classroom. Once this subordinate objective is mastered, the next objective might focus on increasing the appropriate verbal interactions of the behaviorally disordered student with peers who sit close to him.

The consultant's role might be to assist the teacher in identifying the problem, sequencing subordinate objectives, recommending intervention approaches, and evaluating the outcome. The consultation process—the completion of each subordinate objective to criterion—usually takes several months or longer.

Problem-centered consultation. This form of consultation is limited to solving specific and immediate problems. A learning disabled (LD) student who is aggressive, self-injurious, or repeatedly off-task in school might be a candidate for problem-centered consultation. For example, if the LD student consistently provoked his classmates, intervention might be required. The distinguishing feature of problem-centered consultation is that specifically sequenced subordinate objectives are not used. The consultant and the teacher develop a mutual plan to solve an isolated problem. Long-term involvement is not anticipated with this approach.

The present authors feel that the definitions proposed by Brown et al., Parker, and Bergan are compatible, and capable of being integrated. That is, consultation can be considered a mutual problem-solving process, which leads to the resolution of academic, social, or emotional problems of students, and which may or may not involve the achievement of several subordinate objectives.

CONSULTATION MODELS

As stated previously, a consultant's efficiency is usually increased when she operates within a systematic model. The model provides the guidelines within which the consultative services can be delivered. Two models will be presented that represent ways in which school consultation can be conceptualized. A third model will show how school consultation approaches can be applied on a statewide basis. These models are not intended to be all-inclusive. Rather they illustrate how consultation services can be described and evaluated with individuals, small groups, or large populations. Each of the models can be used to solve school-related problems. The models include: the triadic model (Tharp & Wetzel, 1969; Tharp, 1975), the systems model (Stephens, 1977), and the Vermont Consulting Teacher Program (McKenzie, 1972; Egner & Lates, 1975).

Triadic Model

The *triadic model*, in its most basic form, is a linear sequence that portrays the relationship between the consultant, the mediator, and the target (see Figure 1–1).

The triadic model describes a functional sequence for consultation rather than an absolute one. That is, any professional—principal, resource room teacher, supervisor, or psychologist—could serve as the consultant, and a regular education teacher, paraprofessional, or parent could serve as the mediator. The target is the student for whom the consultative service is intended, or any other person with a problem (Tharp & Wetzel, 1969). The mediator has access to the target student and has some influence over him, while the consultant is the person who serves as a catalyst to activate the mediator. The only requirement for serving

Figure 1–1 The consultative triad showing individuals within each role. SOURCE: R. G. Tharp and R. J. Wetzel, *Behavior modification in the natural environment.* (New York: Academic Press, 1969), p. 47. Adapted by permission of the publisher and authors.

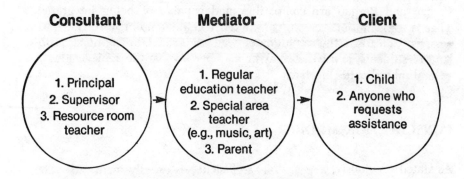

Consultant	Mediator	Client
1. Principal 2. Supervisor 3. Resource room teacher	1. Regular education teacher 2. Special area teacher (e.g., music, art) 3. Parent	1. Child 2. Anyone who requests assistance

as a consultant is that the individual possess the special knowledge, skills, or abilities needed to help the target person.

The consultant has two evaluative measures to index when using the triadic model. The first measure is the extent to which the mediator acquires the knowledge or skill presented by the consultant. The second measure is whether the application of this knowledge or skill affects student performance. It is possible for gains to be obtained on the former dimension when little or no improvement on the latter dimension is realized. As Heath and Nielson (1974) indicate, the relationship between the specific performance of the teacher and achievement of the student is uncertain.

Applied example. Suppose that a regular classroom teacher (the mediator) approached the resource room teacher (the consultant) to help her with an educable mentally retarded student (the target) in her seventh-grade class. The student was off-task frequently and his work performance was extremely low. To help the classroom teacher, the resource room teacher showed her a short film that demonstrated how to use differential reinforcement. Specifically, the film depicted a teacher attending and praising a student when he worked, and ignoring the student when he was off-task. After watching the film together, the teachers discussed how this approach could be used with Dan, the educable mentally retarded student.

The regular class teacher initiated the program with Dan after obtaining a week of baseline data. The data served as a comparative measure of Dan's performance prior to the intervention.

During evaluation the consultant could determine the extent to which

Figure 1–2 Hypothetical data that shows the mean percentage of Dan's off-task behavior during the baseline and praise-plus-ignore condition. The praise-plus-ignore procedure, learned during the consultation process, reduced the percentage of Dan's off-task.

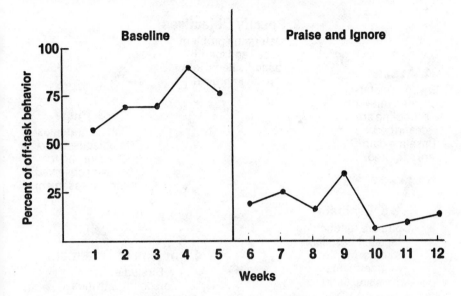

the teacher learned the praise-plus-ignore procedure by observing, or having the teacher self-record, her performance in the classroom. Figure 1–2 shows the hypothetical results of the consultation with Dan.

Systems Model

Stephens (1977) described a *systems model* for consulting with school personnel. His model is an extension of his directive teaching approach (Stephens, 1976). His consultation model involves five phases: assessment, specification of objectives, planning, implementing treatment, and evaluation.

Assessment. Baseline data are collected on target behaviors; for example, the number of student talk-outs that occur during the day. Factors which may affect a planned intervention are determined and alternative strategies are considered. Data are collected for a period of time, usually three to five days, to use as a basis for comparing treatment effects. Also, during baseline antecedent and consequent conditions are identified which might play a role in the planned intervention. For instance, talk-outs might be related to the time of day, subject area, or lack of reinforcement.

Figure 1–3 A schematic view of consulting procedures (Stephens's model) SOURCE: T. M. Stephens, *Teaching skills to children with learning and behavior disorders.* (Columbus, Ohio: Charles E. Merrill, 1977), p. 427. Reprinted by permission of the publisher.

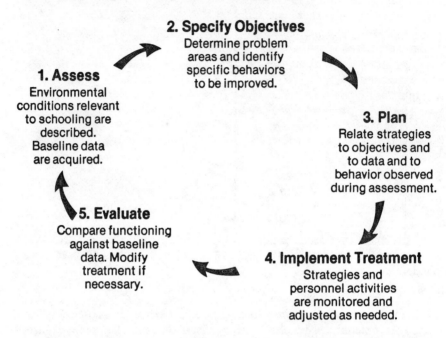

Specify Objectives. During this phase problem areas are specified and rank ordered from most severe to least severe. Behaviors to be modified are identified and operationally defined. An operational definition for talk-outs might be any verbalization made by the student without the teacher's permission.

Planning. Strategies that are intended to reduce or increase the level of target behavior are outlined. Strategies are chosen so as to be consistent with the teacher's style of instruction or management, yet still powerful enough to obtain the desired change in behavior.

Implementation. The main strategy is initiated, and direct and daily measurement of the target behavior is continued so that modifications in the treatment approach can be adjusted. An example of a direct and daily measure of talk-outs would be the number of inappropriate verbalizations made by the student each day.

While the teacher is probably the primary person responsible for implementing a strategy in the school, both the teacher and consultant share the responsibility for monitoring the day-to-day progress of the student.

Evaluation. At this stage of the consultation process, data are analyzed across baseline and treatment conditions. Again, the consultant and the teacher share responsibility for data analysis. The essential questions to be answered are: Was there a treatment effect, and was any change that occurred after the treatment condition satisfactory as far as the teacher was concerned?

Stephens's model is an example of a systems approach, because subsequent to the evaluation stage the process loops back to Step 1—Assessment. That is, if the planned treatment did not have the desired effect, further assessment may have to be conducted. If the plan was effective, baseline data are then collected on the next behavior targeted for change. A feature that the systems approach shares with other models of consultation is that the consultant helps the teacher devise her own criterion-referenced assessments or coding devices. Helping teachers rather than simply supplying an existing assessment gives them a vested interest in their projects. They feel like an integral component, and acquire skills so that once the consultant is gone they will be able to function independently.

Applied Example. A regular education teacher approached a special education supervisor regarding the withdrawn behavior of a language-impaired student mainstreamed into her math class. The teacher was interested in increasing the student's verbal participation in class. Baseline data were collected on the number of initiations the student made to the teacher or her peers (Assessment). Verbalizations were defined as any vocal comment made to the teacher or peer for the purpose of asking a question or responding to a question (Specify Objective). A plan was outlined which would reinforce the whole class for increased verbalizations by the language-impaired student (Plan). The number of verbalizations was recorded each day for several weeks to note any trends in the data (Implement Treatment). To evaluate whether the class reinforcer was effective, it was terminated briefly, and later reinstated (Evaluate). After the program was over the consultant and the teacher concluded that when the class reinforcer was in effect the verbalizations of the language-impaired student increased. When the reinforcer was withdrawn verbal production decreased (see Figure 1-4).

The Vermont Consulting Teacher Program

Both the triadic model and Stephens's model can be used to solve a range of school-related problems. These models have been employed by

Figure 1–4 The number of verbal initiations and responses made by a language-impaired student during math class (hypothetical data)

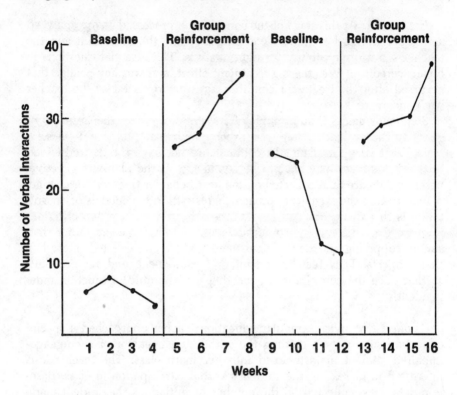

individual consultants in many parts of the country. The *Vermont Consulting Teacher Program*, however, is a collaborative effort of local school districts, the Vermont State Department of Education, and university personnel aimed at providing consultative services statewide to regular education teachers who have handicapped children in their classrooms. The program is behaviorally oriented and assumes that all children and teachers are capable of learning skills, that teacher effectiveness can best be measured as a function of student growth, and that the systematic use of behavior analysis—procedures to determine the extent to which planned treatment affects performance—will provide the most appropriate methods of comparison (Egner & Lates, 1975).

The Vermont model for providing consulting service to regular education teachers is shown in Figure 1–5.

Within the four-phase model is a ten-step behavioral consultation process that is implemented with the specific objective of skill acquisition by the classroom teacher (see Table 1–1).

Figure 1–5 The Vermont Consulting Teacher Program model to provide special education in the regular classroom. SOURCE: A. Egner and B. J. Lates, The Vermont consulting teacher program: Case presentation. In C. A. Parker (Ed.), *Psychological consultation: Helping teachers meet special needs.* (Minneapolis, Minnesota: Leadership Training Institute/Special Education, 1975), p. 32. Reprinted by permission of the publisher.

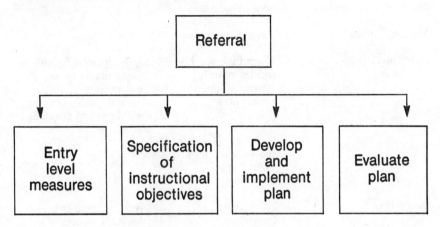

The key feature of the Vermont program is that the consulting teacher must individualize the program to meet the specific needs of the regular educator.

One unique aspect of the Vermont program is the way in which evaluation of student performance is conducted. A "minimum rate of learning" is established for a given content area. For example, a school district or community might determine that a given set of hierarchically arranged instructional objectives must be mastered within a certain time frame. That is, by the end of fourth grade students must be able to complete two-step word problems, three-digit multiplication with regrouping, and long division with remainders. Students who fall below the minimum rate of learning curve not only become eligible for the supportive services of the consulting teacher, but also the minimum rate line becomes the benchmark by which future progress is determined. The trend of the student's progress compared to rate line provides the index by which services are begun, changed, or terminated (Egner & Lates, 1975).

Advantages. The Vermont program offers several advantages for consultants who work with regular education teachers. First, the program is data-based. Student performance, not categorical labels, determines eligibility for service, and entrance and existing criteria are measured

Table 1–1 Relation of Behavioral Model and Skills Acquired by Classroom Teacher during Consulting Steps

BEHAVIORAL MODEL	CONSULTING STEPS	SKILLS ACQUIRED BY TEACHER
Eligible learner	1. Referral procedure	
Entry level	2. Consulting teacher meetings for baseline diagnosis procedures	Defining target behaviors in measurable terms, measuring behavior reliability, collecting, recording, and graphing data daily
	3. Consulting teacher/ teacher meetings to establish eligibility	
Instructional objectives	4. Parent meeting for written permission	Involving parents in education process
	5. Consulting teacher classroom objectives	Writing individual instructional objectives
	6. Decision-making process for intervention	and procedures involving parents
Teaching/learning procedures	7. Parent information meeting for intervention procedures	
	8. Implementation of intervention procedures	Following teaching/ learning procedures precisely
Evaluation	9. Evaluation of intervention procedure	Identifying possible reinforcing consequences in the classroom
	10. Follow-through or confirmation	Responding to changes in behavior of the child

SOURCE: A. Egner and B. J. Lates, The Vermont consulting teacher program: Case presentation. In C. A. Parker (Ed.), *Psychological consultation: Helping teachers meet special needs* (Minneapolis, Minnesota: Leadership Training Institute/Special Education, 1975), p. 33. Reprinted by permission of the publisher.

Figure 1–6 *Hypothetical data showing Sam's rate of growth in math.*

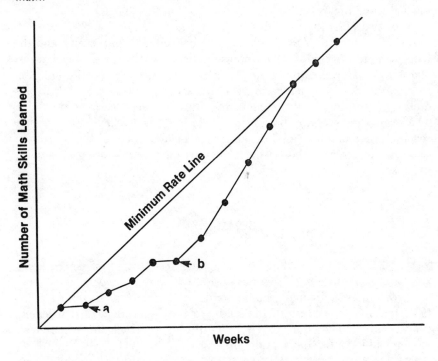

against the minimum rate line. Second, teachers and parents are active participants in the program. Recall in the consulting steps (Table 1–1) that parents provide their input to the program prior to implementation of a given plan. The Vermont program has also proven to be a cost effective approach. Consultants are only employed for the students who need help. These services are thus allocated more efficiently.

Disadvantages. The primary disadvantage of the program is that it requires the specification of minimum levels of achievement within certain time frames. To successfully implement the program, a task analysis of objectives must be arranged hierarchically. Also, general consensus must be reached by knowledgeable individuals on reasonable time frames to learn objectives. Given the responsibilities which regular teachers currently have, it is unlikely that many would spontaneously translate existing curriculum objectives, which are usually stated globally, into behavioral objectives. If the objectives were generated on a district-wide basis, teachers might be more willing to use the approach.

Applied Example. Figure 1–6 presents hypothetical data which show how a student's progress can be determined with the Vermont Consulting Teacher Program.

Note that after the second week Sam became eligible for the consulting teacher program (see point a). The consultant, the parents, and the teacher jointly decided that intensive drill on the math facts to be learned would suffice to bring Sam's performance up to criterion. Unfortunately, this did not happen, and a second intervention—drill plus cross-age tutoring—was implemented during week six (see point b). The second intervention produced the desired result. Sam's performance reached the minimum rate line, and the special services of the consultant were no longer required. Using drill plus cross-age tutoring effectively increased Sam's rate of growth.

SUMMARY

School consultation is defined as an interactive process in which a consultant and a consultee share responsibility for the outcome. Some consultation approaches may not be conducted effectively in school situations because the nature of the student's problem indicates that a long process is involved. Fortunately, most problems which arise in schools are amenable to the consultation process.

Consultation is most effective when it is done systematically. Three models were presented which offer the practitioner a choice of action to follow. Two of the models, the triadic and the systems model, describe the consultation process. The Vermont Consulting Teacher Program describes the application of a consulting teacher's approach on a statewide basis.

Questions

1. Define consultation.

2. Distinguish between developmental and problem centered consultation.

3. Of the three models of consultation, which one(s) offer(s) the consultant and the teacher the opportunity to measure individual student progress across time?

4. Who could serve in the role of the mediator in the triadic model?

5. Relate Stephens's model of consultation to his model of directive teaching.

6. How is the minimum rate line used in the Vermont Consulting Teacher Program?

7. Cite one advantage and one disadvantage of each of the models presented in the chapter.

Discussion Points and Exercises

1. Conduct a meeting with teachers at the elementary, junior high, and senior high levels. Determine from them their views on what consultation should involve. Compare their perception of the consultation process with the definitions presented in this chapter.

2. Using the Vermont Consulting Teacher Program as a model, conduct a pilot study within your own district or region to determine the usefulness of the minimum rate line. Evaluate your results.

3. Identify a classroom-related problem. Apply Stephens's model. Evaluate whether the model provides sufficient guidelines for school consultation.

REFERENCES

BERGAN, J. R. Behavioral consultation. Columbus, Ohio: Charles E. Merrill, 1977.

BERGAN, J. R., & TOMBARI, M. L. Consultant skill and efficiency and the implementation and outcomes of consultation. *Journal of School Psychology*, 1976, *14* (1), 3–14.

BROWN, D., WYNE, M. D., BLACKBURN, J. E., & POWELL, W. C. *Consultation: Strategy for improving education*. Boston: Allyn and Bacon, 1979.

CAPLAN, G. *The theory and practice of mental health consultation*. New York: Basic Books, 1970.

EGNER, A., & LATES, B. J. The Vermont consulting teacher program: Case presentation. In C. A. Parker (Ed.), *Psychological consultation: Helping teachers meet special needs*. Minneapolis, Minnesota: Leadership Training Institute/Special Education, 1975.

HEATH, R. W., & NIELSON, M. A. The research basis for performance-based teacher education. *Review of Educational Research*, 1974, 44, 463–484.

MEYERS, J. A consultation model for school psychological services. In J. P. Glavin (Ed.), *Ferment in special education*, New York: MSS Information Corporation, 1974.

McKENZIE, H. S. Special education and consulting teachers. In F. Clark, D. Evans, & L. Hammerlynk (Eds.), *Implementing behavioral programs for schools and clinics.* Champaign, Illinois: Research Press, 1972, 103–125.

MEYERS, J., MARTIN, R., & HYMAN, I. *School consultation: Readings about preventive techniques for pupil personnel workers.* Springfield, Illinois: Charles C Thomas, 1977.

MORSE, W. C. The helping teacher/crisis teacher concept. *Focus on Exceptional Children*, 1976, 8 (4), 3–11.

NELSON, C. M. & STEVENS, K. B. Mainstreaming behaviorally disordered children through teacher consultation. Paper presented at the Third Annual Conference on Severe Behavior Disorders of Children and Youth. Tempe, Arizona, November, 1979.

PARKER, C. A. *Psychological consultation: Helping teachers meet special needs.* Minneapolis, Minnesota: Leadership Training Institute/Special Education, 1975.

SANDOVAL, J., LAMBERT, N., & DAVIS, J. M. Consultation from the consultee's perspective. *Journal of School Psychology*, 1977, 15 (4), 334–342.

STEPHENS, T. M. *Directive teaching of children with learning and behavioral handicaps (2nd Ed.).* Columbus, Ohio: Charles E. Merrill, 1976.

STEPHENS, T. M. *Teaching skills to children with learning and behavior disorders.* Columbus, Ohio: Charles E. Merrill, 1977.

THARP, R. G. The triadic model of consultation: Current considerations. In C. A. Parker (Ed.), *Psychological consultation: Helping teachers meet special needs.* Minneapolis, Minnesota: Leadership Training Institute/Special Education, 1975.

THARP, R. G., & WETZEL, R. J. *Behavior modification in the natural environment.* New York: Academic Press, 1969.

WIEDERHOLT, J. L., HAMMILL, D. D., & BROWN, V. *The resource teacher: A guide to effective practices.* Boston: Allyn and Bacon, 1978.

2

Providing Consultation Services to Students, Teachers, and Administrators

Consultation services to students, administrators, or staff can be direct or indirect. The consultant can work individually with a student, a teacher, or administrator to change their behavior, or he can work indirectly with one of them to change the behavior of a third party. Regardless, it is necessary for the consultant to have a clear idea of the problem to be solved, options for solving it, available resources, and evaluation techniques, prior to initiating the consultation.

The purpose of this chapter is to provide strategies and techniques which a consultant could use to assist students, teachers, or administrators. The chapter will highlight the how-to aspects of direct and indirect service to these individuals, as well as the role and function of related-service personnel and suggestions for the consultant interested in facilitating interactions with these professionals.

Objectives

After reading this chapter, the reader should be able to:

1. list and discuss two indirect services which consultants can provide to students.

2. list and discuss four direct consulting services which can be provided to teachers.

3. identify ten related-service professionals and describe their roles and responsibilities.

4. state two recommendations for facilitating interactions with related-service professionals.

5. state the major purpose of school consultation at an administrative level.

6. relate from experience how school consultation could be used to solve a classroom or other school-related problem.

Key Terms

Direct service	Consulting teacher
Indirect service	Educational diagnostician
Covert modeling	Speech clinician
In-service training	School psychologist
Related-service personnel	School social worker
Support staff	Occupational therapist
Individualized Education Program	Physical therapist
	Art, music, dance, recreation staff
Itinerant teacher	School bus driver

PROVIDING CONSULTATION SERVICES TO STUDENTS, TEACHERS, AND ADMINISTRATORS

According to Meyers (1974) consultation services can be provided to students, teachers, and administrators directly or indirectly. *Direct service* is provided when the recipient is the intended target and a mediator is not used. *Indirect service* is provided when the recipient acquires a skill or additional knowledge from the consultant, and that skill or knowledge is applied to a third party.

Direct Service to Children

Direct service to children includes any task where the consultant (for example, a school psychologist or resource room teacher) actually works with the student without a mediator. Conducting individual assessments, performing an interview, providing counseling, and, in some cases, an in-class observation would be examples of direct service.

According to Bergan (1977) direct service to students is usually carried out subsequent to a referral. Additional information is required, and the consultant is called upon to obtain that information and to communicate it to those professionals (or parents) with whom the student interacts.

Let us assume that June, a learning disabled, seventh-grade student, was referred to a resource room teacher because of adjustment problems in the classroom. After a discussion with the classroom teacher, the resource room teacher was able to determine that June's adjustment problem involved her interactions with other students during small group activities. She did not finish her portion of an assignment and consequently her group was not able to complete the whole task. As a result, she was ignored by her peers.

In this example, the direct service the consultant provided was on two levels. First she conducted an observation of the small group activity to ascertain the type of assignment June was to complete and the nature of the interactions she was having with her peers. Next she discussed the situation with June directly. During the interview June indicated that she felt uncomfortable performing several of her tasks. She had to read, take notes, and compile her portion of the project for the other group members. She wanted to do her assignment, but felt frustrated at being so slow. The consultant suggested that June tape portions of the assignment (the assignment required report writing) so that she could complete the work within the deadline. The plan worked smoothly. Although June still had trouble with the reading portion of the group assignment, she used a tape recorder to make notes on major points which she later transcribed and edited for her report. Her peers reacted positively since June's assignment was completed within the required time along with their reports.

Advantages of direct service. Bergan (1977) indicates that direct service to students offers several advantages for the consultant. First, the consultant serves as an advocate by acting as the mediator between the student and the teacher. Hence, the student perceives the consultant as a colleague. In this sense the student becomes the consultee and a mutual plan is decided upon in the same way as it might be were the teacher the consultee. Second, it gives the student the opportunity to engage in decision making. In June's case, she discussed the use of the tape recorder with the consultant. A final advantage is that the student gains a skill that can be applied in this situation and possibly in other situations as well.

Another example of direct service to children which may have far-reaching implications was shown in a study conducted by Graubard, Rosenberg, and Miller (1971). In this study students were taught techniques to gain and maintain the teacher's attention during classroom activities. Specifically, students were taught how to establish eye contact with the teacher, ask for additional assistance, nod approvingly when the teacher spoke, say "ah, hah" during a teacher explanation, and reinforce the teacher for praising them.

Teaching countercontrol techniques to the student had the effect of increasing appropriate teacher-student interaction. The obvious advantages of this technique are that students can apply these procedures in other settings, such as the home, and it is a cost-effective way to teach several students a functional coping skill.

Disadvantages. The main disadvantage of providing direct service to individual students is the time factor. Few consultants have the time to meet students on an individual basis.

Also, if the classroom teacher receives direct service for all the student behaviors for which she may need assistance, the teacher may never learn how to use preventative measures herself. A teacher involved in the consultation process increases her opportunities to learn, and provides the consultant with more time to work with other teachers.

Despite the cost factors involved and the potential loss of efficiency, direct service to individual students should be offered when the need arises. In cases where other professionals can be called upon to help, a referral can be made. Otherwise, the consultant might be the only person who is able to solve the student's problem.

Direct Service to Teachers

Direct service to teachers can be conducted with an individual teacher, small groups of teachers, or whole school staffs. The intent of direct consultation could be to help a teacher prevent or solve a particular student problem, increase the teacher's level of awareness regarding curriculum issues, or conduct observations and evaluations of teacher performance. The goal of direct consultation is to improve a teacher's skill so that she will be more proficient in dealing with student problems. Newcomer (1977) states, "The (consultant's) ultimate goal is not to remediate a particular child's learning problems, but to prevent certain problems from developing and provide the regular educator with the additional skills and competencies required to undertake remedial activities independently." (p. 161)

Direct consulting service to regular education teachers is maximally effective when the teacher wants to change his behavior. This perception by the regular teacher is a precondition to effective consultation. The consultee (the teacher) perceives the situation to be outside his direct control and he requests assistance. To be absolutely clear on this point, the consultee may have the skills required to do the job, but because of extraneous factors, these skills are not evident. For example, a regular educator may be able to provide individualized instruction to his students if the class size is not too large. If additional students are added to his roster, especially if these students have handicaps, the teacher's ability to provide individualized instruction may decrease, and the services of a consultant must be requested to solve the problem.

Direct consulting services can be rendered in several ways: conducting observations in classrooms, modeling, providing in-service training, conducting evaluations, and providing referrals for support services within and outside the school system.

Conducting classroom observations. Consultants can be of great assistance to regular educators when they conduct classroom observations for the purpose of quantifying and qualifying student and teacher behavior. A consultant can serve as another pair of eyes and ears and help a teacher determine who is receiving his attention and under what circumstances.

Skinner (1979) conducted a study which illustrates this point. A regular education teacher expressed interest in having an observer in her classroom because she was concerned about the uneven amount of attention students in her classroom were receiving. Baseline data were collected on six students in the classroom (two high achievers, two low achievers, and two learning disabled). After five sessions, the consultant met with the teacher to discuss the observational findings. The teacher felt that student 3, one of the learning disabled students, was not receiving enough teacher-initiated statements, while student 2, a nonhandicapped student, was receiving a disproportionate share of initiations when compared to the other students. The teacher indicated that the remaining four students were receiving an appropriate amount of initiations.

Beginning with week six of observation for student 3 and week eleven for student 2, the consultant met with the teacher to show her the data on her initiations. Figure 2–1 shows that the observation plus feedback phase was successful in modifying the teacher's interactions with each of the two students. The student who had received too many initiations was now receiving less and vice versa.

Skinner's approach to resolving this teacher's problem was successful for several reasons. First, his observational data was accurate and reliable. Second, he was able to relate to and interact with the classroom teacher. Third, he had consulting experience. As V. L. Brown (1977) stated, few professionals who express a desire to become consulting teachers have preservice training in consultation, or have the skill to provide realistic alternatives for a range of management problems. Skinner was able to combine his experience and skill to resolve the teacher problems.

Modeling. Modeling is an effective procedure to use when the teacher has some prerequisite skills already in her repertoire, holds the model in esteem and perceives the person as competent (Bandura, 1971). Modeling can be performed at any state in the consultation process. The consultant merely instructs the teacher to imitate what he does. For example, a consultant could model how to dispense tokens or plan daily lessons.

Another form of modeling, referred to as surreptitious or covert modeling, also may have the potential for affecting teacher performance (Brown, Reschly, & Wasserman, 1974). During *covert modeling* the consultant performs a desired classroom behavior in the presence of the teacher, but without necessarily saying or implying to him "watch what I do and you do the same." According to Brown et al. (1974) this procedure can be effective, even though no specific directional prompts are issued. The main advantage of surreptitious modeling is that the chances for a potentially negative "expert-subordinate" relationship between the consultant and the teacher are reduced or eliminated. Since verbal prompts are not given, the teacher is not made to feel inferior or incompetent, feelings which Oldridge (1977) indicates teachers may have during the consultation process.

Figure 2–1 Percent of teacher-initiated statements to a normal and a learning disability student during baseline and intervention.
Source: Skinner, M. E., Effects of an in-service program on the attitudes, knowledge, and student-teacher interaction patterns of regular classroom teachers. Unpublished masters thesis, The Ohio State University, 1979, p. 55. Used by permission.

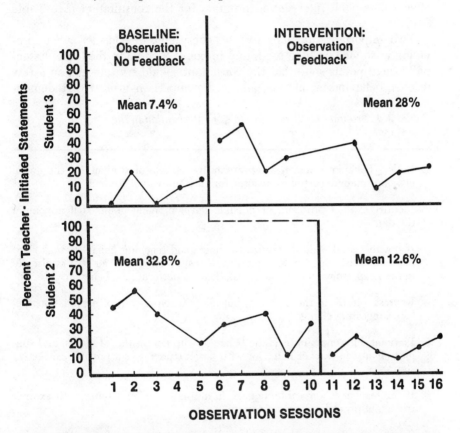

Conducting in-service training. The need for continued teacher *in-service training,* defined as the process whereby additional skills are acquired to maintain or improve instructional effectiveness, is well recognized (Stephens, 1978; Cooper & Hunt, 1978). However, few educators agree on the best method to provide it. Shaw and Shaw (1972), however, state that regardless of the method for delivering in-service, the training will only be effective when the participants want to learn a new skill or method. If participants are forced to attend in-service programs for which they have no interest, it is unlikely that learning will be efficient.

On the other hand, consultants can provide teachers with in-service training by giving them reliable and credible feedback as soon after the teaching act as possible (Brophy & Good, 1974). Brophy and Good's research seems to indicate that an effective in-service consultation strategy is to make teachers aware of their established, but inappropriate, behavior or interaction patterns with students. Brophy and Good offer a nine-point intervention program for the consultation (see Table 2–1).

Two important functions for the consultant to consider when providing in-service training are found in points 2 and 3 in the table. Essentially these points state that the consultant should try to focus on a few teacher behaviors at a time, and find comparison groups that demon-

Table 2–1 Brophy and Good's Model for Intervention in the Classroom.

1. Collect behavior data on a representative sample of students or the entire class but maintain separate records for each individual student.

2. Identify explicit problems or possible developmental points that appear in the data.

3. If possible, find contrast groups to show good teaching behavior, making it possible to ask teachers to extend to new situations behavior that is already in their repertoire rather than to ask them to perform new behaviors.

4. Express interest in the problem, but allow teachers to give explanations before suggesting changes.

5. Pinpoint differences in teaching behavior with contrasting students, and suggest change in teacher behavior with target students as a possible corrective step.

6. If the teacher is agreeable, engage in mutual problem solving until explicit treatment procedures are agreed upon.

7 Specify exactly what the teacher will do to attempt to change student behavior

8. Arrange to get posttreatment data to evaluate success in changing teacher and student behavior and to examine the data for radiation effects.

9. Hold a debriefing session with the teacher to review the results of the study and to gain valuable clinical data from the teacher (Brophy & Good, 1974, pp. 292–295).

From *Student-Teacher Relationships: Causes and Consequences* by Jere E. Brophy and Thomas L. Good. Copyright © 1974 by Holt, Rinehart and Winston, Inc. Reprinted by permission of Holt, Rinehart and Winston.

strate good teaching technique, communicating to the teacher that she already has some of the skills the consultant is trying to reinforce. A teacher is more likely to have confidence in a consultant who reinforces him for the positive instructional behaviors he has instead of criticizing him for what he lacks.

If positive instructional behaviors do not occur or occur only occasionally, the consultant might try to reinforce approximations of the desired behavior. (For example, "I noticed the way John smiled when you publicly praised his accomplishment in science. I bet that same strategy would work for Mario, who also seems to like your attention.") The consultant is attempting to extend a demonstrated positive approach to another situation where the likelihood of success is high. The essential message the teacher gets when she receives in-service consultation using Brophy & Good's approach is that she has teaching competencies and skills, and they can be employed in other situations to prevent or solve problems. The teacher does not perceive an "expert-subordinate" relationship because the consultant has de-emphasized his role in the process (Meyers, 1974), and has reinforced the teacher for appropriate instructional behavior.

Conducting evaluations. Consultants who assist teachers with evaluation procedures perform a direct service of immeasurable importance. Not only can a functional evaluation plan determine whether a given treatment or intervention was effective in solving a current problem, but the data collected during the course of the program might prove helpful in future situations (Alpert, 1977). For example, suppose a teacher successfully implemented a peer-tutoring activity with a hearing-impaired student in the class. The knowledge gained during the course of the study of such things as tutor-student pairs, the length of the tutoring sessions, or the procedures used during the tutoring session could be invaluable if the teacher decided to use a peer-tutoring program with other students.

The key element in conducting evaluations is to decide whether the planned intervention worked. Are the student, the class, or the teacher "better" than they were prior to the intervention? How much better are they? A second key element is that evaluation helps to determine when to change a given intervention approach or when to terminate it. From an instructional standpoint, much teacher and student time would be saved if teachers had reliable timetables for knowing when to make these decisions.

By discussing the types of questions the teacher is seeking to answer the consultants will be in a better position to recommend an evaluation plan. Some classroom-related questions might be answered using an interview format or questionnaires. Other questions might require more systematic analysis and several common research designs might be used (e.g., reversal, multiple-baseline, pre-posttest).

Referral services. The consultant may not be able to solve many classroom-related problems, even with the assistance of a sensitive and competent teacher. Therefore, it is important for the consultant to be able to refer the teacher to other professionals who may be in a position to help. An example is the case where a student's hyperactive behavior in the room might be based on neurological or organic problems. The consultant might recommend that the child be tested for hypoglycemia, a condition which produces excessive motor behavior in some children. Also, in the case where a student's problem in school extends into the home and disrupts the family life, counseling services might be recommended. Consultants who work within specific geographical regions should be thoroughly familiar with the referral resources of the community including child protective services, mental health agencies, parent-assistance programs, and counseling services. Of course, the consultant should know which related-service personnel in the school or district might share in the consultation process.

Related-Service Personnel

Related-service personnel, so-called support staff (physical, occupational, speech therapists, counselors, bus drivers, etc.) can play an essential role in the implementation of a student's Individualized Education Program (IEP). As defined in the *Federal Register,* a daily government document that publishes rules and regulations for federal programs, the term *related services* means:

> transportation and such developmental, corrective, and other supportive services as are required to assist a handicapped child to benefit from special education and includes speech pathology and audiology, psychological services, physical and occupational therapy, recreation, early identification and assessment of disabilities in children, counseling services, and medical services for diagnostic or evaluation purposes. The term also includes school health services, social work services in schools and parent counseling and training. (*Federal Register*, 42, 163, 8/23/77, 42479).

The scope can be extended to include art, music, dance, or other cultural or supportive services, if such are required to assist the child with meeting identified needs as determined by the multifactored team and prescribed in the *Individualized Education Program* (IEP), a written document that specifies the services handicapped students should receive to meet their instructional needs.

An almost limitless number of professionals could be employed to provide related services. For example, counseling services might be delivered by a guidance counselor, social worker, or school psychologist, and in each case the type of service delivered might be direct or indirect. The amount of direct and indirect service seems to be increasing as the effort to facilitate the instruction of handicapped children in the mainstream of the educational system increases. Below are several examples of related-service staff and what they do. A description of the roles and responsibilities for each professional is provided. Subsequently, suggestions for facilitating interactions with related-service personnel are offered.

The Itinerant Teacher. The *itinerant teacher* is not usually responsible for direct instruction in classrooms. He provides direct service to the handicapped student, but the student remains a member of a regular or special class where the classroom teacher has primary responsibility for his education. Rather than having the student leave the regular class to receive instruction, as is the case with a resource room, the itinerant teacher comes to the student.

Itinerant teachers may serve several schools and travel a considerable distance. Visits to classrooms can be arranged on a regular or as-needed basis.

Itinerant teachers have worked with visually impaired and mildly handicapped populations. They provide visually impaired students with instruction in braille or mobility training. They also offer indirect service to the handicapped student by supplying materials or specialized equipment, such as a braille machine, tape recorder, or language master. Similarly itinerant teachers help teachers of mildly handicapped populations to plan and execute in-class remedial and compensatory strategies.

The Consulting Teacher. Like the itinerant teacher, the *consulting teacher* provides indirect service to the exceptional student. Usually, no supervisory function is assumed by the consulting teacher so as not to interfere with communication between education personnel. Rather the consulting teacher provides the regular classroom teacher with instructional techniques, knowledge about exceptional children, and strategies that might be employed to improve student academic or social performance.

Certification programs for consulting teachers exist in several states, for example, Vermont, New Jersey. The requirements for certification usually involve a master's degree, teaching experience, and training in consultation.

The Educational Diagnostician. With mandated IEP's specifying each handicapped student's level of academic function and procedures for reevaluation, the *educational diagnostician* is becoming more evident in public school systems. Basically, the role of this related-service person is to conduct educational evaluations, using standardized and criterion-referenced assessments and observation techniques. Educational evaluations may encompass testing in the basic academic areas of reading and math, as well as the so-called "underlying correlates of learning" (for example, visual and auditory perception). Such information may be used to confirm a handicapping condition, or to develop an individualized educational program.

The Speech Clinician. A *speech clinician* is a highly trained professional capable of providing direct or indirect service to handicapped individuals. Indirect service can be in the form of advice or assistance to the regular classroom teacher in identifying speech or language-impaired children, or maintaining therapeutic programs for students currently in a program. Direct service to children with articulation or language difficulties as well as more severe disorders of speech and language is also a function of the speech clinician. Students who receive service may be multihandicapped, as in the case of a mentally retarded student who also has a concomitant speech or language problem, or they may only have one disability such as a speech or language impairment. Services are usually provided in individual or group therapy sessions as well as through consultation with the student's teacher.

The School Psychologist. The *school psychologist* is usually involved in providing evaluation services, such as intelligence testing, although in recent years, other services, such as counseling, curriculum planning, and in-class observation, have been emphasized. With these responsibilities the school psychologist assumes a major role in placement decisions. He or she may provide therapy for students and parents, as well as assist in the general adjustment of a handicapped child to a specific educational program. School psychologists have played an important role in the reintegration process. Also, their role has expanded to matters related to classroom management and parenting.

The School Social Worker. The *school social worker*, a major resource in programming for exceptional students, serves as a link between educational personnel and the family, as well as between the school and community agencies. Social workers provide assistance to handicapped students at home and in school. They supply counseling on a regular or crisis basis, and usually offer recommendations in the development of educational programs for students.

The Occupational Therapist. The *occupational therapist* conducts individual and group activities designed to increase the student's physical, social, psychological, and cognitive development. The occupational therapist may teach a child to match shapes and colors, fit puzzle pieces together, button clothes and tie shoes, and do other important daily tasks. Some occupational therapists are based in schools; others conduct therapy in clinics or private facilities.

The Physical Therapist. A *physical therapist* works closely with a physician. Treatment is provided in the area of motor performance and focuses on correction and prevention of physical problems. These professionals help individuals recover from or compensate for physical defects, diseases, or injuries. Therefore, it is apparent that the services of a physical therapist would be used more extensively with physically or severely impaired students than they might for mildly handicapped students. Physical therapists are prepared to give direct service to handicapped students by conducting therapeutic procedures, such as heat treatments, massage, exercise. They also provide indirect service by supervising training in the development and coordination of movement or consulting with the classroom teacher on techniques designed to foster independence. Like their counterparts in occupational therapy, physical therapists are based in schools or clinics.

Art, Music, Dance, and Recreational Staff. Art, music, dance, and *recreational staff* provide handicapped students with skills in the so-called specials areas. In some cases, the handicapped student participates in the specials curriculum because the class as a whole is scheduled in the area. In other instances, these subjects or skill areas are specified in the student's IEP because they are designed to meet an identified need. Nevertheless, the consultant should know the goals and objectives of these programs, and the roles of the professionals who run them, so that an appropriate program can be planned and delivered to the student.

The School Bus Driver. The *school bus driver* is often the forgotten member of the educational team. This is unfortunate for several reasons. First, in some parts of the country, handicapped children are transported long distances to school, forcing them to spend considerable time on buses. In some cases, students may spend up to two and a half hours traveling to and from school each day. For students with learning deficiencies or handicaps, this can mean wasted time, unless that time is properly programmed and managed.

Second, many school bus drivers, especially drivers of handicapped students are genuinely interested in helping. Given direction from a consultant, the driver may be able to extend school learning experiences or activities on the bus. For example, the driver may be able to verbally interact with a student who has language difficulties, thereby providing another source of stimulation.

Third, when drivers are not consulted for their ideas or when they are not asked to participate in a student's program, the teacher and consultant lose an opportunity to train the child for generalization of skills from the classroom to the bus.

Finally, drivers can play an active role in the referral process, can help to determine the effects of medication, and can serve as a liaison with parents. Their cooperation in the overall management program for the student can be invaluable.

Facilitating Interactions with Related-Service Personnel

One way consultants can facilitate interactions with related-service personnel is to be knowledgeable about their jobs. By being sensitive to their roles and functions, the consultant will be in a better position to know which professional might offer the maximum amount of service.

Second, interaction can be facilitated if the IEP program integrates the positive recommendations made by related-service personnel. Not all recommendations from all related-service providers need to be included in the IEP, but the major recommendations should be addressed.

Third, interactions can be facilitated if a program is planned and implemented which reflects a common orientation. Situations become strained when the IEP goals and short-term objectives reflect different orientations and philosophies. The program becomes fragmented, and strategies that are recommended by one individual might be counterproductive for another.

Anecdote 2–1 indicates how an educational consultant facilitated the interaction of several related-service professionals prior to an IEP meeting. The purpose of the pre-IEP meeting was to prepare in-house recommendations so that a sample document could be mailed to the guardian prior to the meeting. The student to be discussed at the conference was a behaviorally disordered adolescent who resided at a county child protective care facility.

Anecdote 2–1

EDUCATIONAL CONSULTANT (*chairing a pre-IEP meeting with a guidance counselor, speech pathologist, school psychologist, and social worker*): "Thank you for attending the meeting this afternoon. I realize that everyone's schedule is full this time of year. Let's begin with Danny O'Rourke."

SPEECH PATHOLOGIST (*speaking for the other participants*): "Fine. Let's get started."

EDUCATIONAL CONSULTANT: "As I am sure you are aware, Danny is a behaviorally disordered youth residing at the Dawn County Child Protective Services facility. He's lived there for eight months. Since the IEP conference will be the first meeting with Danny's legal guardian this year, I'd like to review last year's IEP and ask for your recommendations."

GUIDANCE COUNSELOR (*reviewing previous IEP*): "Since Danny didn't arrive at our school until spring, we couldn't accomplish all the initial objectives prescribed for him. I'm in favor of addressing these objectives again this year—at least for the short term."

EDUCATIONAL CONSULTANT: "Are there any objectives in particular which seem more important than others?"

GUIDANCE COUNSELOR: "Yes, I'd like Danny to be able to identify personal strengths and weaknesses so that I could begin to show him how his personality characteristics might affect his on-the-job performance after graduation. He is an adolescent. We need to focus on career expectations."

SCHOOL PSYCHOLOGIST: "I agree. Danny still is all bottled up. He has difficulty communicating his feelings. I don't think he thinks of himself in very positive terms."

SPEECH PATHOLOGIST: "You're right about his communication problem. However, I think it goes beyond any psychological disability he has. My observations indicate that he has a problem expressing his concerns and ideas. Not only does he have a slight articulation problem, but he also has difficulty sequencing his verbalization. He jumps from thought to thought. I'd like to continue individual therapy."

EDUCATIONAL CONSULTANT: "How about you, Fran? What goals do you think are appropriate for Danny?"

SCHOOL PSYCHOLOGIST: "I'd like to get Danny involved in group therapy as soon as possible, but it may be premature to begin in September. I'd like to see him individually to work out some of his problems."

EDUCATIONAL CONSULTANT: "What is your target date for beginning group therapy?"

SCHOOL PSYCHOLOGIST: "January."

EDUCATIONAL CONSULTANT: "Fine. Louise, you work directly with the county child care facility. What are your thoughts?"

SOCIAL WORKER: "I'd like to see Danny start out-patient care from a nearby mental health clinic as soon as possible. I think it will be difficult for Danny to achieve any measurable goals if only a school approach is used. Holidays and Christmas vacation come along quickly, and these breaks can stall gains. I'd like to see Danny receive services from the mental health clinic now, if he is eligible."

EDUCATIONAL CONSULTANT: "OK. I'll leave it to you to check his eligibility for these services."

SPEECH PATHOLOGIST: "It sounds like we are going to initiate basically the same plan for Danny this year, although some changes have been suggested."

EDUCATIONAL CONSULTANT: "True. But I'd like to suggest that we consider the recommendations made by Danny's classroom teacher at the end of last year. In her summary remarks, she indicated Danny was responding very well to a contingency contract she had negotiated. She stated that he liked the flexibility of deciding his tasks and rewards. I'd like to continue this approach. Specifically, I'd like to recommend that each of us use some form of contingency contract with Danny, at least initially, to test its effectiveness."

SPEECH PATHOLOGIST: "That's fine with me. I can draw up a contract for Danny for several skills in therapy."

SCHOOL PSYCHOLOGIST: "I can as well."

GUIDANCE COUNSELOR: "I'm not that fond of strict contracts. I prefer a less structured approach, but I'm willing to give it a try for a short time, especially if the teacher found it effective."

SOCIAL WORKER: "Since I don't work directly with Danny, it's purely academic to me."

EDUCATIONAL CONSULTANT (*following up on the social worker's comment*): "Except that if a mental health agency becomes involved, it might be important for it to consider using some form of contracting, if it eventually provided direct service."

SOCIAL WORKER: "I see your point."

EDUCATIONAL CONSULTANT: "In sum, we're recommending basically the same goals as last year and we'll each try a contingency contracting approach using the teacher's program as a model. Am I correct?"

TEAM: "Yes."

EDUCATIONAL CONSULTANT: "I'll mail our sample to Danny's legal guardian so that he'll be able to review it prior to the IEP meeting. At that time we can finalize our program, and with the guardian's approval begin shortly thereafter. Thank you for your help."

This anecdote shows how a knowledgeable consultant using reliable information (the teacher's experience with contracting) set the stage for a consistent approach by the support team. While the details of the contract were not specified, consensus was reached that this strategy should be initiated. Of course, Danny's legal guardian would have the opportunity to provide suggestions as well, and the formal details of the IEP (long and short-term goals, duration of service, amount of service) would have to be identified.

The facilitating of interactions with related-service personnel is continued during the IEP implementation phases. It is important that the educational consultant monitor the progress of the student within individual disciplines and across settings. For example, if Danny were making gains in individual speech therapy sessions, were these gains evident in the classroom or at the child care facility? If gains were evidenced in therapy but not in the classroom, a revised plan might focus on generalization training.

Direct Services to Administrators

Administrators often seek the advice of supervisors, principals, and consultants to help solve problems related to policy design, short and long-term planning, in-service training programs for teachers, services to handicapped and minority children, and a host of other topics.

Before consultation can be provided, the consultant must have a clear idea of the terminal objective the administrator has in mind. She must be certain that the objective is measurable, and she must know the time frame in which the administrator wants the problem solved. For example, the administrator might state in broad terms that she wants all of the teachers in the district competent in certain classroom management techniques. The following dialogue illustrates how a consultant determined the terminal objective, a procedure to measure it, and the time constraints for achieving the objective.

Anecdote 2-2

ADMINISTRATOR: "Ruth, I asked you here today to talk over a situation I've felt many of our teachers need assistance with."

CONSULTANT: "I'll be glad to help if I can."

ADMINISTRATOR: "I feel we could use a refresher course on classroom management. I've noticed that several teachers at the high school were unable to handle the inappropriate behavior in their classes."

CONSULTANT (*Attempting to determine the terminal objective*): "I agree that appropriate classroom management techniques are important. Which ones did you have in mind—individual or group approaches, positive or aversive techniques?"

ADMINISTRATOR (*Hesitantly*): "Well, all of them."

CONSULTANT (*Narrowing the range*): "That's a tall order. Do you feel that we need to concentrate on group strategies to help the high school teachers with the whole class?"

ADMINISTRATOR: "I think that would be appropriate."

CONSULTANT: "Fine. I'll work up a plan for an initial in-service program on positive group strategies for managing secondary level classrooms. (*Attempting to determine time constraints*) Incidentally, what time frame did you have in mind for the teachers acquiring the competencies?"

ADMINISTRATOR: "I'm thinking of this program as long range. By the end of the year would be appropriate."

CONSULTANT: "That's good. I'll be able to plan several mini-conferences—maybe lunch bag seminars—which will follow-up on the information presented during the initial conference."

ADMINISTRATOR: "Great idea."

CONSULTANT: "Thank you. That leaves one more question to be resolved. What are your thoughts on evaluating the year-long in-service program?"

ADMINISTRATOR: "As I stated, I'd like to see better behaved students in the classes."

CONSULTANT: "If students raised their hands to respond to teacher questions, waited their turn to speak, and asked permission to leave their seats, would you think their overall behavior would have improved?"

ADMINISTRATOR: "Without question. You cited three very troublesome matters for our teachers."

CONSULTANT: "I'll plan a two-phase evaluation procedure. The first phase will assess the knowledge gained after the workshop series is over. I'll prepare a simple assessment device, and interview several teachers to obtain their reactions to speakers, audiovisuals, and the rest. Next, I'd like to set a schedule of short observations in each teacher's class to obtain reliability data. I'm confident the teachers can get the bulk of the data on these behaviors themselves. The real improvement you're looking for must occur in the classroom if our program is to be any success at all. My conferences with them will focus on the student's change of behavior before and after the in-service."

ADMINISTRATOR: "That sounds very comprehensive."

CONSULTANT: "Thank you, but there is one other thing."

ADMINISTRATOR: "What's that?"

CONSULTANT: "I'll be meeting with the teachers collectively and individually to inform them of the purpose, scope, and expectations, and to obtain their views on the program. Also, it is important that they view this series of workshops and observations as a chance to improve and extend their management skills. They must understand my role in this process as that of a facilitator. I'll do my best to insure that the 'evaluation' stigma which is sometimes created by these projects is avoided."

ADMINISTRATOR: "I'll do everything I can to help."

CONSULTANT: "I'm sure you will."

Aside from obtaining necessary information from the administrator (the terminal objective, time contract, and evaluation procedure), the consultant shared vital information with her. She told the administrator that she viewed the teachers' reaction to the in-service plan as important. Also, she smartly established her facilitating role with the administrator and the teachers in the consultation process. As Hughes (1980) has indicated, consultants must avoid alienating any organizational or philosophical factions within the school. Obtaining consensus and avoiding confrontations are important objectives for the consultant.

In our hypothetical example, the consultant indicated by her questions and responses that she was going to prepare a plan in concert with the teachers' perspectives that would help to improve the classroom management skills of the teachers. In this situtation the consultant is acting clearly in the role of a facilitator.

Consultants can perform other functions at the administration level as well. For example, they may assist with establishing and maintaining open communication between teachers and administrators. They may serve as a resource for innovative program planning, applying for and receiving grants-in-aid for experimental education research projects. They may participate in advisory meetings to design district-wide policy on a range of topics from corporal punishment in the classroom to the dress code.

Although the reasons for the interaction between the administrator and the consultants may vary, the nature of the interaction should follow a consistent path: determine the goals, identify resources, establish the consultant role, implement the program, and evaluate the results.

SUMMARY

This chapter emphasized that consultant services can be provided directly or indirectly to students, teachers, and administrators. While it is usually an inefficient use of the consultant's time to work with an individual student for an extended period of time, it is recognized that cases exist where the consultant, as the only resource or support person with the requisite knowledge and experience, may have to do so. Teachers can benefit from the direct service of a consultant to solve a host of classroom-related problems, especially if in-service training is provided on a mutually-recognized problem.

The role and function of support personnel within the school were described because these professionals may also share in the consultation process. The consultant working with individuals who may have different orientations must be willing to listen to these professionals and determine the best course of action to be taken. Each of these professionals, when included in the IEP process, plays a critical role. Suggestions were made to the educational consultant for facilitating positive interactions with related-service staff and administrators.

Questions

1. Identify three ways a consultant can provide direct service to teachers. State your reaction to three services.

2. List and discuss the type of data a consultant must possess prior to initiating effective consultation at the administrative level.

3. Discuss the pros and cons of providing consultation directly to children.

4. Choose three in-school, related-service personnel. Identify their potential role in the consultation process.

5. What are the key features of Brophy and Good's intervention model?

6. Outline two means by which educational consultants can facilitate positive interactions with school bus drivers.

7. Discuss how an educational consultant might enhance cooperation between diverse groups of professionals, especially as it relates to IEP development.

8. Why do you think the recommendations from related-services personnel need to be integrated into a comprehensive program reflecting a specific orientation?

Discussion Points and Exercises

1. Why is it important for the consultant to establish his role in the consultation process before service is delivered?

2. Conduct a meeting with elementary and secondary level teachers to obtain their views on in-service workshops. Solicit from them alternatives to the traditional lecture format of in-service workshops.

3. Establish your own criteria for providing one-to-one consultation service to a student. Discuss these criteria with other related-service personnel.

4. Compile a list of referral agencies in your community. Conduct a meeting with key staff of these agencies to determine the type of service they provide, eligibility requirements, and free procedures.

5. During an IEP conference, collect data on the number of recommendations offered by related-service personnel. Categorize these data. Determine if data represent a comprehensive, integrated approach to remediating the student's assessed need.

6. Follow up the IEP conference conducted in item five above to determine the extent to which program recommendations are actually implemented. If recommendations are not followed, determine reasons for the delay or the revision.

REFERENCES

ALPERT, J. L. Some guidelines for school consultants, *Journal of School Psychology*, 1977, *15* (4), 308–319.

BANDURA, A. *Social learning theory.* New York: General Learning Press, 1971.

BERGAN, J. R. *Behavioral consultation.* Columbus, Ohio: Charles E. Merrill, 1977.

BROPHY, J. E., & GOOD, T. L. *Teacher-student relationships: Causes and consequences.* New York: Holt, Rinehart and Winston, Inc., 1974.

BROWN, D., RESCHLY, D., & WASSERMAN, H. Effects of surreptitious modeling upon teacher classroom behaviors. *Psychology in the Schools*, 1974, *11* (3), 366–369.

BROWN, V. L. "Yes, but . . ." A reply to Phyllis Newcomer. *The Journal of Special Education*, 1977, *11* (2), 171–177.

COOPER, J. O., & HUNT, K. P. A cooperative approach to inservice training. *Viewpoints in Teaching and Learning*, 1978, *54* (4), 61–69.

Federal Register, Vol. 42, No. 163, Paragraph 121a.13, August 23, 1977.

GRAUBARD, P. S., ROSENBERG, H., & MILLER, M. B. Student applications of behavior modification to teachers and environments or ecological approaches to social deviancy. In E. A. Ramp & B. L. Hopkins (Eds.), *A new direction for education: Behavior analysis.* 1971, vol. 1, The University of Kansas: Support and Development Center for Follow Through, Department of Human Development, Lawrence, Kansas, 1971.

HUGHES, J. A case study in behavioral consultation: Organizational factors. *School Psychology Review*, 1980, 9 (1), 103–107.

MEYERS, J. A consultation model for school psychological services. In J. P. Glavin (Ed.), *Ferment in special education*, New York; MSS Information Corporation, 1974.

NEWCOMER, P. L. Special education services for the "mildly handicapped": Beyond a diagnostic and remedial model. *The Journal of Special Education*, 1977, *11* (2), 153–165.

OLDRIDGE, O. A. Future directions for special education: Beyond a diagnostic and remedial model. *The Journal of Special Education*, 1977, *11* (2), 167–169.

SHAW, S. F., & SHAW, W. K. The in-service experience plan, or changing the bath without losing the baby. *The Journal of Special Education*, 1972, *6* (2), 121–126.

SKINNER, M. E. Effects of an in-service program on the attitudes, knowledge, and student-teacher interaction patterns of regular classroom teachers. Unpublished masters thesis, The Ohio State University, 1979.

STEPHENS, T. M. A rationale for training of teacher educators. *Viewpoints in Teaching and Learning*, 1978, *54* (4), 10–19.

3

Working with Teachers
in the Mainstreamed Classroom

Handicapped students are being placed in regular classrooms at an increasing rate. Regular education teachers who previously believed that exceptional children and youth were the sole responsibility of special educators are now faced with what Toffler (1970) described as "future shock." Many regular educators feel unprepared to assume the responsibility for teaching these students. Nevertheless, Public Law 94–142 clearly states that handicapped children and youth are to be educated with their normal peers to the maximum extent possible.

Unfortunately, most regular education teachers, and many special education teachers, have only a vague understanding of the intent of the federal and state legislation. For example, many regular education teachers feel that all students who are now enrolled in self-contained classrooms will be integrated in the regular classroom. Further, many regular education teachers feel that they will be the sole person in charge of the student's education, and, consequently, they will be held accountable for the student's rate of progress—or lack of it.

In this chapter the concept of mainstreaming will be defined, as well as the concept of the least restrictive environment. Additionally, variables which influence the degree to which integration in the regular classroom is successful will be discussed with an emphasis on techniques a consultant can recommend to the regular educator to enhance the mainstreaming process.

Finally, a composite decision-making model will be discussed, which outlines intervention techniques a consultant can suggest to maintain mainstreamed students in the regular classroom.

41

Objectives

After reading this chapter, the reader will be able to:

1. define the term *mainstreaming.*

2. cite components of the least restrictive environment.

3. cite the two components of the least restrictive environment as published in the *Federal Register.*

4. cite two variables which affect the quality of teacher-student interactions in the classroom.

5. distinguish between the concepts of mainstreaming and the least restrictive environment.

6. provide examples of variables which affect education within mainstreamed classrooms.

7. state two strategies for teaching a regular class teacher how to manage exceptional and normal students within the classroom.

Key Terms

Mainstreaming	Social relationships
Temporal integration	Countercontrol
Instructional and social integration	Modeling
Eligibility	Peer tutoring
Least restrictive environment	Programmed instruction
Opportunity to respond	Individualized instruction
Teacher-student interaction	Feedback
Proportional interaction	Cues

MAINSTREAMING VERSUS THE LEAST RESTRICTIVE ENVIRONMENT

Distinguishing the terms: Mainstreaming and least restrictive environment. To discuss the terms *mainstreaming* and *least restrictive environment*, a definition of each must be provided. The terms have been used interchangeably. However, there are clear differences between them.

Mainstreaming. According to Kaufman, Gottleib, Agard, and Kukic (1975) *mainstreaming* is ". . . the temporal, instructional, and social integration of eligible exceptional children with normal peers based on an on-going, individually determined, educational planning and programming process and requires clarification of responsibility among regular and special education administrative, instruction, and supportive personnel" (1975, p. 4). Embedded in this definition are a number of major conditions or concepts that many professionals in special and regular education have failed to implement to the fullest. Let us examine some of the key concepts of Kaufman et al.'s definition of mainstreaming.

Temporal integration. This term is defined as the total amount of time a handicapped student spends with nonhandicapped peers expressed in "periods per day" or "academic subject areas." For example, a student might be mainstreamed for math, but remain within a self-contained classroom or resource room for other academic or vocational subjects, or the student might spend a two week trial period in a regular third grade. If at the end of the two weeks he seems to be progressing satisfactorily, the placement is made final. Although the latter strategy has often been used, Stephens (1977) cautions against the use of trial placements for exceptional students. He feels that trial placements can be more detrimental than beneficial to students if the placement is not successful. Further, Stephens states that such placements show a lack of adequate planning on the part of a placement team. It would be better if more planning were done by the team prior to integrating the exceptional student.

It is the opinion of others that temporal integration is not sufficient (Kaufman et al., 1975; Keogh & Levitt, 1976; MacMillan & Becker, 1977). In a review of research concerning the mainstreaming of mentally retarded children, Corman & Gottlieb (1978) concluded that ". . . research on the academic achievement of integrated educable mentally retarded (EMR) pupils has yielded inconsistent results" (p. 270). Furthermore, they state that the social acceptance of retarded students by nonhandicapped peers is not related to the amount of time retarded students spend in the integrated classroom.

Instructional and Social Integration. The next key concept in Kaufman et al.'s definition of mainstreaming is that of instructional and social integration. To the maximum extent possible, the exceptional child should have the opportunity to benefit from academic instruction and social contact with his normal peers.

Instructional integration is viewed by Kaufman et al. (1975) as instruction so arranged for the handicapped child that he partakes in the same educational activities as his normal peers but is not required to participate in areas that are too difficult for him. This may possibly be achieved by presenting information at a suitable level, through various modalities, and modifying the expected response. For example, a physically handicapped high school student may be able to successfully participate in a class science lesson if the teacher carefully structures the tasks. The physically handicapped student might have to describe the steps of an experiment and predict the outcome, while another student manipulates the apparatus, and a third student takes notes on process and writes up the results.

If a student were unable to be integrated in the normal classroom for academic subjects because he lacked certain prerequisite academic skills, then an effort should be made to integrate him in nonacademic areas, such as recess, special subjects, and physical education. Every alternative should be explored to program as much of the student's day with his normal peers as possible.

Consultants are usually more successful integrating handicapped students in nonacademic subject areas when they stress the following points to the regular or special teacher. First, the handicapped student, although lacking many prerequisite academic skills, may have adequate social skills to perform satisfactorily. Second, other students (for example, the low achieving nonhandicapped) may have similar traits to the handicapped student, and the teacher has managed their behavior successfully. Finally, a resource person is available and willing to assist if the situation warrants it.

The second concept, *social integration,* is included because it is realized that school offers more than just academic experiences. Since many mildly handicapped children have difficulty establishing and maintaining adequate social relationships with normal peers (Bryan, 1974a; Bryan & Bryan, 1977; Iano, Ayers, Heller, McGettigan, & Walker, 1974), one of the objectives of mainstreaming is to provide occasions where such relationships can develop.

The consultant can recommend a number of strategies to the regular and special classroom teacher to foster social integration, even prior to a student's placement in a regular setting. For instance, a peer group activity involving handicapped students and a regular class could be suggested. Games, athletic events, or playground activities could be arranged to maximize positive social exchanges between the two groups.

Eligibility. The final concept in the Kaufman et al. definition is *eligibility*, the criteria for placement. What does it mean to be eligible for a mainstreaming placement? Who determines eligibility?

Eligibility for placement of a handicapped student in a mainstreamed setting is determined by a multidisciplinary evaluation team including the student's regular teacher, the special education teacher, the school psychologist, the parents, and other persons with knowledge in the area of suspected disability (*Federal Register*, Vol. 42, no. 163, 121a 533, August 23, 1977).

For a consultant to provide effective service to eligible handicapped students, he must be thoroughly knowledgeable regarding district placement criteria. Of course, since these criteria are derived from state program standards, state laws, or federal statutes, the consultant must be grounded in these areas as well.

Least Restrictive Environment

It is interesting to note that nowhere in either Public Law 94–142 or the rules and regulations which accompanied the statute is the term *mainstreaming* used. Rather, Public Law 94–142 and the regulations speak to the issue of an educational experience within the context of the least restrictive environment (LRE).

According to the final rules and regulations of Public Law 94–142 published in the *Federal Register*, the *least restrictive environment* has essentially two components. First, to the maximum extent possible the student is to be educated with his normal peers; and second, he should only be removed from that setting when the nature of his disability precludes an adequate educational experience even when supplementary learning aids are used (*Federal Register*, Vol. 42, no. 163., 121a 550 (1), (2), August 23, 1977).

The terms *mainstreaming* and *least restrictive environment* may seem identical. However, there are subtle differences in interpretation and practice which greatly affect the way educational personnel and parents perceive the two concepts.

It seems that regular educators perceive mainstreaming to be a process whereby all exceptional children are integrated into regular classrooms. While Edwin Martin was Deputy Commissioner for the Bureau for the Education of the Handicapped in 1974, he cautioned that mainstreaming should not be a "pell-mell" process. Nevertheless, regular education teachers seem confused about the whole notion of integration. In short, regular educators are frequently less than enthusiastic about the prospects of having to teach handicapped children. Although reasons for the lack of enthusiasm are as varied as the teachers themselves, there are some common concerns.

Teacher Concerns

First, many regular educators feel that they lack the specialized training needed to teach handicapped students. This opinion is evident in a survey conducted by McGinity and Keogh (1975) whereby only 27 percent of forty-four teachers interviewed felt knowledgeable about the characteristics of exceptional students.

Second, though recommended support services can help the regular educator teach the exceptional learner, it is acknowledged that support services vary across schools and districts. Many regular educators are not familiar with such services or how to locate them. They are concerned that exceptional students will be simply dumped in their classrooms and they will have to sink or swim with the added challenges.

Third, the regular education teacher is concerned about accountability. Before a regular teacher accepts a child into his classroom he wants to know to what extent he will be held accountable if the student does not make reasonable gains.

The consultant needs to impress upon regular educators that the rules and regulations of Public Law 94–142 specify that neither the teacher nor the school district will be held accountable if a handicapped student does not achieve the goals prescribed in his IEP. However, educational personnel are required to show "good faith" in their efforts to accomplish IEP goals and objectives. Despite Public Law 94–142, legal suits have been brought against schools by nonhandicapped, illiterate graduates of high schools who claim they are not educated or trained for a career. Results of such litigation may set precedents for handicapped students who, in the future, may challenge the educational process by claiming that their IEP goals were not consistently attained.

Finally, many regular education teachers feel they should share the instructional responsibility for the exceptional student with support personnel. Included in the instructional responsibilites would be planning, teaching, and evaluation. Many special educators advocate shared instructional responsibility with regular educators (Turnbull & Schulz, 1979).

Consultants can plan an active role in the instructional process by recommending appropriate teaching strategies, materials, and evaluation techniques. At the secondary level the offering of options for grading, credit hours, and class scheduling would be beneficial. The consultant's main task would be to act as a liaison or resource person for the regular educator.

Parent Concerns

Parents have a paradoxical view of the benefits to be gained from integration of handicapped children with normal peers. On one hand, parents may see the integration process as a positive step. For too long they may have watched their son or daughter in a self-contained classroom, the object of ridicule by other students. The pain which they may have felt when their child was called "dummy" or "retarded" is real. Parents may feel that an integrated program with normal children will have a number of advantages. First, they may believe that the amount of ridicule will be reduced, since their child would be participating in a "normal" curriculum. Second, parents may believe that the normal students will be a good influence. They envision their child modeling the appropriate academic and social behavior of the normal students, rather than the reverse. Finally, some parents may view the integration process as a valuable experience for the regular students. These parents feel the regular student will become sensitive to the individual differences of students and grow to view exceptional children as "children with a handicap" rather than "handicapped children."

Conversely, parents are often apprehensive about integration programs. They know the regular students may not accept their handicapped child. Further, they are aware that their child may precipitate problems in the regular classroom because of immaturity or lack of social skills (Bryan, 1974a; Bryan & Bryan, 1977). Parents are also concerned that, given the increased ratio of students to teacher, their child may not receive the individualized assistance and special instructional programming he may have been receiving in the less populous self-contained classroom. Of course, closely related to the last concern is the parent's apprehension that his child may not have the same response opportunities as normal peers in the classroom. Parents who are aware of the general nature of classroom interaction realize that the student who survives the pitfalls of education in the day-to-day world is usually the student with the fastest answer, passive and compliant in the room, and who reinforces the teacher (Brophy & Good, 1974). Handicapped students frequently have characteristics or qualities opposite to those expected by teachers and to the extent that a child's behavior differs from the norm the parent will be apprehensive about mainstreaming.

Some of the techniques and activities that consultants and supervisors could use in dealing with these common concerns will be discussed further in this chapter and in greater detail later in the text.

Defining the Least Restrictive Environment

The criteria for a least restrictive environment, published in the *Federal Register,* can only be viewed as guidelines. They are vague and open to varying interpretations. In one sense, a general guideline permits school districts in different parts of the country to exercise a certain degree of latitude in establishing programs for exceptional students. Yet, so general a guideline makes it extremely difficult for a placement team within a local education agency to determine the specific criteria for reentry and maintenance within a regular environment.

Heron and Skinner (1981) have proposed a definition of least restrictive environment that is consistent with research studies that have been completed within the last ten years. The use of their definition facilitates data collection on the effectiveness of the integration effort. Further, the definition proposed by Heron and Skinner (1981) is consistent with Kenowitz, Zweikel, and Edgar's (1978) concept of the least restrictive environment for severely and profoundly handicapped students. Heron and Skinner favor a movement toward programming options and social interactions with nonhandicapped populations rather than thinking exclusively in terms of placement alternatives. Their definition reads:

> The least restrictive environment is defined as that educational setting which maximizes the learning-disabled student's opportunity to respond and achieve, permits the regular education teacher to interact proportionally with all the students in the classroom, and fosters acceptable social relationships between nonhandicapped and learning-disabled students.

This definition has three essential components: opportunity to respond and achieve, proportional interaction between teachers and students, and acceptable social relationships between normal and exceptional students. Each component along with supporting documentation will be addressed in the next sections.

Opportunity to respond and achieve. A variety of reinforcing consequences (for example, free time [Osborne, 1969; Long & Williams, 1973]; praise [Madsen, Becker, & Thomas, 1968; Cossairt, Hall, & Hopkins, 1973], and tokens [McLaughlin & Malaby, 1972; Iwata & Bailey, 1974]) can be used to increase performance in academic or social areas.

It has only been within the last few years, however, that educational researchers began investigating variables that set the occasion for academic or social responses. Put another way, there have only been a handful of efforts to investigate the effects of antecedent, rather than consequent, events on academic and social performance in the classroom.

For example, Massad and Edsil (1972) found in working with elementary pupils, that the students' *opportunity to respond* to the teacher had a greater effect upon their ability to learn a language skill, such as a grapheme-phoneme relationship, than the use of positive reinforcement alone.

Similarly Broden, Copeland, Beasley, and Hall (1977) found that inner-city high school students participated more frequently in class discussion when the teacher restated the questions to them. Further, when the time between when a teacher finished asking a question and the time a student responded with the answer was increased from 4.5 seconds to 15 seconds, the amount of student hand raising also increased. Both tactics are measures designed to increase student response opportunities. Again, specific reinforcement procedures were not employed, merely the opportunities for response were increased.

In an effort to determine if student opportunity to respond was equal across educational settings, Bryan, Wheeler, Felcan, and Henek (1976) compared regular and special education classrooms. It was found that response opportunities were not equal across these settings. Specifically, the learning disabled students employed in the study had more response opportunities in the special education classroom than they did in the regular classroom. While these data should be regarded as preliminary, the potential exists in the regular education setting for a handicapped student to experience fewer response opportunities than might be found in a more traditional special education setting.

If a consultant were assisting a placement committee with its decision, the environment in which increased opportunity to respond and achieve was greatest should be given priority. Likewise, current research seems to indicate that there is a positive correlation between achievement and self-esteem (Duncan & Biddle, 1974). As students progress through the public school it becomes important that they achieve, otherwise they lose interest in the educational process and their performance reflects their lack of interest.

Data exist which quantify the type, number, and ratio of *teacher-student interactions*, defined as any verbal or nonverbal encounter, within the regular classroom (Duncan & Biddle, 1974). Unfortunately, the volume of data on teacher-student interactions in mainstreamed classrooms does not begin to match the data in regular education classrooms without handicapped children.

A series of studies by Bryan and her colleagues (1972–1979) represents the most consistent research effort to determine the effects of the presence of learning disabled students on teacher-student interaction in the regular classroom. Taken as a whole, her data suggest that learning disabled students receive a disproportionate amount of teacher attention. Specifically, LD students show fewer initiated statements to teachers, receive more negative comments from the teachers (warnings, criticism) and take up more of the teacher's time than do nonhandicapped students. Chapman, Larsen, and Parker (1979) found similar results in a study with first-grade children with one exception. Not only did the LD students receive more teacher criticism and warnings, but they also had fewer initiations to the teachers.

Heron and Skinner (1979), on the other hand, found that teacher-student interaction varied across regular classrooms in which LD students were integrated. One of the most important variables in determining quantity and quality of teacher-student interactions was the teacher.

The crux of the issue, however, is not whether mildly handicapped students receive more or less teacher initiations or teacher praise; it is whether each student receives enough attention to maintain and increase performance. As Brophy and Good (1974) report, two teachers might issue equal amounts of praise, yet one teacher might be distributing her praise to only a small minority of students. This is not proportional interaction.

Proportional interaction. Proportional interaction means that all of the students receive the teacher's attention for appropriate behavior on a consistent enough basis to maintain performance. One way to quantify how much interaction is sufficient, at least for the handicapped students, is to find out before placement in the regular classroom what the rate or percentage of teacher interactions is in the old class. If the observations indicate that the student receives fifteen direct initiations from the teacher each day in the self-contained or resource room, ideally at least fifteen initiations should be provided in the regular classroom.[1] The essential contribution that this component of the definition provides is that the regular teacher is relieved of any psychological pressure to provide *equal* amounts of attention to all students. Rather, it provides a data-based context to determine if a student is likely to receive an appropriate amount of teacher attention. Also, it could serve to allay any fears parents might have that special education students would take the teacher's attention away from the task of educating their children.

Social relationships. Anyone who has worked with handicapped and nonhandicapped students together realizes that the *social relationships*

---

[1] Two points need to be underscored regarding the number of initiations expected from regular education teachers to mainstreamed students. First, although it is difficult to deliver fifteen direct initiatives to the handicapped student in the regular classroom where thirty-five other students may be competing for the teacher's attention, it is not impossible. Second, the initial level of interactions would lessen as soon as the handicapped student's performance could be maintained with fewer direct contacts.

(i.e., verbal and nonverbal interactions), between the two groups can sometimes be strained. As stated previously, several researchers (Bryan & Bryan, 1977; Goodman, Gottlieb, & Harrison, 1972) have found that handicapped students, both learning disabled and educable mentally retarded, are often rejected, ostracized, or actively ignored by their normal peers in the regular classroom. They are also less accurate perceivers of their social status within the classroom than their normal peers (Bruininks, 1978). For example, the handicapped students often rate their social status in the classroom higher than the actual social status attributed to them by their nonhandicapped classmates. On the other hand, Kirby and Toler (1970) found that contingent upon the implementation of direct intervention approaches, the behavior of normal peers can be changed so that a favorable position is held toward the exceptional student.

It is realized that all interactions between nonhandicapped and exceptional students will not be positive and supportive. That situation does not exist in a regular classroom even if handicapped students are not integrated. The consultant should be aware of the social climate within a classroom to effectively assist the placement team with its decision. For example, it might not be desirable to place a handicapped student in a classroom if the student were actively disliked or mistreated by other students. Since peer acceptance can have a tremendous effect on academic performance and self-concept (Schmuck & Schmuck, 1975), and a positive relationship between peer status and academic achievement exists in the classroom (Lilly, 1970), the consultant must be sensitive to the social dynamics of the class.

Many supervisors face situations in schools where special education students do not get along with regular students. To place a handicapped student in a regular classroom is a decision that has to be made carefully. The responsibility of being a supervisor or consultant precludes the random placement of students in compromising learning environments where nonhandicapped students do not accept and are not likely to work with them.

Heron and Skinner's definition of the least restrictive environment has a number of advantages over previous definitions for the supervisor or consultant. Specifically, the consultant is able to find out across three dimensions (measurable outcomes, teacher benefits, and parent benefits) whether the environment is least restrictive. Heretofore such documentation was not possible.

Measurable outcomes. All three components of the definition (response opportunities and achievement, proportional interaction, and appropriate social exchange) are measurable. Placement team members are in a better position to determine whether a regular education setting is least restrictive if the consultant helps to provide data across these dimensions. The placement decision can be made on the basis of a more objective analysis, rather than an intuitive notion about the efficacy of a particular classroom.

Further, once integration has been completed the consultant can monitor the process more closely if measurable data are available for comparison. By noting differences that may arise across the three areas, the consultant is able to recommend specific interventions to the classroom teacher. For instance, suppose that prior to the integration of a handicapped student, it was found that the regular education teacher distributed her interactions equally to all students. Once the handicapped student was mainstreamed, however, the teacher began to interact differentially with all students. She gave the handicapped student more attention than was needed and the nonhandicapped students less attention than they needed to maintain performance. In this case, the consultant might recommend to the teacher that she reemploy the same techniques she used to distribute her attention prior to placement. These might include walking around the room regularly to monitor student seatwork, using prompting strategies more effectively during class discussion, or praising all the students, not just a select few, on a regular basis.

Teacher benefits. As stated previously, the classroom teacher will not have to be under the psychological pressure to provide one-to-one instruction for the handicapped student. If proportional attention is provided in sufficient amounts to maintain the performance of students at an acceptable level, teacher anxiety should be reduced.

Also, successful integration of a handicapped student may set the occasion for the regular educator to use a wider variety of content and teaching materials, as well as instructional techniques in both academic and nonacademic areas. As a result the teacher may become more sensitive to the unique learning style of the handicapped student and, with guidance from the consultant, begin to see how each student's needs can be addressed systematically.

Finally, by addressing the three areas in the definition the consultant will be able to focus on preventative measures the regular teacher can use to reduce possible classroom management problems as well as enhance the learning atmosphere. Presently, consultants spend a disproportionate amount of time trying to help teachers solve problems that might have been prevented.

Parent benefits. Parents of handicapped students would be likely to accept Heron and Skinner's definition because of the multiple criteria used. In the past, their children have been placed in special classrooms usually on the basis of low achievement scores or poor social behavior. With the new definition the opportunity arises for children to participate in some of the regular curriculum and for the parents to monitor their child's progress. For example, during parent-teacher conferences the parents would be able to ask direct questions about the academic achievement of their child, the level of teacher-student contacts, and social acceptance. The conference would be more structured, and the parents would be able to establish whether the goals of their child's individualized education program were being addressed.

In summary, the terms *mainstreaming* and *least restrictive environment* are not synonymous. While the terms may be interchangeable in everyday use, the professional should approach them with care when making placement and evaluation decisions.

VARIABLES AFFECTING EXCEPTIONAL CHILDREN WITHIN A REGULAR CLASSROOM

Composition of Mainstreamed Classrooms

Mainstreamed classrooms are usually composed of one or more handicapped students. Seldom does the regular education teacher find more than 10 percent of the students in his class identified as handicapped.

The high ratio of regular education students to handicapped students may be deceiving. At first glance it might appear as though only a small percentage of the class will need individualized programs or assistance. Unfortunately, the reverse is almost always the case. Within any regular classroom, even without the inclusion of handicapped children, a range of abilities, skills, and interest levels exists. For example, in a given fifth-grade classroom some students will be doing sixth- or even seventh-grade work, while other students may be doing third-grade work or lower. The majority of the class, however, would fall somewhere in between, as average fifth graders. So, even if handicapped children were never integrated into regular classrooms, a heterogeneous population would already exist there.

The important point here is that the inclusion of the handicapped student may not always serve to extend the heterogeneity of the class. In many cases, the student is integrated for only those subject areas where he can successfully achieve. So, the teacher may have an easier time instructing the handicapped student than he does, say, a low achiever, who has been in the classroom all along. A physically handicapped student who has no loss of cognitive functioning is an example of someone who would be able to perform the intellectual tasks, if not the motor ones, without imposing unduly on the teacher.

Another consideration may be the fact that unidentified handicapped children are in the classroom already. Functionally, therefore, the teacher has to deal with their individual learning needs, regardless of whether or not they are labelled "handicapped."

Teacher attitude. An attitude is defined as a predisposition to behave in a certain way. In the classroom, teacher attitude towards the handicapped student can greatly influence the success or failure of the mainstreaming effort. Numerous studies have been conducted which substantiate the affects of teacher attitude and mainstreaming (Yates, 1973; Shotel, Iano, & McGettigan, 1972; Moore & Fine, 1978).

These studies seem to indicate that when a handicapped student is placed in the regular classroom, teachers may be pessimistic about the student's chance for academic or social success and may even doubt the efficacy of such an integration process. Given these factors, a climate may be established for self-fulfilling prophecies (Jackson, 1968). That is, the handicapped student may do poorly in the regular classroom simply because the teacher acts differentially toward the student. For example, if the student had a learning disability the teacher might give him fewer learning trials, thereby precipitating lower performance.

Changing Teacher Attitudes

One of the more difficult tasks which faces a consultant is to change a teacher's attitude toward having a handicapped student in the classroom. The task is hard for two reasons. First, the teacher may not have much experience with handicapped individuals. Unless there is a handicapped sibling in his family, it is unlikely that he has had much day-to-day exposure to this population. Second, the teacher's preservice course or practicum work in elementary or secondary education probably did not prepare him to teach the handicapped student.[2]

The consultant has a number of options for changing the attitude of the regular educator. These include using the principal as a resource, conducting a pilot study, implementing team teaching, generating parent support, and countercontrol.

Using the principal. By virtue of the principal's position as administrative and instructional leader in the school, she has achieved status with

[2] Current or proposed standards in twenty-five states require course work on educating handicapped students as part of state certification (Smith & Schindler, 1980).

respect to her teachers. In most cases, the principal is perceived as a trustworthy individual, and teachers are usually willing to follow her lead.

A consultant can capitalize on this status and ask the principal to approach the teachers and listen to their concerns about mainstreaming handicapped students. The principal can reassure the teachers that support services and instructional materials are available to assist with the process.

Further, after integration has taken place, the consultant could recommend to the principal that she visit the regular educator's classroom and reinforce the teaching efforts there. The visits need not be long in duration, but they would confirm in the teacher's mind the personal commitment of the principal to see this worthwhile process implemented.

Conducting a pilot study. Despite Stephens's (1977) caution that placements within a regular classroom should not be done on a trial basis, the consultant may choose to implement a pilot study to demonstrate that a regular educator has the instructional knowledge to successfully teach in a mainstreamed setting. For example, the consultant might come to an agreement with a regular educator to conduct a study to determine if a handicapped student could function adequately within one of the classroom reading groups. If the regular educator felt that integration was not possible, the data obtained in the pilot study might persuade her that the handicapped student could indeed learn in the reading group. Thus, the teacher's attitude might change.

Implementing team teaching. Team teaching is a common instructional strategy used in classrooms. It involves two or more teachers who share instructional and evaluative responsibilities for a group of students. By pairing an experienced teacher of the handicapped with a less experienced teacher, the less experienced teacher could gain the skills of the experienced teacher. The experienced teacher could model appropriate planning, instructional, and management techniques, and provide the opportunity for the less experienced teacher to practice these skills in a supportive environment. After gaining confidence and experience with teaching the handicapped student, the teacher's attitude toward integration might be more favorable. Also, she might be more likely to maintain her positive attitude in situations where team teaching was not used.

Generating parent support. Many educators feel isolated from parents. They perceive the tasks the student completes in school as separate from tasks the student completes at home.

By establishing lines of communication between the educator and the parent, the consultant could bridge the gap in the student's program. Moreover, the teacher could perceive that the parents were concerned about their child's performance and willing to work cooperatively with her to help the student.

Countercontrol. *Countercontrol* refers to a specific procedure whereby students are trained to systematically employ behavioral principles to change teacher behavior (Graubard, Rosenberg, & Miller, 1971). Specifically handicapped students might be taught ways to increase the rate of praise by a teacher or decrease the rate of criticism or warnings. In short, they would reinforce the teacher for positively attending to them. While it is acknowledged that countercontrol raises a number of ethical issues, nevertheless a consultant might want to use a modified version of it where teacher resistance has to be changed by a subtle, cost-effective, and systematic procedure.

In summary, the consultant has a variety of options at her disposal for changing a teacher's attitude toward the handicapped. The consultant should not hesitate to use these techniques individually or collectively.

Teacher-Student Interaction in Mainstreamed Classrooms

Very little research has been conducted in the past on teacher-student behavior in regular classrooms where handicapped students were enrolled. Since 1970, however, educational researchers have been investigating the effects of handicapped children on teacher behavior in the classroom.

The quantity and quality of teacher-student interactions in the mainstreamed class are important variables for the consultant to consider. Not only must the consultant be able to adequately index the level of teacher-student interaction, but to apply the correct intervention if the level is not appropriate. A superficial view of the interaction data might give the consultant a false representation of the true interaction pattern in the classroom.

Student-Student Interaction in Mainstreamed Classrooms

Sociometric data collected in mainstreamed settings has yielded some interesting results. For example, Shotel, Iano, and McGettigan (1972) found that EMR children were frequently rejected or actively ignored by their normal peers. They had fewer friends than normal children, and the likelihood of their acquiring new friends in the regular classroom was slim.

Bryan (1974–1977) conducted a series of sociometric studies to determine if the attitudes of normal children toward mildly handicapped children affected their acceptance. In one study, using a population of 1,200 third, fourth, and fifth-grade students in classrooms with at least one learning disabled student, Bryan administered a sociometric scale designed to ascertain social acceptance and social rejection within the classroom. Social acceptance was defined with respect to answers to the following questions: "Who is your favorite friend? Who is fun to be around? Which student in the classroom does everybody like?" Social rejection, on the other hand, was defined with respect to answers to: "Who is not your friend? Who is worried and scared? Which student does nobody want to have around?"

The results indicated that, in general, the learning disabled student received fewer votes for social acceptance and more votes for social rejection than his nonhandicapped peers. Second, white LD females were the most frequently rejected population in the study. White LD boys and girls were rejected more often than black LD boys and girls.

Bruininks (1978) found that LD students, especially boys, rated themselves higher in social status in the regular classroom than the normal children of the same sex rated them. Nonhandicapped students were more accurate in their estimation of their social status in the classroom than the LD children. These findings tend to support Bryan's research. That is, LD students are less socially acceptable than normal students in regular classrooms.

Peterson, Dammer, and Flavell (1972), indicate that LD students may miss subtle communication cues, and that poor role taking (the ability to assume the role of the other person) may account for much of the difficulty mildly handicapped children have with nonhandicapped peers. In short, mildly handicapped students may be unable to perceive the normal student's dislike for their inappropriate behavior, and normal students may be unable to comprehend the unique needs and problems of the mildly handicapped (Kitano, Steihl, & Cole, 1978).

Given the results of these studies, the consultant might be well advised to recommend Kitano et al's. role-taking training be used to foster better social relationships between normal and exceptional students. The role-taking training could increase student sensitivity toward each group's needs and feelings and add a positive dimension to mainstreaming in terms of improved self-esteem for LD's and better social relationships between LD and normal students.

Further, the consultant or supervisor might be able to assist the handicapped student, either directly or indirectly, to discover his social status within the classroom, develop specific behaviors that would positively affect his status, and train him to regulate his behavior.

Data obtained by Bruininks (1978), Kitano et al. (1978) and Bryan and Bryan (1977) indicate that both the verbal and nonverbal behaviors of LD students seem to adversely affect their status and acceptability in the classroom. Thus, the consultant and the regular education teacher need to examine the nature of the verbal and nonverbal exchanges between the handicapped and nonhandicapped students. After an analysis of the data they could jointly plan and implement a program designed to teach each group to recognize and engage in socially acceptable and positively reinforcing verbal and nonverbal exchanges. Presumably if mildly handicapped students were taught to use verbal and nonverbal signals in a constructive fashion their status within the classroom would be enhanced. A number of factors affecting teacher-student and student-student interaction have been presented. Later in this chapter, specific educational alternatives will be offered within a decision-making model for the consultant to use in helping the classroom teacher reduce or eliminate some of the more troublesome factors.

MAINTAINING MILDLY HANDICAPPED STUDENTS WITHIN THE REGULAR CLASSROOM

If an appropriate placement for a handicapped student has been made, what is a consultant to do if the mainstreamed child begins to present problems in the regular classroom that were unanticipated? The following decision-making model offers the consultant a systematic approach to solve the problem.

A Decision-Making Model

Heron (1978) has constructed a decision-making model which supervisors, principals, consultants, or even the teachers themselves can use to solve an array of problems related to integrating the handicapped (See Figure 3–1).

Rationale. The strategies which are listed under each major target population (for example, exceptional child, normal child, and teacher) are arranged hierarchically. The least intrusive technique is listed first, followed by more intrusive measures. More important, the strategies

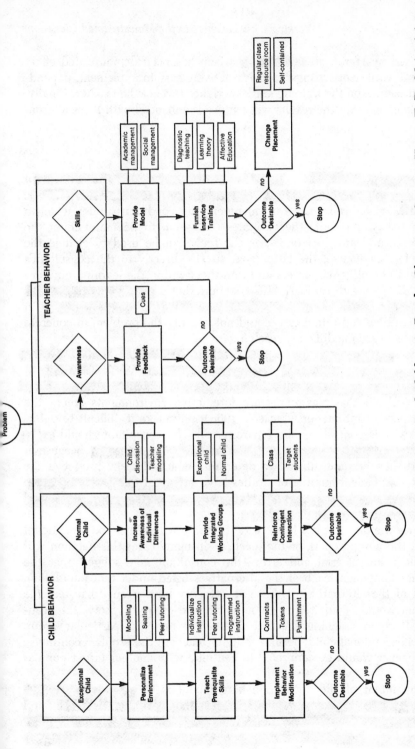

Figure 3–1 Process Approach for Maintaining Mainstreamed Children in Regular Classrooms. SOURCE: Heron, T. E., Maintaining the mainstreamed child in the regular classroom: The decision-making process. *Journal of Learning Disabilities,* 1978, 11(4), p. 213. Reprinted with permission.

proposed by Heron are data based. Each has been demonstrated effective in a variety of settings, each is relatively easy to implement, depending, of course, on the training and experience level of the teacher. Finally, the likelihood that the results will endure is enhanced with these alternatives.

Employing the model. To use the model effectively the consultant must be able to do two things. First, she must be able to identify the problem. Specifically, she can document the conditions under which a given behavior occurs, the variables that seem to be maintaining the behavior, and any variables that she feels can be used to change the behavior. Of course, the latter goal speaks directly to the consultant's ability to identify reinforcers and punishers within the learning environment. Bergan and Tombari (1976) report that a consultant who is able to identify the problem is more likely to come up with a solution. In their study, a consultant who could not identify the problem in concrete terms had extreme difficulty resolving it.

The second task the consultant must perform is to identify the most probable agent for change. In the regular classroom there are three change agents—the exceptional child, the normal child, and the teacher. It is realized that classrooms are interactive environments where the rapid pace of interaction (Jackson, 1968) may make it difficult to determine who is controlling the environment. The consultant should resist the temptation to apply multiple strategies simultaneously because it would then become difficult to determine which strategy produced the effect. A sufficient number of studies have indicated that increases in the teacher's use of a specific technique produce positive, consistent, and enduring effects on student behavior.

Once the decision has been made to begin with either the exceptional child, the normal child, or the teacher—in many cases this decision will be the result of trial and error—the consultant may suggest that the teacher implement each of the alternatives listed under that population. If all of the alternatives within one category have been exhausted, the teacher would be advised to go on to the next group to resolve the problem. If upon reaching the last alternative under a particular group (e. g., exceptional child, normal child, or teacher) the problem continues, the teacher would be counseled to continue with another target population.

The intent of the decision-making model is to provide supervisors with functional alternatives to offer regular education teachers, and preclude the premature removal of a mainstreamed student from a regular setting before a series of alternatives has been systematically attempted.

EDUCATIONAL STRATEGIES FOR EXCEPTIONAL
CHILDREN AND YOUTH

There have been a considerable number of mildly handicapped children
and youth who have been successfully integrated in the regular classroom
at the elementary and secondary level. Successful entry can be attributed
to such factors as the teacher's attitude and ability to provide a specific
remedial approach to solve a specific academic or social problem. A
number of common educational problems are presented in the following
section, as well as teacher strategies and procedures which have been
used successfully.

To illustrate the function of Heron's model, only those instructional or
behavior management strategies referred to in the model will be presented. Readers are referred to Chapter 9 for a more elaborate description of behavior management approaches.

Personalizing the Learning Environment: Alternatives
for the Exceptional Student

Adelman (1971) indicated that a potentially effective strategy to use to
reduce the level of inappropriate social behavior or increase the level
of appropriate academic behavior might be to personalize the learning
environment of the handicapped student. The student would be presented with tasks in a more individualized and structured fashion than
ever before. In short, the handicapped student would have the feeling
that he was receiving the teacher's personal, undivided attention. Three
alternatives which a consultant could recommend to a classroom teacher
to personalize the environment will be discussed: modeling, seating
arrangement, and peer tutoring.

Modeling. One of the most effective techniques that can be used to
teach new behaviors in a personalized fashion is modeling. Unfortunately,
it is an educational strategy many teachers do not use. Simply stated,
when one uses a *modeling* approach, the target student imitates the
behavior of the model.

Bandura (1969) and Stephens (1977) have cited the positive, efficient,
and constructive effects of modeling. In general, it has been found that
modeling works best when the student (or for that matter the teacher) is
able to perform much of the required behavior. Modeling the behavior
serves as a cue to perform the complete sequence efficiently. For example, Blankenship (1978) demonstrated that a modeling plus feedback

approach reduced the number of inversion errors made by students during subtraction computation. Essentially, what Blankenship did was write a problem, such as $37-9 = $ ————, and then verbalize each step of the procedure in front of the student. The student was then able to complete several examples independently.

Another interesting result was that the modeling procedure only involved an average of thirty-five seconds per day per child. Additionally, Blankenship noted that the skills acquired by a majority of the students during training generalized to higher order math problems.

Seating. The physical size, configuration, and arrangement of seats within a classroom may be important factors in learning new behaviors. This may be especially true for low-achieving or handicapped students. Low achievers, for example, tend to improve academically as their seats are moved from the back of the room toward the front. As a rule, the closer they come to the teacher and the closer they come to the stimuli to which they have to attend, the better their performance becomes.

If a teacher were interested in increasing the verbal behavior of a handicapped student during "show and tell" or classroom discussion times, the consultant might suggest that a student with high verbal ability sit across the table from a student with low verbal skills, rather than beside him. Studies done in group dynamics and sociometry (e.g., Steinzor, 1950) indicate that communication flows across the table rather than around it. Apparently, the low verbal student picks up gestural, facial, and verbal messages from the high verbal student, thereby increasing his likelihood of an oral response.

Peer tutoring. For many teachers the term *peer tutoring* means one student helping another student with a given subject area or problem. The scenario in the classroom usually unfolds as follows: "Sally, will you give Kristin a hand with her science project?" or "Bill, will you help Meg with her multiplication facts?"

While this type of approach may offer relief to the overworked teacher and frustrated student, the effects are only temporary because the student will probably need help for the same problem again in the future. Further, since the teacher does not have control over the instruction, it is difficult to tell whether any substantial teaching has taken place.

Alternatively, Parson and Heward (1979) and Heron, Heward, and Cooke (1980) have developed and field-tested a peer-training program which consultants could teach to regular education teachers in a short time. Teachers, in turn, can instruct students in the essential components of peer tutoring—preparation, prompting, praising, testing, and plotting behaviors.

A classwide peer-tutoring program can be established after students have participated in a thirty-minute orientation session and three to five thirty-minute training sessions. During training, tutors learn to gather the necessary materials such as flash cards, pencils, and folders. Next, they learn to use a two-step prompting strategy that provides the student with another chance or gives him the correct answer to the item he failed to identify. Then, tutors learn to praise their student for correct responses on an intermittent basis (after every three correct responses), and at the end of the tutoring session. Tutors also learn to conduct a brief test, and to record the results of the test on a cumulative graph.

The training can be conducted with either large or small groups using modeling, role playing, practice, and feedback. Parson and Heward (1979), Heron et al. (1980), and Ellis (1980) indicate that this systematic training approach can be very effective in teaching tutoring skills to children. After training, tutors were able to perform all behaviors independently. A minimum of teacher involvement was necessary to maintain performance.

Teaching Academic Skills

Since comprehensive data are collected during the multi-factored evaluation prior to placement, it is reasonable to suspect that the teacher would have an accurate indication of the student's academic strengths and weaknesses. Unfortunately, if the data were derived exclusively from norm-referenced (standardized) tests, an unbalanced view of the student's performance might be obtained, because these tests usually indicate the student's frustration level. The teachers would have to translate the test findings into daily lessons.

It is possible that a student could be placed in a regular classroom lacking specific prerequisite skills. The consultant might recommend to the classroom teacher that programmed instruction, individualized instruction, and peer tutoring[3] be implemented to improve academic performance.

Programmed instruction. *Programmed instruction* refers to the logical arrangement of material into small steps; at each step the reader obtains information, responds to it, and receives feedback on his performance. At one time, programmed instruction was hailed as the savior of the American educational system. It seemed as though technology was finally coming to the classroom in the form of programmed readers, mathematics texts, science curricula and a host of other programmed materials. For reasons that are complex and beyond the scope of this book, suffice

[3] The reader is referred to Heward, Heron, and Cooke (1980) for a discussion of "tutor-huddle," a key element in a classwide peer-tutoring system.

it to say that programmed materials have remained a supplemental rather than a primary source of instruction.

Nevertheless, it should be recognized that programmed texts offer several advantages for the teacher and the student. First, if the programmed materials are written competently, students can progress at their own paces. Within a heterogeneous class, a resource like a programmed text for teaching specific reading skills allows the teacher to give instruction to individual students without impeding the learning rate of others. Second, student frustration with difficult concepts or skills could be reduced if the frames within the programmed text build on skills or knowledge previously learned and do not proceed too rapidly from skill to skill. Finally, programmed texts usually progress gradually so that the correct response for an item helps the student answer the next item, or they provide an answer key for students to refer to. In either case, the student is able to check his own responses.

Individualizing instruction. Ask 100 professionals what they mean by individualizing instruction and you are likely to obtain 100 different responses. In this book, *individualized instruction* refers to a teacher's skill in structuring learning tasks that match student comprehension and response capabilities. For example, if a student had a short attention span and was easily distracted, the consultant might suggest that lessons be presented which are varied in format, of short duration, and limited in abstract content. The mode of presentation and the expected mode of response are integral components of individualizing instruction.

Further, a teacher may require different responses from different students based on his knowledge of the task and response requirements. For instance, if the teacher were having difficulty instructing a geography class at the junior high school level, the consultant might recommend that he require one student to supply an answer to a question, whereas another student would only have to choose among alternative answers. In the former case a recall response is required; in the latter instance a recognition is required. The authors define individualizing instruction as the teacher providing the least intrusive, yet most powerful, prompt to increase the probability that a student will respond correctly. The issues of individualized instruction at the elementary and secondary level are addressed more completely in Chapters 6 and 7.

Implementing Behavior Management Techniques

The use of behavior management techniques in regular and special classrooms has increased since 1968. The use of a behavioral approach in special education settings has been shown to be consistently effective (see Kazdin & Craighead, 1973). Three behavior management strategies that have been used successfully at the elementary and secondary level will be discussed below. A more thorough description of these and other behavior management approaches will be found in Chapter 9.

Contracts. Contingency contracting is a term used to define a situation in which teachers (or parents) and students negotiate task and response requirements. Contracts can either be verbal or written, although most educators (e.g., Homme et al., 1969; Dardig & Heward, 1976) recommend the written contract because of the documentation it provides.

In essence, a contract is a "when-then" statement of agreement: "When you finish your math assignment, then you will earn fifteen minutes of recess." Another term for contracting is "Grandma's Law."

Tokens. Numerous authors have demonstrated the efficacy of token reinforcement programs in changing academic and social behavior. The essential feature of the token economy is that the student receives an interim reward (a token, chip, or check mark) which can later be exchanged for a back-up reinforcer. For example, a behaviorally disordered student may earn three check marks for good academic behavior which can be exchanged for three minutes of free time at the end of the period. Token programs have been successful with students who do not respond to conventional reinforcers in school, such as grades or teacher praise, and who have a long history of academic or social failure. For a review of token systems the reader is referred to Chapter 9 in this text, Axelrod (1971), and Kazdin and Bootzin (1972).

Punishment. The term punishment has a number of meanings for the educator. According to Sulzer-Azaroff and Mayer (1977) the common definition of punishment refers to physical pain. Heron (1978), however, indicated that if a functional definition of the term were employed at least three procedures could be considered punishing: (1) contingent application of an aversive stimulus; (2) contingent removal of a specific amount of reinforcement; and (3) contingent removal of the opportunity to earn reinforcement for a specific time period. If the likelihood of an inappropriate response is decreased after the application of any of these procedures, then punishment has taken place. Conversely, if one of these procedures is employed and the student's undesirable behavior continues, then punishment has not taken place.

ALTERNATIVES FOR NORMAL STUDENTS

One reason for the variability of behavior in the classroom is that all students enter the learning environment with different needs and expectations. Competent teachers attempt to address these needs. However, in doing so they often times precipitate problems. For example, students, especially in junior and senior high school, are not always able to reconcile the teacher's differential treatment of their peers. That is, the teacher might require neater papers, faster answers, and more participation from one student, and a different set of responses from others. Students often complain that the teacher is unfair, or that he likes one student more than another. Unfortunately, some students are unwilling to accept the teacher's actions. Hence, the sensitivity they might have to individual differences is compromised.

Increasing Awareness of Individual Difference

As stated previously, Kitano et al. (1978) indicated that a prerequisite skill for developing effective interaction may be the ability to assume the role of the other person. According to Kitano et al. there is little research that indicates that normal children without training are able to comprehend the needs and feelings of handicapped children. Some strategies that have been shown to be effective in increasing student awareness of individual differences will be addressed below.

Class discussion. Class discussion can be an effective way to increase student awareness of individual differences. Using the *Peabody Language Development Kit* (PLDK), or the kit, *Developing Understanding of Self and Others* (DUSO), a consultant might recommend that the teacher structure discussions on the nature of individual difference without pointing out a particular child in the class. For instance, if the teacher were interested in having the normal students reduce the amount of badgering they inflict on a handicapped student, he might present a lesson from one of the kits that portrays a handicapped student attempting to play with friends. Using a scene that shows a handicapped child being ridiculed by the other children on the block, the teacher might open the discussion by asking a question such as, "How would you feel if you were teased by your friends?"

Teacher modeling. Modeling can be an effective procedure to employ when many of the prerequisite behaviors exist in the student's repertoire. So, a consultant might suggest that the teacher model appropriate verbal and nonverbal interactions with exceptional and normal students.

Provide Integrated Working Groups

One way to increase the probability of mainstreaming students is to set the occasion whereby exceptional students can work on projects with normal students. Bruininks (1978) indicates that cooperative learning in small groups fosters social integration and academic achievement. For example, the consultant might plan a newspaper project with the regular teacher where each student in the group, handicapped and nonhandicapped, was given tasks within his capabilities. If the exceptional student was a good artist, she might be art editor, while the nonhandicapped students might serve as proofreaders, sports editors, or circulation editors. Each group would see the other contributing a portion of work toward a common goal.

Exceptional child. The benefits derived by the exceptional child while participating in a small, integrated working group are many. First, it provides the opportunity for the exceptional student to gain public recognition from his peers for his contribution to the project. Second, it fosters the notion that school is not an environment where ridicule and rejection are constantly encountered. Third, as a member of the group, the handicapped student would not be fully responsible for the group effort. His successful participation in the project could be assured if the teacher structured the requirements with the exceptional child's abilities and deficits in mind.

Normal child. In any social or academic situation where the less skilled or less talented are paired with the more skilled or more talented, it is frequently assumed that the former group will derive all of the benefits of the interaction while the latter will not derive any. Unfortunately, this misconception continues to exist despite some fairly conclusive evidence to the contrary (Greenwood, Sloan, & Baskin, 1974).

Davis (1972), for example, noted that academic gains were made by student tutors as well as student tutees. Also, according to Kitano et al. (1978) nonhandicapped children may need role-taking training to increase their sensitivity to the unique needs and problems of the mildly handicapped. Such training might serve to teach them about the differences which exist among people, and provide them with practice in dealing with these differences on a day-to-day basis.

Reinforce Contingent Interaction

Sometimes it is necessary for the consultant to suggest that the regular teacher structure situations so that the class as a whole or individual students earn reinforcement. Under these circumstances students would earn free time, classroom privileges, or be excused from assignments (negative reinforcement) contingent upon an interaction with a mainstreamed student.

Consultants, of course, realize that the encounters between mainstreamed and normal students may not be of long duration, perhaps just saying "hello" or asking to borrow a pencil. Therefore, the teacher needs to be aware of this behavior so that the rewards are appropriately dispensed.

Class. Having the whole class share the reward earned by a student who interacted with an exceptional child is an excellent way to foster social acceptance of the mainstreamed child in the classroom. (See Chapter 9, group contingencies for more detail.) Operationally, this contingency would establish that classroom reinforcers could be earned and pooled for each positive encounter with the mainstreamed student. At best, peer group pressure would be exerted to earn reinforcers for the class. At worst, the exceptional student would be tolerated, rather than actively abused. If an individual within a group behaves negatively toward another person or group of persons and is subsequently rewarded for behaving positively, it is likely that his attitude will become more consistent with his behavior (Goldstein & Sorcher, 1974).

Target students. Frequently, the successful entry of mainstreamed students is impeded by one or two normal students who hold high status in the class, and exert a great deal of influence over it. In this case, the consultant might recommend that the teacher consider a reinforcement approach for these individuals alone. The contingencies mentioned beforehand could be applied in much the same manner. The only difference is that the rewards are now earned by individuals. (See Chapter 9, individual contingencies for more detail.)

ALTERNATIVES FOR THE TEACHER

Thus far, we have discussed educational strategies that the consultant can recommend to the classroom teacher for consideration. If all the procedures suggested have been tried without success, the consultant's last alternative would be to provide strategies directed toward changing the behavior of the classroom teacher himself. While the prime targets mentioned earlier have been the students in the classroom, now the emphasis for intervention is on the regular classroom teacher.

Providing Feedback

Brophy and Good (1974) cite three reasons why the teacher's awareness of classroom interaction is frequently low: (1) the rapid pace of classroom events; (2) poor preservice training; and (3) lack of conceptual understanding by teachers of what should be going on in the classroom. Unfortunately, these three deficiencies combine in a way that makes for reactive teaching rather than proactive teaching. In reactive teaching, the teacher simply responds to behavior that occurs in the classroom. In proactive teaching the teacher is constantly anticipating events and structuring tasks to maximize instruction.

Many regular education teachers are unfamiliar with the patterns of classroom interaction, and consequently give more attention to some students than to others. As Brophy and Good suggest, there are a host of variables which contribute to the disproportional interaction which occurs in the classroom. They also state that if teachers received *feedback,* information pertinent to improving their skills, the patterns of interaction they are displaying in the classroom would change. It is as if they were saying to themselves, "Oh, I didn't know I was doing that!" Data reported by Heron and Skinner (1978) would substantiate this position. Although some techniques are more intrusive than others or require the assistance of ancillary personnel in the classroom, there are a number of ways of providing in-class feedback to teachers. All present cues to the teacher during the instructional period rather than after it.

Cues. Educational researchers have demonstrated that providing verbal or nonverbal cues to teachers as they work can have a profound impact on the quality of instruction which takes place. A *cue* is any prompt or instruction that sets the occasion for a behavior to occur. For example, Van Houten and Sullivan (1975) reported a procedure where contingent upon a preestablished buzzing of the school intercom a praise statement was issued to a target student in the class. This audio cue served as a prompt to remind the teacher to praise the target student in the class.

Other cueing strategies have used similar approaches with a similar result. Where school intercoms are unavailable or the teacher feels that the buzz would be too distracting, an alternative approach could be recommended by the consultant. Or the teacher can simply use a tape recorder with a blank tape. Every five minutes (or whatever other interval the teacher would prefer), he makes a sound on the tape. The blank tape continues and again at the next five-minute interval the sound is repeated. This process continues until the tape is expended. Then the teacher rewinds the tape which has all the intervals present. When the teacher begins instruction, he starts the tape recorder, and the audio cues are delivered at the established intervals.

It should be realized, however, that often the regular education teacher may need to have his skills expanded to more adequately serve the needs of the exceptional student. In no way should this statement be construed to mean that regular education teachers are unskilled. However, some teachers, although willing to accept mainstreamed students into their classrooms, lack the diagnostic and prescriptive teaching skills necessary to do a competent job.

The consultant faced with this challenge has two alternatives. He can provide a model for the regular classroom teacher to imitate, or he can enhance skill development in the teacher through additional in-service training.

Modeling. As stated previously, modeling can be an effective instructional strategy when the teacher already possesses many of the component behaviors in his repertoire. The modeling procedure involves having the consultant demonstrate the appropriate instructional behaviors for the teacher to imitate. Subsequently, the teacher receives feedback on how well the behavior was imitated.

Furnish in-service training. Every school district must provide a program of continued education for its teachers. Most school districts or regions provide at least one in-service day per year where teachers attend professional meetings to enhance their teaching skills. Where teachers have a voice in establishing the in-service program, the training is usually beneficial.

For in-service training to be optimally effective, teachers must have the opportunity to practice the skills presented, and they must receive feedback and reinforcement for their attempts and accomplishments. It cannot be assumed that skills learned in one instructional setting—in-service training—will automatically be transferred to another instructional setting—the classroom. As Baer, Wolf, and Risley (1968) state, "generalization should be programmed rather than expected or lamented" (p. 97).

SUMMARY

The subtle difference between the terms *mainstreamed classroom* and *least restrictive environment* were discussed. A new definition for least restrictive environment focused on observable and measurable behaviors within the classroom. The issue of teacher-student interaction in the least restrictive environment was presented as a variable which seems to affect successful mainstreaming.

The consultant's role in facilitating the integration process was discussed as were specific strategies a consultant could recommend to a regular educator. Finally a decision-making model for maintaining handicapped students in the least restrictive environment was described. Techniques which a consultant could suggest were presented within this model.

Questions

---

1. How do Kaufman et al. define the term *mainstreaming?*

2. According to the regulations published in the *Federal Register*, the least restrictive environment is defined by two criteria. Name these criteria.

3. List two reasons why parents might be anxious about having their son or daughter integrated in a regular classroom.

4. Differentiate between the Heron et al. definition of least restrictive environment and the criteria set by the *Federal Register.*

5. Give a brief synopsis of the research on teacher-student interaction in the regular classroom, especially with mildly handicapped children present.

6. What factors contribute to the social rejection mildly handicapped students frequently experience in the regular classroom?

7. Given that social interactions between mildly handicapped students and normal students are often strained, what suggestions have been offered to improve this situation?

8. Outline three functional recommendations a consultant could offer to a regular education teacher to help manage the academic and social behavior of a handicapped student.

9. Describe Heron's model for maintaining mildly handicapped children in the regular classroom.

Discussion Points and Exercises

---

1. How would service delivery to mildly handicapped students be enhanced (or impeded) if Heron et al.'s definition of the least restrictive environment were employed?

2. In-service training for regular education teachers is essential if integration programs are going to be successful. Discuss how a consultant could determine the in-service needs for her teachers.

3. It is sometimes said that regular education teachers, though competent with normal students, lack the skills to serve the mildly handicapped. What skills and attitudes are essential for a teacher if mainstreaming is to be a successful educational alternative?

4. Counter an argument offered by a regular educator who stated that the handicapped should be educated in separate facilities using specially trained teachers and unique equipment.

5. Observe in a classroom the interaction patterns which exist among students. Then choose two students, one who is receiving a disproportionate amount of teacher's attention and one who is not. Suggest to the regular education teacher that he shift his pattern of attention to meet the assessed needs of all students.

6. Conduct a sociometric analysis of a regular classroom using a peer-nominating procedure to determine degree of social acceptance and rejection within the class. Compare these data with classroom observations. With the teacher design an intervention to reduce or eliminate the degree of social rejection. Use modeling and integrated working groups for your intervention.

7. Collect data on teacher attitudes toward accepting handicapped children and youth in the classroom. Arrange to have the school principal visit mainstreamed classrooms regularly to reinforce teaching efforts. Reassess the teachers to note the effect of the principal's visit.

8. Present a fifteen-minute videotape to a group of regular educators, perhaps junior high science teachers, depicting a science class with a handicapped student. Ask the teachers to identify the positive teaching behaviors (prompts, reinforcers, etc.) that the instructor used, and to state how the lesson could have been presented differently. Focus the teachers' attention on specific instructional techniques that were used to enhance the lesson.

REFERENCES

ADELMAN, H. The not so specific learning disability population. *Exceptional Children*, 1971, 37 (7), 528–533.

AXELROD, S. Token reinforcement programs in special classes. *Exceptional Children*, 1971, 37, 371–379.

BAER, D., WOLF, M., & RISLEY, T. Some current dimensions of applied behavioral analysis. *Journal of Applied Behavior Analysis,* 1968, 1, 91–97.

BANDURA, A. *Principles of behavior modification.* New York: Holt, Rinehart & Winston, 1969.

BERGAN, J. R., & TOMBARI, M. L. Consultant skill and efficiency and the implementation and outcomes of consultation. *Journal of School Psychology,* 1976, 14, 3–14.

BLANKENSHIP, C. S. Remediating systematic inversion errors in subtraction through the use of demonstration and feedback, *Learning Disability Quarterly,* 1978, *1* (3), 12–22.

BRODEN, M., COPELAND, G., BEASLEY, A., & HALL, R. V. Altering student responses through changes in teacher verbal behavior. *Journal of Applied Behavior Analysis,* 1977, 10, 479–487.

BROPHY, J., & GOOD, T. *Teacher-student relationships: Causes and consequences,* New York: Holt, Rinehart & Winston, 1974.

BRUININKS, V. L. Actual and perceived peer status of learning disabled students in mainstreamed programs. *Journal of Special Education.* 1978, *12* (1), 51–58.

BRYAN, T. An observational analysis of classroom behaviors of children with learning disabilities. *Journal of Learning Disabilities.* 1974a, 7, 26–34.

BRYAN, J., & BRYAN, T. The social-emotional side of learning disabilities. *Behavior Disorders.* 1977, 2, 141–145.

BRYAN, T., WHEELER, R., FELCAN, J., & HENEK, T. "Come on Dummy": An observational study of children's communication. *Journal of Learning Disabilities,* 1976, 9, (10), 661–669.

CHAPMAN, R. B., LARSEN, S. C., & PARKER, R. M. Interaction of first-grade teachers with learning disordered children. *Journal of Learning Disabilities,* 1979, 12 (4), 20–25.

CORMAN, L., & GOTTLIEB, J. Mainstreaming mentally retarded children: A review of research. *American Journal of Mental Deficiency,* 1978, 3, 251–275.

COSSAIRT, A., HALL, R. V., & HOPKINS, B. L. The effects of experimenter's instructions, feedback, and praise on teacher praise and student attending behavior. *Journal of Applied Behavior Analysis,* 1973, 6, 89–100.

DARDIG, J., & HEWARD, W. L. *Sign here: A contracting book for children and their parents.* Kalamazoo, Michigan: Behaviordelia, 1976.

DAVIS, M. Effects of having one remedial student tutor another remedial student. In G. Semb (Ed.), *Behavior Analysis and Education—1972.* Lawrence: University of Kansas, Department of Human Development, 1972.

DUNCAN, M., & BIDDLE, B. *The study of teaching.* New York: Holt, Rinehart & Winston, 1974.

ELLIS, D. E. Peer tutoring: The effect of praise on the academic achievement and social structure of a first-grade classroom. Unpublished masters thesis, The Ohio State University, 1980.

Federal Register, Vol. 42, No. 163, paragraph 121a. 533, August 23, 1977.

Federal Register, Vol. 42, No. 163, paragraph 121a. 550 (1), (2), August 23, 1977.

GOLDSTEIN, A. P., & SORCHER, M. *Changing Supervisor Behavior,* New York: Pergamom Press, Inc., 1974.

GOODMAN, H., GOTTLIEB, J., & HARRISON, R. The social acceptance of EMR's into a nongraded elementary school. *American Journal of Mental Deficiency,* 1972, 76, 412–417.

GRAUBARD, P. S., ROSENBERG, H., & MILLER, M. B. Student applications of behavior modification to teachers and environments or ecological approaches to deviancy. In E. A. Ramp & B. L. Hopkins (Eds.), *A new direction for education: Behavior analysis,* 1971, Lawrence: University of Kansas, 1971, 80–101.

GREENWOOD, C. R., SLOANE, H. N., JR., & BASKINS, A. Training elementary aged peer behavior managers to control small group programmed mathematics. *Journal of Applied Behavior Analysis,* 1974, 7, 103–114.

HERON, T. E. Maintaining mildly handicapped children in the regular classroom: A decision making process. *Journal of Learning Disabilities,* 1978, 11, 210–216.

HERON, T. E. Punishment: A review of the literature with implications for the teacher of mainstreamed children. *Journal of Special Education,* 1978, 12, 243–252.

HERON, T. E., & SKINNER, M. E. Mainstreaming the learning disabled child: Effects on teacher-student interaction and student classroom behavior. Paper presented at the Kentucky Federation Council for Exceptional Children Conference, April, 1979.

HERON, T. E. & SKINNER, M. E. Criteria for defining the regular classroom as the least restrictive environment for LD students. *Learning Disability Quarterly,* 1981, 4 (2), 115–121.

HERON, T. E., HEWARD, W. L., & COOKE, N. L. A classwide peer tutoring system. Paper presented at the Sixth Annual Meeting of the Association of Behavior Analysis, Dearborn, Michigan, May, 1980.

HEWARD, W. L., HERON, T. E., & COOKE, N. L. Tutor huddle: Key element in a classwide peer tutoring system. *The Elementary School Journal,* 1981, (in press).

HOMME, L., CSANYI, A., GONZALES, M., & RECHS, J. *How to use contingency contracting in the classroom.* Champaign, Illinois: Research Press, 1970.

IANO, R., AYERS, D., HELLER, H., McGETTIGAN, J., & WALKER, V. Sociometric status of retarded children in an integrative program. *Exceptional Children,* 1974, 40, 267–271.

IWATA, B. A., & BAILEY, J. S. Reward versus cost token systems: An analysis of the effects on students and teacher. *Journal of Applied Behavior Analysis,* 1974, 7, 567–576.

JACKSON, P. *Life in Classroom.* New York: Holt, Rinehart & Winston, 1968.

KAUFMAN, M. J., GOTTLIEB, J., AGARD, J. A., & KUKIC, M. B. Mainstreaming: Toward an explication of the construct. *Focus on Exceptional Children,* 1975, 7, 1–12.

KAZDIN, A. E., & BOOTZIN, R. R. The token economy: An evaluative review. *Journal of Applied Behavior Analysis,* 1972, 5, 343–372.

KAZDIN, A. E., & CRAIGHEAD, W. E. Behavior modification in special education. In L. Mann and D. Sabatino (Eds.), *The first review of special education.* Philadelphia: JSE Press, 1973.

KENOWITZ, L. A., ZWEIKEL, S., & EDGAR, E. Determining the least restrictive educational opportunity for the severely and profoundly handicapped. In N. G. Haring and D. D. Bricker (Eds.), *Teaching the Severely Handicapped.* Volume III. Columbus, Ohio: Special Press, 1978.

KEOGH, B. K., & LEVITT, M. L. Special education in the mainstream: A confrontation of limitations? *Focus on Exceptional Children,* 1976, 8, 1–11.

KIRBY, F. D., & TOLER, H. C. Modification of preschool isolate behavior: A case study. *Journal of Applied Behavior Analysis,* 1970, 3 (4), 309–314.

KITANO, M. D., STEIHL, J., & COLE, J. T. Role taking: Implications for special education. *Journal of Special Education,* 1978, 12 (1), 59–74.

LILLY, S. *Classroom sociometry: A research related review of theory and practice.* Eugene, Oregon: Northwest Regional Special Education Instructional Materials Center, 1970.

LONG, J. D., & WILLIAMS, R. L. The comparative effectiveness of group and individually contingent free time with inner-city junior high school students. *Journal of Applied Behavior Analysis,* 1973, 6, 465–474.

MACMILLAN, D. L., & BECKER, L. D. Mainstreaming the mildly handicapped learner. In R. D. Kneedler and S. G. Tarver (Eds.), *Changing perspectives in special education.* Columbus, Ohio: Charles E. Merrill, 1977.

MADSEN, C. H., BECKER, W. C., & THOMAS, D. R. Rules, praise, and ignoring: Elements of elementary classroom control. *Journal of Applied Behavior Analysis,* 1968, 1, 139–150.

MARTIN, E. W. Some thoughts on mainstreaming. *Exceptional Children,* 1974. 41, 150–153.

MASSAD, V. E., & ETSEL, B. C. Acquisition of phonetic sounds by preschool children. Effects of response and reinforcement frequency. In G. Semb (Ed.), *Behavior Analysis and Education–1972.* Lawrence: The University of Kansas, Department of Human Development, 1972.

MCGINITY, A. N., & KEOGH, B. K. *Needs assessment for in-service training: A first step for mainstreaming exceptional children into regular education.* Technical Report, University of California, Los Angeles, 1975.

MCLAUGHLIN, T., & MALABY, J. Reducing and measuring inappropriate verbalizations in a token classroom. *Journal of Applied Behavior Analysis,* 1972, 5, 329–333.

MOORE, J., & FINE, M. Regular and special class teachers' perceptions of normal and exceptional children and their attitudes toward mainstreaming. *Psychology in the Schools,* 1978, 15, 253–259.

OSBOURNE, J. G. Free-time as a reinforcer in the management of classroom behavior. *Journal of Applied Behavior Analysis,* 1969, 2, 113–118.

PARSON, L. R., & HEWARD, W. L. Training peers to tutor: Evaluation of a tutor training package for primary learning disabled students. *Journal of Applied Behavior Analysis,* 1979, 12, 309–310.

PETERSON, C. L., DAMMER, F. W., & FLAVELL, J. H. Developmental changes in children's response to three indications of communicative failure. *Child Development,* 1972, 43, 1463–1468.

PUBLIC LAW 94–142. Education of All Handicapped Children Act of 1975. 94th Congress, 1st session, 1975.

SCHMUCK, R. A., & SCHMUCK, P. A. *Group Processes in the Classroom.* Dubuque, Iowa: William C. Brown, 1975.

SHOTEL, J., IANO, R., & McGETTIGAN, J. Teacher attitudes associated with the integration of handicapped children. *Exceptional Children,* 1972, 38, 677–683.

SMITH, J. E., & SCHINDLER, W. J. Certification requirements of general educators concerning exceptional pupils. *Exceptional Children,* 1980, 46, (5), 394–396.

STEINZOR, B. The spatial factor in face to face discussion groups. *Journal of Abnormal Social Psychology,* 1950, 45, 552–555.

STEPHENS, T. M. *Teaching skills to children with learning and behavior disorders.* Columbus, Ohio: Charles E. Merrill, 1977.

SULZER-AZAROFF, B., & MAYER, R. *Applying behavior analysis procedures with children and youth.* New York: Holt, Rinehart & Winston, 1977.

TOFFLER, A. *Future shock.* New York: Random House, 1970.

TURNBULL, A. P., & SCHULZ, J. B. *Mainstreaming handicapped students: A guide for the classroom teacher.* Boston: Allyn and Bacon, 1979.

VAN HOUTEN, R., & SULLIVAN, K. Effects of an audio cueing system on the rate of teacher praise. *Journal of Applied Behavior Analysis,* 1975, 8, 197–202.

YATES, J. Model for preparing regular classroom teachers for mainstreaming. *Exceptional Children,* 1973, 39, 471–472.

4

Working with Teachers in Self-Contained Special Education Classrooms

---

Despite the active efforts to mainstream handicapped students, placement within self-contained special education settings may sometimes be more appropriate for them. For example, a regular education placement of a deaf student, who has not fully mastered communication techniques with hearing individuals, may not necessarily be supportive. The student's learning potential could be seriously compromised without the special instruction offered by a teacher in a self-contained classroom.

Special education classrooms have fewer students, specially trained and certified teachers, and often special equipment so that the unique learning needs of the students can be met. Programs in self-contained classrooms vary widely depending on the disabilities of the students, but one common objective is to provide intensive, diagnostic-prescriptive instruction so that students will be able to compensate for their specific disabilities. For example, a blind or visually impaired student may receive mobility and orientation training so that he will be able to function within a sighted world.

Since the ultimate goal of placing a student in a self-contained classroom is to eventually move him to a less restrictive setting—a process referred to as normalization—the emphasis in this chapter will be on techniques a consultant can use with special educators to develop functional Individualized Education Programs and increase generalization and maintenance of skills. Ways in which a consultant can assist the special education teacher with academic and social programming will also be addressed.

77

Objectives

After reading this chapter the reader will be able to:

1. cite a rationale for self-contained classrooms within the service delivery hierarchy.

2. define the term *self-contained classroom* and provide two examples.

3. identify several educational areas in need of assessment (e.g., academic achievement, learning style, and preferred reinforcers).

4. distinguish between an annual goal and a short-term objective.

5. provide four suggestions for programming for generalization within the self-contained classroom.

Key Terms

Self-contained classroom	Short-term objective
Mastery	Response generalization
Learning style	Situational generalization
Preferred reinforcer	Intermittent schedule of
Annual goal	reinforcement

DEFINITION OF SELF-CONTAINED CLASSROOMS

According to Turnbull and Schultz (1979) *self-contained classrooms* are instructional settings which serve students who have substantial handicapping conditions and for whom placement in less restrictive settings is inappropriate. Wallace and McLoughlin (1979) state that the self-contained special education classroom is only one placement option on a continuum. According to these authors the self-contained class offers instruction which differs in kind and intensity from other alternatives. Self-contained classrooms exist for all types of handicapping conditions (blind, learning disabled, physically impaired, etc.).

Advantages of self-contained classrooms. Self-contained classrooms are usually structured to minimize distraction and increase individualized attention (Heward & Orlansky, 1980). Since the entire academic program is usually taught by one teacher, the student does not have to relate to several adults during the course of the day. For many learning and behavior disordered students who have difficulty establishing and maintaining social relationships, the one teacher can be an advantage.

In instances where special classes are formed categorically, that is, separate classes for each handicapping condition, a specific educational orientation may prevail (Stephens, 1977). A specific instructional or educational orientation, such as diagnostic-prescriptive teaching, may be of benefit to students for whom conventional approaches have failed.

Disadvantages of self-contained classrooms. Several authors have indicated that one of the main disadvantages of self-contained placements for handicapped students is the likelihood that the assignment may be permanent (Stephens, 1977; Wallace & McLoughlin, 1979; Heward & Orlansky, 1980). The apprehension about permanent placement is especially critical if poor or minority group students are placed in this setting because of the stigma which such placements have acquired (Wiederholt, Hammill, & Brown, 1978). Wallace and McLoughlin (1979) indicate that the teaching responsibilities of the self-contained special education teacher are not nearly as comprehensive as that of the resource room teacher. Generally speaking, self-contained special education teachers have fewer direct contacts with regular educators insofar as their students are concerned.

Despite some inherent drawbacks with the self-contained classroom, it continues to be an option for some handicapped students. Smith and Arkans (1974) indicate that it should not be abandoned on the hierarchy of service delivery alternatives.

Assuming that a handicapped student is considered for placement within a self-contained classroom the consultant can provide invaluable assistance to the IEP team by helping it develop, implement, refine, and evaluate the student's individualized program.

HELPING TEACHERS TO DEVELOP THE INDIVIDUALIZED EDUCATION PROGRAM

Before an Individualized Education Program can be implemented successfully three major steps must be taken. First, an initial assessment of the student's performance levels must take place. Second, assessment data must be analyzed so that annual goals and short-term objectives can be determined and resources identified to meet these goals. Third, an IEP meeting must be planned and conducted to develop the specific program which will be aimed at remediating the student's known deficits.

Consultants and supervisors can be of service to special educators in each of these areas. For example, a consultant can recommend that a draft of the IEP be mailed to the parents prior to the meeting so that they can share the team's view of the program. Figure 4–1 illustrates a working draft of this kind.

Also, the consultant can indicate to teachers how complex, and sometimes confusing, information can be integrated so that a functional program can be developed and presented to the parents. Finally, the consultant can assist in recommending related services, and provide technical assistance with developing and evaluating the IEP long and short-term goals.

Conducting the Initial Assessment

According to Wiederholt, Hammill, and Brown (1978) assessment refers to the range of tasks which a teacher performs to obtain data to enhance instruction. These tasks include administering and interpreting norm and criterion-referenced tests, conducting observations in the classroom, interviewing the students, the teacher, or the parents, and using analytic teaching approaches. Since each of these methods for obtaining reliable and valid assessment data has been discussed comprehensively by other authors (e.g., Wiederholt et al., 1978; Wallace & Larsen, 1978; Cooper, 1981), and a consultant usually provides service after the initial assessment, the rest of the chapter will focus on ways a consultant can assist special educators with the following tasks: integrating assessment data, conducting and planning individual programs, and promoting generalization and maintenance.

Figure 4–1 Sample Individualized Education Program (IEP).

Student's Name _____ Date _____

Conference Participants _____ Birthdate _____

_____

_____

Present Education Levels:

    Academic achievement: Reading: Math: Other:

    Emotional maturity:

    Self-help skills:

    Social adaptation:

    Prevocational skills:

    Vocational skills:

    Psychomotor skills:

    Other:

Special education and   Date started   Expected duration
related services

_____ _____ _____

_____ _____ _____

_____ _____ _____

Instructional Area

    Annual goal(s):

    Short-term objectives:

    Instructional methods/materials (optional):

    Evaluation of instructional objectives:

    _____ test, materials, evaluation procedures to be used

    _____ criteria for successful performance

Date for review and/or revision _____

Person responsible for maintenance and implementation: _____

Signature of Parent/Guardian _____ Date _____

Signature of Team Members _____ Date _____

_____ Date _____

_____ Date _____

Integrating Assessment Data and Writing Goal Statements

Conducting the assessment is only half the battle, the other half is to integrate the data so that a functional program can be written. Figure 4–2 shows a summary sheet for Arlene that profiles the student's level of performance, her learning style, preferred reinforcers, objectives for instruction, materials and techniques, and evaluation measures.

Determining strengths. An academic or social strength is that skill or cluster of skills which allows the student to perform independently. According to Stephens (1977) a student functions independently when he is able to complete ninety to ninety-five percent of his assigned tasks without assistance. The term *mastery* is usually reserved for completed tasks which are above ninety-nine percent correct. Strengths can be delineated using a variety of formats. For example, Arlene is able to read competently at the 1.5 reading level on word recognition and comprehension. A general rule of thumb is that the independent level is approximately two levels below the grade equivalent score on the test. Also, she has mastered all blends and consonants in the initial, medial, and final positions (see Figure 4–2).

Determining weaknesses. Technically speaking, performance at an eighty percent success criterion could be considered an instructional level. This means that the student has sufficient knowledge or skill to profit from instruction. The cut-off score to determine a level is somewhat flexible and depends upon the skill to be mastered and the teacher's criterion for success. So, weaknesses are, in a practical sense, those areas or skills which may not be fully developed and which may need further remediation and instruction. In the example shown in Figure 4–2, Arlene has difficulty with words ending in final *e*, and with words that change the *y* to *i* before adding *ly*. In addition, she has difficulty with inferential questions and identifying word parts.

Learning style. According to Barbe and Swassing (1979) students have one of four basic *learning styles*—visual, auditory, kinesthetic, or mixed. While conducting assessments the teacher should note the mannerisms or behaviors the student uses to complete the task because such information can be used in educational programming. Hawisher and Calhoun (1978) indicate that teachers need to consider the number of tasks that are assigned to students, and the rate and mode with which these tasks are to be completed. Students unable to complete a task presented in one fashion might be able to do it when presented differently. For example, a learning disabled student may be unable to supply an

Figure 4–2 Diagnostic Summary Sheet.

Student's name: Arlene M.   Birthdate: 7/6/70
Date: 9/5/80   Grade level: 5th/Resource
Teacher's name: Mr. Franks   room

Reading Strengths
- Reading recog. level, 3.5
- Reading comprehension, 3.0
- Mastered all initial, medial, and final consonants and blends.
- Reads with inflection.

Reading Weaknesses
- Difficulty with inferential questions.
- Unable to apply final e rule
- Unable to identify word parts (syllables)
- Unable to apply plurals to y ending words.

Learner Style

Arlene's performance is enhanced when tasks are issued one at a time, rather than altogether. Seems to rely heavily on visual cues. Providing modes of response which allow her to write or demonstrate might be helpful.

Preferred Reinforcers

Arlene clearly enjoys free time in class. Throughout assessment she stated that playing with games (Battleship, checkers, bingo) were her favorite activities.

Annual Goals
1. By June, Arlene will be able to answer a variety of inferential questions based on her reading series.
2. By June, Arlene will gain proficiency with the application of the final e rule to sight vocabulary.
3. By June, Arlene will be able to identify word parts for polysyllabic words.
4. By June, Arlene will be able to use plurals correctly.

Short-Term Objectives
1. After reading a story (at least 100 words) on her independent level, Arlene will be able to answer three inferential questions with 100 percent accuracy (Target date—11/9/80).
2. Given ten words ending in final e Arlene will be able to apply the final e rule nine percent of the time (Target date—10/10/80).
3. Given ten compound words, presented visually, Arlene will be able to correctly syllabicate eight of them (Target date—9/21/80).
4. Given ten "y" ending words, Arlene will be able to write the correct plural form at ninety percent criterion (Target date—10/5/80).

Materials and Techniques
1. Basal reader
2. Practice worksheets
3. Use visual presentations, expect writing or demonstration responses.

Evaluation Measures
1. Tracking sheet showing date of mastery of each short-term objective.
2. Direct and daily measurement.

answer that requires him to fill in the blank. However, if the student is provided with several visual alternatives, his performance may improve.

Other questions might be: if a student is asked to pronounce a word, does he attempt to sound it out? Does he appear to look at only the first part of the word and then seemingly guess at the rest? If a student consistently uses one modality (visual, auditory, or kinesthetic) to solve problems on the assessment, the teacher might infer that this sensory channel is the preferred learning modality. Instruction might be facilitated if conducted through this modality. However, the consultant must caution the teacher against wholeheartedly assuming that this is the preferred modality because she could be in error.

According to the teacher's perception, Arlene's performance seems to be enhanced when tasks are well-paced for her. Giving too many assignments at one time apparently resulted in a poorer performance. Also, providing Arlene with writing or demonstration responses seemingly increased her accuracy (see Figure 4–2).

Preferred reinforcers. *Preferred reinforcers* are rewards which students choose more frequently than other reinforcers. Teachers can determine preferred reinforcers in three ways. First, the teacher can ask the students what they like. Valuable time and energy can be saved when teachers ask students what they would prefer to do contingent upon task completion. Second, the teacher can watch students to see what they like to do during free time. Third, teachers can set up a forced-choice situation. For example, the teacher might say, "John, you can play a game, read a book, or help Mark with his math." If John chooses to read a book, the teacher might infer that reading was the most reinforcing activity given these options. The other two activities might also be reinforcing, but the teacher now knows which is the most powerful of the three.

The teacher during the course of the assessment was able to determine that Arlene's preferred reinforcers included games and activities such as bingo, Battleship, and checkers (see Figure 4–2).

Annual goal. An *annual goal* is defined as a statement of the behavior the student is expected to achieve within a calendar year. It is anticipated that annual goals for each major need identified in the evaluation and placement procedures will be attained through the implementation of the IEP. Examples of annual goals for Arlene are included on the Diagnostic Summary Sheet (see Figure 4–2).

Short-term objectives. Simply stated, a *short-term objective* is an intermediate step between the child's current level of performance and the annual goal. These steps are measurable and act as benchmarks for indicating progress toward the annual goal. They are less detailed than daily instructional objectives, which usually require more specific outcomes or products. The number of short-term objectives that is identified depends on several factors including the number of annual goals, the complexity of the task to be learned, and the criteria established for success. Short-term objectives are written to project student accomplishment within a specified unit of time (for example, a report card period, quarterly, or bisemester). Examples of short-term objectives for Arlene are included on the Diagnostic Summary Sheet (see Figure 4–2).

Materials/approach/evaluation. After conducting the assessment the teacher must make a decision about the method, duration, and location of instruction, the materials that will be used, and the process that will be used to evaluate the effectiveness of the instructional program. Since Arlene has difficulty with inferential questions, the teacher has elected to use the basal reader and individual worksheets (see Figure 4–2). Finally, the regular classroom may be selected as the site for reading instruction because of the student's ability to perform well in this setting.

Evaluation. Evaluation of all short-term objectives should be based on measurable performance levels. Turnbull et al. (1978) recommended that continuous or direct and daily measurement be employed to increase the likelihood that short-term objectives will be achieved systematically. Reviewing short-term objectives on a periodic basis, but at least on an annual basis, will help to insure student progress. Common measures that can be used to note educational progress can be divided in two main groups, permanent product measures and observational recordings (see Chapter 8 for a description of measurement approaches).

Planning and Conducting the Individualized Education Program

According to McDaniels (1980) the IEP serves six important functions. First, it is a communication vehicle for the parents and the school. Each party helps to write the IEP, and each understands the needs of the child and the goals of the program. Second, the IEP serves as the basis for resolving problems between the parents' desires for programs and the school's wish to serve the child. Third, resources are allocated based on the prescription in the IEP. Fourth, the IEP is a management tool for teachers; it enables them to provide appropriate education and related services. Fifth, the IEP is a compliance and monitoring document. It allows parents, schools, and governmental agencies to determine whether the child is receiving the appropriate service. Finally, the IEP can serve as an evaluation device to determine student progress, although teachers are not held accountable if IEP annual goals or short-term objectives are not reached by prescribed time lines.

The first three and the last functions of the IEP listed above are important for the consultant to stress to special and regular education teachers. However, the consultant must also emphasize to teachers that parents must be made to feel a part of the IEP process. Too often, parents attend an IEP meeting only to find the document has already been prepared without them. Either directly or indirectly they get the message that the educators have decided the best course of action and parental input is not needed. Anecdote 4–1 is an example of how a consultant helped a special education high school teacher plan an appropriate IEP meeting.

Anecdote 4–1

CONSULTANT: "I understand that you'll be meeting with the Wilson family next week to discuss Fred's IEP."

TEACHER: "That's correct. I was hoping that you might be able to give me some suggestions on the best way to approach the parents with the IEP goals."

CONSULTANT: "I'd be glad to help. Let's start by reviewing Fred's progress."

TEACHER (*handing the Diagnostic Summary Sheet to the consultant*): "I've already begun to list what I believe are appropriate long-term goals and short-term objectives, as well as the instructional approach and materials I'd like to use."

CONSULTANT: "Good."

TEACHER: "I don't want to complete the entire IEP document because I'm afraid the parents might feel that I don't want their suggestions."

CONSULTANT: "I couldn't agree with you more. Maybe we could outline the program, the services to be rendered, and their duration on the IEP for the parents. Put it in the mail along with a short cover letter explaining the draft so that they can review it before the meeting. Then we'd have a working draft to refer to during the actual meeting. Any changes that the parents recommend could be added, and if they felt strongly that any of our plans were inappropriate, we'd be able to discuss our reasoning."

TEACHER: "That sounds fine."

CONSULTANT: "I'd like to suggest that the annual goals and short-term objectives we list for Fred be written so that the emphasis is on application of skills and concepts in real-life situations. I think the parents would appreciate the career education emphasis and goals which will lead to better survival skills for Fred."

TEACHER: "I hadn't thought of that. We have units on careers, community living, and leisure, but I've never written them directly into an IEP."

CONSULTANT: "It's certainly something to consider, especially in Fred's case. He'll be graduating from high school this year, and it will be important for him to be able to apply the skills you are teaching to many situations. A career education emphasis might increase his chances of getting a job."

TEACHER: "What happens if the parents refuse to sign the IEP?"

CONSULTANT: "You've raised a good question. The parents are *not* obligated to sign the IEP. Many do, of course, but there is no rule which says they must. What is required is that both parties—parents and educators— agree on the most appropriate program. Hopefully, if both parties are prepared for the meeting, we'll be able to reach consensus. We inform the parents that they'll receive a copy of the IEP for their records."

TEACHER: "Thanks so much for your help."

CONSULTANT: "I'll try to attend the meeting, but sometimes too many professionals at the IEP meeting inhibit the dialogue. If you have any questions before or after the meeting, please feel free to give me a call. Remember, it's important for the parents to have the opportunity to express their views. Let them talk."

TEACHER: "I'll do that. Thanks again."

In this anecdote the consultant provided three key recommendations that should greatly enhance the productivity of the conference team, and strengthen Fred's performance after the conference as well. First, the consultant suggested that a working draft be mailed to the parents so that they would be better prepared to discuss Fred's program at the conference. Several school districts currently provide this service and, according to anecdotal information, parents are responsive to this approach. Second, the consultant suggested that the annual goals and short-term objectives for Fred be written with a career education focus. Given Fred's impending graduation, it is critical that he have the opportunity to practice the survival skills he will need after leaving school. Finally, the consultant reminded the teacher to give the parents the opportunity to talk. Goldstein, Strickland, Turnbull, and Curry (1980) indicated that the two most frequent speakers at an IEP conference were the resource room teacher and parent. However, the resource room teacher spoke twice as often as the parent. Parents must be given every opportunity to discuss their concerns, and parents whose verbal participation is low should be encouraged to express themselves.

GENERALIZATION AND MAINTENANCE OF SKILLS IN THE SELF-CONTAINED CLASSROOM

Another way a consultant can help after the IEP conference is to show the teacher effective ways to promote generalization and maintenance of the student's skills. This is an important task because the student needs to use the academic or social behavior learned in the classroom in other areas or settings.

Since many handicapped learners need specially designed materials and have to function in a variety of home and school settings, it is imperative that the special educator have built-in instructional strategies for promoting generalization and maintenance. The consultant can help to increase the special educator's awareness that generalization and maintenance can be part of the lesson plan.

The first step toward increasing a teacher's awareness is to let her know that generalization can be considered in two ways—response generalization and stimulus or situational generalization.

Response Generalization

Response generalization occurs when a student is able to complete not only a task for which he has been trained, but also a task for which no training has been received (Lovitt, 1977). A learning disabled student who is able to say the word *cow* (the trained word), and the word *cowboy* (the untrained word) has generalized his sight vocabulary response from a simple word to a compound word without instruction. This is an example of response generalization.

Smith and Lovitt (1973) provided an example where training of *b–d* reversals which occurred in the initial position ("bog" for "dog") spontaneously generalized to medial and final positions as well. Their experiment involved taking data on the number of reversals the pupil made with words that began and ended with the letters *b* and *d*. After collecting these data, training was begun on words beginning with the letter *d* (the most errors occurred with this letter). Shortly after instruction no reversals were noted for either initial *d*'s or *b*'s, and the teacher wanted to test for generalization. She asked the student to copy words from dictation onto three separate lists: single syllable words with initial or final *b* or *d*, and words with *b* or *d* in the medial position. The results indicated that response generalization had occurred. The student was able to write the correct letter (no reversed *b*'s for *d*'s or vice versa) in either the initial, medial, or final position.

Fortunately for this teacher, response generalization occurred spontaneously. She did not have to program her instruction to insure that it occurred. More often than not, however, generalization does have to be programmed. As Baer, Wolf, and Risley (1968) indicated, it is better to program for it than to lament its nonoccurrence.

Stimulus or Situational Generalization

Stimulus or *situational generalization* can be defined as the student's ability to perform a behavior learned in one setting in a different setting. For example, if a deaf student trained to use sign language in a self-contained classroom used signs to communicate at home, situational generalization would have occurred.

To cite another common example, if a learning disabled student, who spent part of his day in a self-contained classroom for academic subjects and part of his day in a regular classroom for nonacademic subjects, was trained to raise his hand to get the teacher's attention in the self-contained classroom, and later did the same in the regular classroom, situational generalization would have occurred.

PROMOTING GENERALIZATION AND MAINTENANCE

According to Sulzer-Azaroff and Mayer (1977) generalization is most effectively promoted when the teacher focuses on similar elements to be learned or the common elements across settings, uses an intermittent reinforcement schedule, conducts the training and learning across a variety of settings, and uses more than one trainer to instruct the student. Teachers in self-contained classrooms who systematically program their lessons with these four criteria as guidelines will increase the probability that generalization will occur.

Focusing on Similar Elements

There are several elements which enhance generalization. When the teacher wants to train for response generalization, she should teach in a way that focuses the student's attention on stimuli common to the skill that is known and the skill that is to be learned.

Skill building. Assume that a learning disabled student could perform two digit × two digit multiplication with regrouping, and the teacher wanted to extend the skill to three digit × three digit multiplication. The teacher, by focusing on the elements common to each problem (arranging the numbers according to place value and correctly multiplying and adding the columns) would be training the student for a higher order skill using a response generalization approach.

Likewise, if the teacher were reasonably certain that a handicapped student might be mainstreamed for specific academic periods or specific skill areas she would be wise to consider several variables common to each setting that may affect the success of the program.

Classroom rules. Probably one of the most useful pieces of information a student needs to survive in any classroom are the classroom rules. The student needs to know what is permitted, and what the consequences are for rule infraction. Often handicapped students break rules and suffer the consequences because the rules were not clearly explained or understood. Anecdote 4–2 provides an example of how a consultant helped a teacher in a learning disabilities class program for situational generalization.

Anecdote 4–2

CONSULTANT: "I understand that Matthew will be going to Mr. Hooper's class for part of the day beginning next month."

LD TEACHER: "That's right. He's made excellent progress with his reading and he'll be going to Mr. Hooper's class for one reading period per day."

CONSULTANT: "That's great. I'm sure you're proud of his accomplishment. Do you think Matt will get along in the class without too much trouble?"

LD TEACHER: "I'm sure he'll be able to do the work. What I'm concerned about is his ability to follow directions, to listen, and to obey the rules in the classroom. It's not that I'm lax with the students in here; it's just that the structure of my class is different from what Matt will experience in Mr. Hooper's class."

CONSULTANT: "Maybe we could come up with a few ideas that will make the transition smoother for Matthew."

LD TEACHER: "It's worth a try. I know Mr. Hooper has the students raise their hands to answer questions or for permission to leave the room. I know he insists that when they're finished their work they find an activity and keep busy."

CONSULTANT: "How about having Matt raise his hand for permission to speak or to leave your classroom and begin to set limits on his free time?"

LD TEACHER: "That's fine with me, but what is the purpose?"

CONSULTANT: "While you're working on these behaviors with Matt in your classroom, I'll meet with Mr. Hooper to let him know that you have initiated a point system for hand raising, and I'll fill him in on how your instructional program works with Matt. I'm sure we'll be able to agree on a similar system for Matt while he is in his classroom."

LD TEACHER: "Sounds like Matt's switching to a regular classroom won't be much of a switch if everything stays the same."

CONSULTANT: "The more we can make the classrooms the same, the easier it will be for Matt to make the transition and the greater the likelihood that he will succeed."

Materials. The consultant can make the LD teacher aware of the type and complexity of instructional materials that are used in the regular class. Again, the closer the materials in the LD class are to those in the regular class in terms of interest, readability, level of difficulty, and the skills to be learned, the greater the likelihood of success. Wallace and Kauffman (1978) indicate that one similar instructional method or set of materials may not be enough to achieve the desired objective.

Anecdote 4-3 follows up on the discussion with the LD teacher. The consultant is describing the instructional approach and materials which the LD teacher uses to Mr. Hooper.

Anecdote 4-3

CONSULTANT: "As you are probably aware, Mr. Hooper, Mrs. Todd uses several pieces of instructional hardware in her classroom to help reinforce a skill she has taught. For example, she relies heavily on the tape recorder, audiotape cassettes, and the language master. She uses them for direct instruction and for independent student work."

MR. HOOPER: "That's good. However, in my class I don't rely on these devices for teaching. Basically, I teach the 3 Rs using a traditional approach. Every once in a while I'll use a tape recorder. The students like to hear their own voices.

CONSULTANT: "I understand that your classroom is structured so that when the students complete their assignments they're required to work independently."

MR. HOOPER: "That's right. They usually read a book."

CONSULTANT: "In Mrs. Todd's class the students use the tape recorder or the language master only after they've finished their primary tasks. They work on supplemental skills that need developing. Do you see any problem using that strategy with Matt after he's finished his work in your classroom?"

MR. HOOPER: "Not at all. As long as he is using his time efficiently, it will be fine."

Time and length of instruction. Two other factors, which can be equated across settings, are the time and length of instruction. Many handicapped youngsters have short attention spans and require their instruction in small doses over longer time periods. Also, some handicapped students perform much better in the morning than they do in the afternoon. In this case, heavy academic instruction should probably be scheduled in the morning rather than later in the day.

Type of reinforcement. Also promoting generalization is the type of reinforcement the student receives. For example, if an educable mentally retarded adolescent received points at school for appropriate behavior a similar system could be established at home. Anecdote 4–4 gives an example of how a home point system was suggested to a parent. The anecdote begins with a conversation among the teacher, her supervisor, and the parent.

Anecdote 4–4

TEACHER: "Mrs. Franco, Paul has been doing quite well in math lately. He has advanced to the point where he works independently for up to ten minutes and completes his tasks accurately."

PARENT: "I wish I could say the same for his behavior at home. I try to help him with his homework, but it's like pulling teeth."

TEACHER: "Oh really! Tell us about your sessions with Paul."

PARENT: "Well, after we've worked together for about one-half hour Paul begins to balk. He claims he is tired, has a headache—the typical excuses."

SUPERVISOR: "One strategy which Ms. Roeland and I have found helpful in working with Paul in class is to issue points every ten minutes or so that Paul is working. We've found that he is able to remain on-task for longer periods and his work is much better when we use the point system.

PARENT: "How are the points used once he has earned them?"

TEACHER: "In a variety of ways. They buy Paul classroom privileges. Free time is his favorite."

PARENT: "He has enough free time at home. I don't think it would work at our house."

SUPERVISOR: "Maybe not with free time. But Paul certainly has other things he likes to do—use the car, go to the movies, buy clothes, etc. The points could be exchanged for these privileges quite easily."

PARENT: "I see."

TEACHER: "The real advantage I see is that both of us would be using a similar system to help Paul. By doing so, it's more likely that we'll be successful because Paul will know what is expected and he'll know the consequences."

SUPERVISOR: "We'll be increasing our consistency."

Using Intermittent Reinforcement

When a teacher uses an *intermittent schedule of reinforcement*, some but not all of the appropriate behaviors performed will be reinforced. Reinforcing student performance on an intermittent schedule is more advantageous to the teacher if situational or response generalization is desired.

A consultant working with a classroom teacher should, at the least, increase the teacher's awareness of four intermittent schedules of reinforcement that can be used with relative ease in the self-contained class-room, but will also benefit the student as he advances from one skill or one setting to another. The first two schedules (fixed interval and variable interval) are time-related. That is, reinforcement is issued for a response after a given time period has passed. The second two schedules (fixed ratio and variable ratio) are response-related. That is, the student has to perform behaviors to earn reinforcement.

Fixed interval. A fixed interval (FI) schedule of reinforcement is said to be in effect when the first response following a specific time period is reinforced (Sulzer-Azaroff & Mayer, 1977). For instance, a physically handicapped student who is reinforced on a fixed interval schedule of three minutes (FI 3) for appropriate object sorting would receive reinforcement for the first appropriate object-sorting behavior he completed following the three-minute time frame. If the behavior did not occur immediately after the three minutes, reinforcement would be withheld until it did.

While there are a few advantages the consultant could mention to the special education teacher interested in this schedule (it might be easier logistically for the teacher), there are several distinct disadvantages which the consultant needs to point out. First, the schedule may become too predictable. The student may figure out when reinforcement is likely to occur, and he may work only at that time. Second, because the schedule may be so predictable, little work may be evident soon after reinforcement has occurred. This characteristic pause tends to produce a curve—referred to as a "scallop"—which shows little or no work soon after reinforcement but steady increases in performance toward the end of the interval. Finally, the student can make a great many errors during the interval for which no corrective feedback is obtained. If a behaviorally disordered student were on a fixed interval of twenty minutes (FI 20) for appropriate social behavior, not only would the teacher have to wait at least twenty minutes to deliver reinforcement, but also inappropriate social behavior might go undetected during the twenty-minute interval. In effect, the student might practice inappropriate behavior and receive reinforcement (perhaps from a peer in the form of attention), and completely compromise the system.

Consultants should recommend FI schedules to teachers with advice to make the intervals short. Increases in the time of the interval should only be extended as the student's behavior improves.

Variable interval. When a variable interval (VI) schedule is used reinforcement is delivered for the first response which follows the passage of a varying amount of time (Sulzer-Azaroff & Mayer, 1977). For example, a learning disabled student in a self-contained classroom who is on a VI 10 schedule for assignment completion would receive reinforcement for the first response which occurred following the passage of ten minutes on the average. So, the student could be reinforced after two minutes, six minutes, twenty minutes or twelve minutes—as long as he performed the desired response after the passage of that time limit and the totals averaged ten minutes.

The most striking advantage a VI schedule has over a FI schedule is that it is unpredictable. Reinforcement could occur at any time—varying around a specific average—and the behavior targeted for change is more likely to be sustained during the interval. This is in contrast to the FI schedule where the target behavior is not usually evident during the entire interval, only at the end of the interval.

Fixed ratio. A fixed ratio (FR) schedule simply means that the student has to perform a set number of responses before reinforcement is delivered (Martin & Pear, 1978). For instance, a behaviorally disordered student on a FR 14 for math would have to complete fourteen math calculations before reinforcement would be delivered. Likewise, on a FR 27, the student would have to do twenty-seven problems before earning reinforcement.

One advantage FR schedules have that the consultant can indicate to the teacher is that they are used in both special and regular classes. It is common to hear the teacher say, "When you are finished with your math worksheet, you can come to my desk or you can have free time." For the student who is likely to be mainstreamed into the regular class the consultant might recommend that a FR schedule be introduced with low response requirements, say FR 5, and later expanded to more closely match the response requirements of the classroom he is going to—say FR 30.

Variable ratio. A variable ratio (VR) or "gambler's" schedule provides reinforcement for a varying number of responses (Martin & Pear, 1978). The number of responses required to earn reinforcement varies around a specific average. For instance, a Down's Syndrome student in a special class who is operating under a VR 7 schedule for hand raising would receive reinforcement following an average of seven hand-raising responses. Since the student is just as likely to earn reinforcement after 1 response as she is after 7, or 10, or 100, very high rates of responding occur.

One distinct advantage of the VR schedule is its unpredictability. Students might perform a great many behaviors anticipating that the very next response will be reinforced. Since many handicapped youngsters are integrated in the regular classroom, the consultant would be wise to advise the special education teacher to move to a VR schedule for as many behaviors as possible. The primary reason for suggesting this strategy is that reinforcement occurs at unpredictable times in the regular classroom, and if the handicapped student is already operating under a VR schedule, it is less likely that appropriate behavior learned in the self-contained classroom will be extinguished in the regular setting. More important, generalization and maintenance will be enhanced.

Training Across Settings

A third strategy to promote generalization and maintenance is to teach the student the desired behavior in as many settings as possible. For a handicapped student who spends his entire time in a self-contained classroom there are at least two other settings in which desired behavior can be taught. The first is the home. The second would be any educational setting in which the student could be found (for example, playground, library, lunchroom, field trip sites).

Home. The cooperation of parents can be of great assistance to the teacher who is programming for generalization training in the home. The consultant must make it clear to the teacher that in her explanations of the program to the parents she must use simple language, plenty of examples, and give the parents the opportunity to ask questions.

As discussed earlier, teachers should convey to the parents the importance of following a program similar to the school's so that generalization is fostered. For example, suppose the teacher was using a contracting approach with the student. The parents might be encouraged to use a similar contracting arrangement at home (see chapters 5 and 9 for additional information regarding the use of contracts at school and home).

Field trips. Most students in self-contained classrooms have the opportunity to go on field trips at least once a year. In addition to the practical benefits which such experiences provide, they can also be an excellent occasion for generalization training. One way a consultant can help a teacher increase generalization of student behavior is to role play, actually rehearse, the behavior expected of the students while they are on the field trip.

Anecdote 4–5 indicates how a consultant helped a secondary level teacher of educable mentally retarded children prepare for a field trip to a local restaurant.

Anecdote 4–5

CONSULTANT: "I understand that your class is scheduled to go on a field trip to the Barbeque Warehouse next week."

EMR TEACHER: "That's right. We've been planning the trip for quite some time now."

CONSULTANT: "Tell me about the plans you've made. They sound exciting!"

EMR TEACHER: "Well, we've discussed the importance of good manners in public and the fact that part of assuming adult roles means being able to handle yourself in social situations."

CONSULTANT: "Have the students been responsive to the discussion?"

EMR TEACHER: "Yes, they've talked about their experiences with their parents and friends. Unfortunately, not all of the students have had experience eating in public places. I'm afraid many of them won't know what to do. I'm afraid they might be embarrassed, and for a few of my students public humiliation could be disastrous."

CONSULTANT: "I understand."

EMR TEACHER: "I've tried to explain what will happen and the sequence in which it will happen from the moment we arrive to the time we pay the check. I'm not sure they all understand."

CONSULTANT: "One technique which several other teachers have used successfully is to role play the entire episode from the time the students enter the restaurant to the time they leave. The way most teachers do it is to have roles assigned to each student. They can be the waiter, waitress, bus boy, or cashier. They read from prepared scripts samples of what might be said. For example, a student playing the waiter could approach students at a table to ask them if they would like a menu and if they wanted separate checks. Students switch roles so that they can practice many of the behaviors they'll be required to perform, such as ordering the food, eating politely, and paying the bill."

EMR TEACHER: "I see. That sounds interesting."

CONSULTANT: "It really works because many of the same things you address in the class and role play are actually required in the restaurant.

The students are not surprised by the course of events. One contingency plan I would suggest is to review some things that might go wrong. For instance, how do you attract the waiter's attention if he has forgotten you? So, you practice what is expected and also what is unexpected."

EMR TEACHER (*approaching the consultant in the hallway a week later*): "Hey, the field trip to the restaurant was super! The students did exceptionally well. They even handled an unexpected situation. The waiter gave us the wrong bill!"

CONSULTANT: "That's great. I'm glad to hear that the trip went so well."

Using Multiple Teachers

The final thing that a consultant may suggest to a teacher who is programming for generalization and maintenance is to use multiple teachers. Teachers in self-contained classrooms have numerous personnel resources available to them to help with this important component of generalization training.

Peers. Without question the use of peers can be an effective technique to increase academic or social skills. Numerous studies have shown peers can teach a variety of academic skills (Parson & Heward, 1978; Neidermeyer, 1970). Furthermore, research seems to indicate that the tutors seem to learn as much as the student (Cloward, 1967; Dineen, Clark, & Risley, 1978). Lovitt (1977) indicates that peers are effective as tutors because they may have just learned the skill themselves and are more likely to remember the steps they went through to learn it, and they may be more patient than the teacher. Regardless of the rationale, when teachers are advised by consultants to initiate peer tutoring in the self-contained classroom, the student skills are likely to improve.

Parents. We have already indicated that parents can help to insure that behaviors learned in school are generalized to the home setting. Parents can sometimes be counted on to help at school during the day, and teachers should be alert to the opportunity to include them in instructional programs.

Other teachers. If handicapped students in self-contained classrooms are expected to be integrated in regular classrooms, the consultant needs to set up discussions with both the special and the regular educator to establish a common program for the student. It may be possible for the regular educator to meet with or actually work with the handicapped student before his official entrance into the room. The intent of the preliminary meeting is to build rapport. Once integration has taken place, the student is more likely to succeed, that is, his skills are more likely to be emitted in the presence of the new teacher, if he has had the opportunity to meet him beforehand. Also, the regular educator is made aware of some of the strengths and weaknesses of the handicapped student before he is faced with instructing him in a group.

SUMMARY

Consultants who work with teachers in self-contained classrooms often have to extend their services in two directions. First, they must be able to assist the self-contained teacher with tasks that are required to meet the instructional needs of students within the class. They must be able to plan an active role in the IEP process, recommending assessments, providing technical assistance with administration of the tests, and interpreting the results. Also, the consultant must be familiar with the scope and sequence of the curriculum so that instructional strategies that are jointly determined by the teacher and the consultant facilitate generalization to higher order skills yet to be taught, and help to maintain previously taught skills. Several key strategies are mentioned in the chapter that a consultant can employ to accomplish each of these objectives.

A second task that a consultant might have to perform with the self-contained teacher would occur when a student is to be integrated in a regular classroom. The consultant can provide the needed support for the self-contained teacher in terms of preparing the student for the new environment. For example, she might recommend that a different schedule of reinforcement be used, that instructional materials more closely aligned with the materials in the regular classroom be considered. The important point for the consultant to remember is that she is serving four agents—the child, parent, the special teacher, and the regular teacher. The strategies she recommends must meet with the approval of each teacher and address the instructional needs of the student. Several anecdotes were presented which illustrate ways in which the consultant can perform this liaison task.

Questions

1. State two functions a consultant can perform to help self-contained teachers with the IEP process.

2. Identify and describe two types of generalization.

3. Indicate four common elements that facilitate generalization. Give a classroom-related example of each.

4. Assume that a student is to be moved from a self-contained classroom to a regular classroom. Why is it important for the two environments to be somewhat similar?

5. Define four basic schedules of reinforcement.

6. Describe a situation where instruction within a self-contained special education classroom would be appropriate for a handicapped child.

7. What factors in a student's educational program may require assessment to successfully develop and implement an Individualized Educational Program?

Discussion Points and Exercises

---

1. Prepare a fifteen-minute videotape which depicts a teacher who has conducted a lesson which was programmed for generalization. Have participants identify the key elements in the generalization training. Solicit their ideas on how this approach could be used in their own classrooms.

2. Pick a child with a learning problem in your school. Identify that child's preferred reinforcers.

3. Devise a plan to maintain student academic and social gains across time.

4. The following represents an annual goal for a multiply handicapped, six-year-old student: Sue Ellen will acquire prerequisite skills necessary for handwriting. Develop appropriate short-term objectives and indicate how these objectives might be evaluated.

REFERENCES

BAER, D. M., WOLF, M. M., & RISLEY, T. Some current dimensions of applied behavior analysis. *Journal of Applied Behavior Analysis*, 1968, 1, 91–97.
BARBE, W., & SWASSING, R. H. *Teaching through modality strengths: Concepts and practices.* Columbus, Ohio: Zaner-Bloser, 1979.

BONNING, R. A. *Specific skill series*. New York: Barnell-Loft, 1968.

CLOWARD, R. D. Studies in tutoring. *Journal of Experimental Education*, 1967, 36, 14–25.

COOPER, J. O. *Measuring behavior* (2nd ed.). Columbus, Ohio: Charles E. Merrill, 1981.

DINEEN, J. P., Clark, H. P., & RISLEY, T. R. Peer tutoring among elementary students: Education benefits to the tutor. *Journal of Applied Behavior Analysis*, 1977, 10, 231–238.

GOLDSTEIN, S., STRICKLAND, B., TURNBULL, A. P., & CURRY, L. An observational analysis of the IEP conference. *Exceptional Children*, 1980, 46 (4), 278–286.

HAWISHER, M. F., & CALHOUN, M. L. *The resource room: An educational asset for children with special needs*. Columbus, Ohio: Charles E. Merrill, 1978.

HEWARD, W. L., & ORLANSKY, M. D. *Exceptional children*. Columbus, Ohio: Charles E. Merrill, 1980.

LOVITT, T. C. *In spite of my resistance . . . I've learned from children*. Columbus, Ohio: Charles E. Merrill, 1977.

MARTIN, G., & PEAR, J. *Behavior modification: What it is and how to do it*. Englewood Cliffs, New Jersey: Prentice-Hall, 1978.

McDANIELS, G. Office of Special Education policy paper. DAS information bulletin, #64, Washington, D.C., May 23, 1980.

NEIDERMEYER, F. C. Effects of training on the instructional behaviors of student tutors. *Journal of Education Research*, 1970, 64, 119–123.

PARSON, L. R., & HEWARD, W. L. Training peers to tutor: Evaluation of a tutor training package for primary learning disabled students. *Journal of Applied Behavior Analysis*, 1979, 12, 309–310.

SMITH, D. D., & LOVITT, T. C. The educational diagnosis and remediation of *b* and *d* written reversal problems: A case study. *Journal of Learning Disabilities*, 1973, 6, 356–363.

SMITH, J. O., & ARKANS, J. R. Now more than ever: A case for the special class. *Exceptional Children*, 1974, 40, 497–502.

STEPHENS, T. M. *Teaching skills to children with learning and behavior disorders*. Columbus, Ohio: Charles E. Merrill, 1977.

SULZER-AZAROFF, B., & MAYER, R. *Applying behavior-analysis procedures with children and youth*. New York: Holt, Rinehart and Winston, 1977.

TURNBULL, A. P., & SCHULZ, J. B. *Mainstreaming handicapped students: A guide for the classroom teacher*. Boston: Allyn and Bacon, 1979.

TURNBULL, A. P., STRICKLAND, B., & HAMMER, S. E. IEP's: Presenting guidelines for development and implementation, Part 1. *Journal of Learning Disabilities*, 1978, 11 (1), 40–46.

TURNBULL, A. P., STRICKLAND, B., & HAMMER, S. E. The IEP—Part 2: Translating law into practice. *Journal of Learning Disabilities*, 1978, 11 (2), 67–72.

WALLACE, G., & KAUFFMAN, J. M. *Teaching children with learning problems* (2nd ed.). Columbus, Ohio: Charles E. Merrill, 1978.

WALLACE, C., & LARSEN, S. C. *Educational assessment of learning problems: Testing for teaching*. Boston: Allyn and Bacon, 1978.

WALLACE, G., & McLOUGHLIN, J. A. *Learning disabilities: Concepts and characteristics* (2nd ed.). Columbus, Ohio: Charles E. Merrill, 1978.
WIEDERHOLT, J. L., HAMMILL, D. D., & BROWN, V. *The resource teacher.* Boston: Allyn and Bacon, 1978.

5

Working with Parents of Mainstreamed Students

This chapter describes the role parents of handicapped students are beginning to assume as home-based educators, behavior managers, tutors in the classroom, and partners in the individualized educational program for their children. The chapter discusses ways in which consultants and supervisors can access and involve parents in the education process.

At the outset it should be stated that a comprehensive parent program means that all parents are involved at some level of participation (Kroth, 1980). Consultants, however, should remember that not all parents will be able to participate in all facets of a parenting program. As McLoughlin (1979) indicates, a parent's primary responsibility is to be a parent—not a clinician or an educator or a therapist. This chapter was written with the assumption that the consultant would consider Kroth's Parent Involvement Model and McLoughlin's advice before embarking on any radical parent-training or intervention program.

Objectives

After reading this chapter, the reader will be able to:

1. cite the four levels of Kroth's "Mirror Model of Parental Involvement" from the professional and parent perspective.

2. state several methods to initiate and maintain communication with parents.

3. identify key aspects in the development of parent-training programs.

4. state the four phases of the parent conference as suggested by Stephens.

5. explain two advantages of using parents as tutors in the classroom.

Key Terms

Mirror Model of Parental
   Involvement

Needs assessment

Home-based educators

Home-school communication

Parent conference

Parent training program

Parent tutoring program

WORKING WITH PARENTS
OF MAINSTREAMED STUDENTS

Educational consultants who work with parents of mainstreamed children and youth need to understand some of the societal pressures as well as some of the individual problems such families face. As Lichto (1976) notes, feelings of social isolation or embarrassment, and the potential loss of family or neighborhood assistance may place enormous strains on parents of a handicapped child. Educational consultants need to be sensitive to these pressures so that supports can be provided for the parent and the family. Supervisors and consultants can provide special assistance in such areas as: the development of an effective communication link between parent and professional, the establishment of specific behavior management approaches at home, or guidance with the IEP process.

Educational researchers and practitioners have stated consistently that parent involvement in the educational process is essential (Cooper & Edge, 1981; Heward, Dardig, & Rossett, 1979). Now, Public Law 94–142 assures the opportunity for parental involvement in the education process by mandating that identification and placement decisions be made with the consent of the parents, and safeguards are established to protect the parent's and child's right to due process.

Assuring the opportunity for parent participation and actually obtaining that participation are two different things. Participation can not be mandated, it must be nurtured, encouraged, and reinforced. Kroth's Mirror Model of Parental Involvement provides the consultant with an excellent perspective on the reciprocal nature of the parent-professional partnership. Also, it provides the consultant with an index to determine parent involvement and the level of that participation.

Mirror Model of Parental Involvement

Figure 5–1 shows Kroth's *Mirror Model of Parental Involvement.* Essentially the model is divided into two major areas—professional service and parental service. Within each area there are four levels of participation designated by the term "all," "most," "some," and "few." According to Kroth (1980) lower levels of participation need to be firmly established before higher levels of involvement can be expected. For example, all parents could probably provide information regarding the child's preschool medical and social history. Most parents could provide relevant information during the IEP process or help with an occasional field trip (for example, prepare snacks, donate equipment, or volunteer to assist teachers). Some parents might become strong advocates for services for

Figure 5–1 Mirror model of parental involvement. SOURCE: Kroth,
R. L., The mirror model of parental involvement. *The Pointer,*
1980, 25(1), p. 19. Used with permission of Heldref Publications,
4000 Albemarle Street, NW, Washington, D.C. 20016.

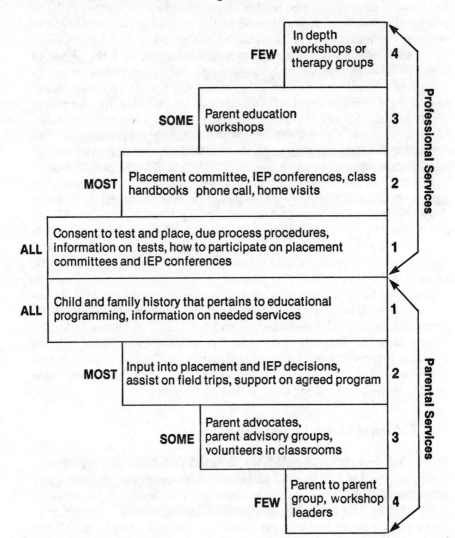

handicapped students. They may attend legislative hearings, initiate parent advisory groups, or volunteer as teacher's aides. Finally, only a few parents might become involved enough to form active parent groups and conduct parenting workshops themselves.

How is this information helpful to a consultant? First, it may dramatically change the way a consultant communicates to a teacher expectations of a successful parent-teacher partnership. Too often a consultant hears from teachers that the parents are not interested because they do not attend meetings or scheduled conferences. Teachers interpret non-attendance as disinterest and may become frustrated because they feel they are working alone to help the handicapped students. These feelings of frustration can build to feelings of resentment toward the child and the parent ("If the parents do not care how their child is doing in my class, why should I?") If the feelings of resentment are translated into social rejection, the student's educational program may be compromised.

Parental nonattendance at scheduled meetings could be for several reasons. The time selected for the conference could have been inconvenient. Both parents may work, or each may work a different shift. Also, the parents may have felt they needed to strike a balance between the help they give their handicapped child and the time they share with each other or other family members. Finally, if the distance was too great to travel or provisions could not be made for competent babysitting, then attendance at meetings might decline.

Second, conducting a *needs assessment* of parent concerns, strengths, and time restrictions either directly through a telephone survey or questionnaire or indirectly by discussion with teachers or principal will help the consultant structure a comprehensive parenting program. Resources and time can be allotted to each level to maximize parent participation at that level, but consultants should recognize that most of the organization and implementation tasks will have to be performed by them until such time as a few parents are able to carry on.

Third, when trying to determine the effectiveness of a school, district, or countywide parent involvement program, single measures of evaluation (such as attendance at meetings or numbers of parents who volunteer as teacher aides or home-based educators) could be abandoned in favor of a more comprehensive index—the percentage of parents who participated at each level in the model. In effect, 100 percent of the parents could have been involved, with differing ratios of parent involvement at each level.

Anecdotes 5–1 and 5–2 describe how a consultant attempted to increase the level of participation of two parents. The first parent was at the *most* level of participation; she provided extensive input for her child's IEP. The second parent was at the *some* level; she had experience providing testimony to state legislative committees. In both cases, the consultant attempted to move the parents' involvement to the next higher level.

Anecdote 5–1

CONSULTANT (*a week after the IEP conference*): "Mrs. Kempe, you really provided several excellent recommendations during Sal's IEP conference."

PARENT: "It's important to me that Sal receive all the necessary services. He is already so far behind. I am especially anxious to see him in the tutoring program."

CONSULTANT: "I was quite impressed with your knowledge of school services. In fact, the reason I'm calling you is to see if you would be interested in helping Sal's teacher implement some of the objectives for Sal and for other children."

PARENT: "You mean help out at school during the day?"

CONSULTANT: "Yes, Sal's teacher indicated he would love to have you as an assistant."

PARENT: "I'm afraid that I will not be able to accept. At the time of the conference I was interviewing for a part-time job, and yesterday I was offered the position."

CONSULTANT: "Congratulations! I can see where your time will be limited during the day."

PARENT: "Yes, it will. Is there anything I could do for the teacher short of coming to the school?"

CONSULTANT: "Maybe we could set something up with you and Sal at home. I'm thinking of helping with a school-related task for only a few minutes each night."

PARENT: "I already do that, but I'm open to ideas on specific things I can do. I often feel lost."

CONSULTANT: "I'll set it up with the teacher. Again, good luck with your new job. I'm looking forward to working with you and the teacher on Sal's home program."

This scenario illustrates several positive consulting behaviors. First, the consultant reinforced the parent for her previous participation at the IEP conference. Second, she included the teacher in the discussion by stating that he was anxious to have the parent assist in the room. Third, she reinforced the parent for getting her job offer. Instead of ignoring the parent's success, the consultant's comment expressed congratulations and empathy for the parent's position (limited time during the day). Finally, the consultant ended the conversation by reiterating that she felt her participation was still of value, and that a home-based program could be explored.

Anecdote 5–2

CONSULTANT: "Lee, I read in the newspaper last night that you provided testimony to the House Education Committee on a bill dealing with special education funding."

LEE: "That's right. It is important that the bill go to the Senate with the amendments I proposed."

CONSULTANT: "I realize you are busy, but I wanted to talk to you because I'd like to capitalize on your experience in an upcoming series of workshops I'm offering."

LEE: "What could I do?"

CONSULTANT: "I'd like you to present your ideas on working with legislators to a group of parents who will be attending. I'd like them to have the total view of educating the handicapped, including the role of the legislator."

LEE: "If the presentation can be scheduled at a time when I'm not required to be in session with the legislators, I'll be glad to do it."

CONSULTANT: "Thank you. I appreciate your help."

In this case, the consultant achieved his objective of having Lee serve as a workshop presenter. Lee was reinforced for his expertise, and his cooperation was obtained for the presentation. Lee may have been inclined to accept the consultant's offer because the time commitment was short, or he felt a social obligation to help. Regardless of why, the consultant attained his goal.

In sum, Kroth's model can be used as a communication vehicle with regular and special education teachers and parents. Feelings of isolation and disillusionment might be prevented when teachers see that parents need not participate in all levels of the model for the total parent involvement program to be successful. Also, when Kroth's model is used with a needs assessment, the consultant is in a better position to recommend parenting resources. Existing networks of communication (school newspaper, Parent-Teacher Association (PTA) meetings, or regional newsletters) can be used to disseminate information about the program. Finally, once success has been achieved with a parent at a lower level of participation, increased involvement at a higher level could be planned and implemented.

Parents as Behavior Managers

All parents change child behavior. They permit some behaviors, inhibit or prevent others, and punish still more. Some parents, however, are more consistent about the behaviors they allow, inhibit, or punish. As a result, they become more effective behavior managers and more effective parents. Learning to become a better manager is not an impossible task for parents. O'Dell (1974) provides a review of programs in which parents have learned to use behavior management approaches in the home. Cooperatively developed plans between school-related personnel and parents have been implemented in the past (Hall, Cristler, Cranston, & Tucker, 1970; Moore & Bailey, 1973).

For example, Hall et al. (1970) found that when parents were given guidelines to follow with respect to executing a management program, inappropriate child behaviors were reduced or eliminated. Specifically, a parent was advised to reduce the amount of time her daughter could stay up at night contingent upon the nonoccurrence of three discrete behaviors. The parents established a rule with the child that for every minute under thirty minutes that she failed to play her clarinet, she would go to bed one minute earlier than her scheduled time.

Immediately clarinet practice increased to the required thirty-minute criterion. Subsequently, the rule was applied to two other problem behaviors with identical results. Within approximately sixteen days the child was engaged in all three tasks at the required criterion level (see Figure 5-2). The parent was satisfied with the results, and the child suffered no apparent side effects.

Shrewsberry (cited in Cooper & Edge, 1981) found that a parent could successfully reduce unpleasant, talking-back behavior by her oldest son. The mother reinforced the youth with a check mark for complying with requests without complaining. When he earned five check marks, he could exchange them for a preferred activity. On occasion when the youth did complain, the mother ignored the back talk.

111

Figure 5–2 Reprinted from Hall, R. V., Christler, C., Cranston, S. S., and Tucker B., "Teachers and parents as researchers using multiple baseline designs." *Journal of Applied Behavior Analysis,* 1970, 3. Used with permission. P. 252.

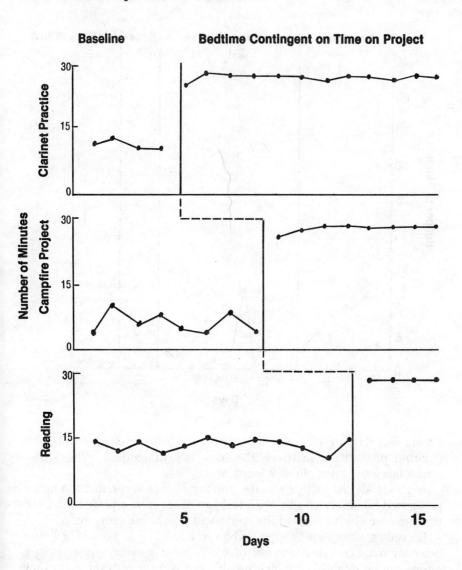

Figure 5–3 The number of times a fourteen-year-old boy talked back following a request. From J. O. Cooper and D. Edge, *Parenting: Strategies and Educational Methods.* Louisville, KY: Eston Corporation, 1981. P. 133. Reprinted with permission.

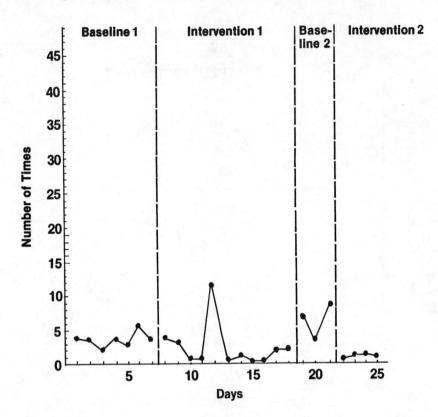

Figure 5–3 shows the results of the study. When the check marks plus ignoring phase were in effect, the back talk diminished. When these conditions were not in effect, it increased.

In this study the mother was the primary change agent, and the father performed reliability checks. With little guidance from a professional, the parents were able to successfully implement the change program.

Consultants can assist parents who are interested in becoming better behavior managers in a number of ways. First, specific workshop programs can be established which provide the parents with the skills they seek. The focus of the workshop might be to train parents to assess the current levels of their children's behavior, plan and execute effective interventions, and analyze the results. More important, the in-service should provide opportunities for parents to practice the skills being taught, receive constructive feedback from a skilled supervisor or consultant, and obtain praise for improved performance.

Second, consultants can provide indirect service to parents by referring them to other sources of support or other resources. For example, many parent associations (for example, Association for Children and Adults with Learning Disabilities) have "parent assistor" programs established to help parents who have child-rearing problems or problems related to their child's performance in school. The parent assistor can serve as a liaison between the parents and another agency (the school), or simply provide information or counseling to the parents.

Finally, the consultant can serve as a mediator between the school and the home. She could try to initiate in the home those behavior management strategies which have been effective in school. The intent, of course, would be to provide a consistent approach at home and at school.

Parents as Home-Based Educators

Teachers and administrators frequently state that there is only so much that can be done at school to increase the academic functioning of a child. As a rule, teachers and supervisors like parents to serve as *home-based educators*, supplementing the instruction their child receives at school, but many do not know how to develop systematic methods for establishing and maintaining parental assistance. While the reasons for the lack of home-school cooperation are numerous (for example, working parents, single parent families, multiple family commitments, and lack of parental enthusiasm), it is still possible to devise useful methods that give parents the opportunity to assist in their child's academic and social development at home.

One method that has worked well in the past has been for the teacher to model instructional strategies for the parents. Then they can incorporate the instructions from the teacher in a home-based program that may improve the child's academic performance (Kroth, 1975; Kroth, Whelan & Stables, 1970).

It should be noted, however, that not all educators favor the use of parents as home-based educators. Barsch (1969) and Kronich (1969) suggest that parents should not attempt home-based education programs. In general, these authors feel that parents of handicapped children may be too anxious, lack the proper education skills, or simply do not have the time to do an adequate job. Further, it is felt that parents may impede the learning process by putting adverse pressure on the child or youth. In short, these authors and others (e.g., Lerner, 1976) suggest that parents remain parents and engage in family recreational or domestic activities, and leave the teaching to professionals.

The present authors are convinced that parents can and should serve as home-based educators if guidance is provided, and they feel comfortable with the task. If parents want to engage in tutoring, and many do, the consultant might conduct mini-training sessions where parents could learn tutoring techniques.

Communication Techniques with Parents

For a functional home-school relationship to develop, the opportunity to communicate must exist. *Home-school communication* is defined as a broad range of oral or written messages between parents and teachers for the purpose of exchanging information and providing training to the parents. There are a number of methods for accomplishing this objective and the following section will describe each one. Documentation to support inclusion of a particular method is provided. The methods are described according to their hierarchy of intrusiveness. The least intrusive technique appears first.

Telephone. Nearly every American family has a telephone or lives close to someone who does. Surprisingly, however, it has only been within the recent past that the telephone has come to play an important role in the home-school communication network.

A number of researchers (Chapman, 1978; Heron & Axelrod, 1976; Varone, O'Brien, & Axelrod, 1972) have used the telephone to increase parent's knowledge of school-related activities, or as a method of structuring home-based instruction. Heron and Axelrod (1976), for example, used a telephone to reinforce inner-city parents for assisting their children with word recognition assignments. The procedure involved calling the parents on the telephone each day to tell them how well their child had done on a previous day's word recognition task, and to ask them to provide the opportunity for their child to learn the next day's ten target words.

The results of the study demonstrated that when parents were given feedback via the telephone for helping with their child's work, the child's performance improved. Conversely, when the parent did not receive such feedback, word recognition performance worsened. Also, the parents reported that they liked the telephone calls. In the past the only time that school personnel had called them was when a son or daughter was in trouble. This positive telephone approach was welcomed. Also, it should be noted that the parents did not receive explicit instructions on how to teach the target words to their children. Yet, at least one parent stated that she told her daughter to "look for little words in the big word, write the words in the air with her eyes closed, and finally write the words in sentences." Each of these decoding strategies is a common instructional method used by classroom teachers.

Varone, O'Brien, and Axelrod (1972) conducted a similar study with children and parents of Hispanic backgrounds. Despite the fact that the parents could not read many of the English words their children brought home from school, gains in word recognition were achieved. Parents simply set the occasion for their child to study the words and to use the words in sentences. Feedback via the telephone maintained parental participation.

In families where both parents work or in single-parent families, the strategy employed by Heron and Axelrod (1976) and Varone, O'Brien, and Axelrod (1972) may have to be modified. In these studies telephone calls were made during the day while the parents were home.

If the telephone system is going to be used to maximum advantage on a school or districtwide basis, it is imperative that consultants find ways to extend this support to more parents. One way is with a telephone-answering service (Bittle, 1975; Chapman, 1978).

Bittle (1975), for example, demonstrated that a telephone-answering service installed in the school, and preprogrammed with information on school-related subjects, could be used as a low-cost method to establish and maintain a parent-teacher communication network, and to improve student performance in school.

As one part of the study students were instructed to take a list of four spelling words home to their parents. The students were scheduled to be tested on the words the following day. In the next step of the study, the teacher not only sent the words home with the student, but also included them on a nightly phone message to the parents. In the third phase the word-list-only condition was reinstated for seven days. Finally, the word-list-and-telephone-message phase was repeated for six days.

Figure 5–4 shows that during the word-list-plus-telephone-message conditions, the percentage of students receiving perfect scores on the spelling test increased substantially over the word-list-alone condition. The results indicate a functional effect between the phone message and student performance. When the spelling words were on the phone message, the level of student performance increased. When the spelling words were removed from the telephone answering service, student performance level dropped.

Chapman (1978) replicated Bittle's study. Her procedure involved taping instructions, requests, and progress notes for the parents on the school telephone-answering service. The parents were free to call after school each day to obtain the data. The results of Chapman's study indicated that more telephone calls were made to the school each day when the messages were available than when they were not (see Figure 5–5).

Figure 5–4 Daily plot of the percentage of students scoring perfectly on daily spelling tests. SOURCE: Bittle, R. G. Improving parent-teacher communication through recorded telephone messages. *Journal of Educational Research*, 1975, 69, p. 91. Reprinted with permission of Heldref Publications, 4000 Albemarle Street, NW, Washington, D.C. 20016.

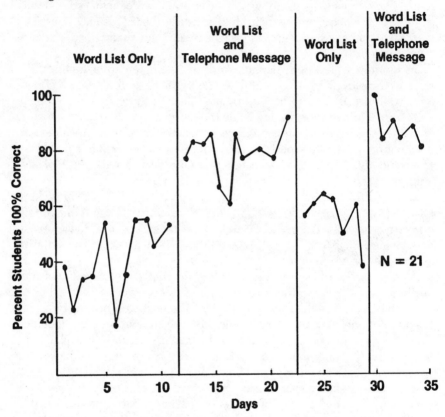

Parents reported that they liked the system because it provided them with essential information on school events.

The telephone system established by Chapman offers consultants a novel way to enlist the cooperation of parents, and it has a number of distinct advantages. First, it is flexible. Daily tapes can be generated in a matter of minutes and updated as necessary, and single-parent families or families in which both parents work can gain access to information after school without having to contact the teacher personally. Second, it is a low-cost item. The cost of the answering service, including installation, is within the budget of most school systems, and maintenance and

Figure 5–5 Number of telephone calls made as a function of recorded messages.

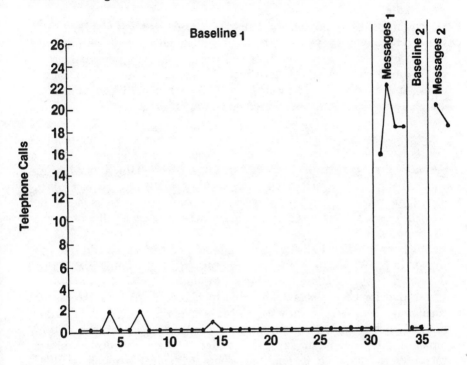

tape costs are low. Third, it is reliable. Handwritten notes are often lost, and parents do not receive the information. Fourth, it is functional. The data indicate that parents will use the telephone to get important information about their child's program, and fifth, since data on individual students are not reported on the tape, confidentiality is assured. Reporting data to parents is reserved for either a private conference or written correspondence.

Notes. Another low-cost technique which has been used repeatedly by classroom teachers over the years is to send notes home with students. The notes, unless they are of the disciplinary nature, usually are aimed at informing the parents of some accomplishment by the student in school.

Hawkins and Sluyter (1970) conducted a study that demonstrated the effectiveness of sending notes home indicating appropriate student academic performance in school. When notes were sent home, student performance improved, and when the notes were later used as tokens, exchangeable for a variety of reinforcers in the home, student performance improved even more. Privileges (staying up later, going to a movie) or the removal of certain tasks (such as putting out the trash) can serve as reinforcers.

Sending notes home with students has a number of advantages. First, it is a tangible reminder from the teacher that the student's performance was acceptable. Second, the note acts as a prompt to the parents to comment on their child's performance. Finally, the note can be used as a token. A number of preprinted notes or award certificates are commercially available and can be used on all grade levels.

Parent conferences. A third opportunity for home-school communication is through the parent conference. According to Stephens (1977) a *parent conference* should be a goal-directed session which provides for the exchange of information between teacher and parent so that educational programming can be enhanced. The parent conference should not be considered a social visit, but rather it should have specific objectives to accomplish.

Stephens (1977) indicates that parent conferences should be conducted in four phases: 1) establishing rapport; 2) obtaining information; 3) providing information; and 4) summarizing. To establish rapport it is imperative for the teacher to be able to place the parents at ease immediately. Teachers are advised to make general statements regarding neutral topics which give the parents the opportunity to speak. For example, the teacher might say, "I'm so glad we have this opportunity to meet. Were you able to find the school without too much trouble?" Opening statements to avoid would include teacher questions on private family matters or controversial school or community issues. Also, to make parents more comfortable the teacher should offer them a beverage and the opportunity to smoke if they wish. The teacher must remember that parents may feel intimidated in the school, and every effort should be made to reduce their anxiety. Anecdote 5–3 illustrates how a regular education teacher established rapport with the parent of a handicapped student who attends her class.

Anecdote 5–3

TEACHER: "Welcome to King Avenue School. It's so nice that you were able to come."

PARENT: "Thank you. I have been looking forward to the meeting.

TEACHER (*offering the parent a cup of coffee*): "Did you have any difficulty finding the school?"

PARENT: "No. The map you included in the announcement letter was perfect."

While usually a teacher conference is scheduled so that the teacher can inform the parent of the student's progress, it would be premature to begin documenting the student's performance right after establishing rapport. A better option for the teacher would be to obtain information from the parent on how the child feels about school, how he performs at home on school-related tasks, and how he gets along with neighborhood children. It is imperative for the teacher to have this data if successful programming is to be accomplished. Of course, the teacher need not continue to ask leading questions of parents to obtain every bit of information possible. Rather, the teacher should wait until there is a natural break in the conversation to provide school-related information to the parents. Anecdote 5–4 describes a scenario where such a break occurs.

Anecdote 5–4

TEACHER: "How does Sally handle money while she is shopping alone?" (*Teacher obtaining information.*)

PARENT: "Not too well. She often does not count her change, and I'm afraid to trust her with large bills."

TEACHER: "Yes, I've observed a similar pattern in the classroom while we were working on paper money, coins, and giving change. Hopefully, we'll begin to see a change in this area because I've introduced a store in the classroom. Students can buy things from the store, like pencils, chalk, and erasers, with play money. To keep whatever they buy, they have to be able to count the change correctly, name the coins they get as change, and give an equivalent value for the coins." (*Teacher providing information.*)

PARENT: "That sounds like the kind of practice she needs."

The dialogue continues with teacher and parent exchanging information until all the teacher's objectives (outlined prior to the conference) are met. Parents should be given every opportunity to ask questions, provide alternatives, and challenge the type of programming their child receives. Teachers need not feel defensive about the educational experiences they are providing, rather they should state as clearly and as straightforwardly as possible the rationale for their approach. If parents object, the teacher should pursue a line of questioning that will elicit from the parents their specific objections. Anecdote 5–5 provides such an example.

Anecdote 5–5

TEACHER: "Are there other questions you have regarding Girard's progress?"

PARENT: "Yes, I don't feel that the math instruction he is receiving is doing him any good. He seems to be going nowhere."

TEACHER (*reflecting the parent's statement*): "You feel that your son has not made adequate progress in math?"

PARENT: "That's right. He continues to have trouble telling time, measuring distances, and dealing with money."

TEACHER: "Let's just explore one of these areas. When Girard arrived in the class in September he could not tell time to the hour, half hour, or quarter hour. Presently, he is able to tell time to the hour and half hour. Have you noticed this at home?"

PARENT: "Well, yes, but he still cannot tell time."

TEACHER: "If I understand you correctly, you mean Girard can not tell time to the quarter hour and the minutes. Is that correct?"

PARENT: "Yes."

TEACHER: "I wish we had been able to make faster progress, Mrs. Carn, but, as I think you see, Girard has made some progress, although not as fast as we would like."

PARENT: "Yes, that's right."

TEACHER: "Since I've had some success with Girard teaching him time to the hour and the half hour, I think I'll continue a similar technique with the quarter hour and minutes. Maybe we can work out a program for Girard at home."

The final phase in the parent conference is the summary. It is important that the parents hear a review of the major points discussed in the conference prior to their departure. The summary provides an opportunity to bring closure to the meeting by restating all the important items of discussion.

More important, perhaps, than simply recounting the major discussion points of the conference, the summary sets the occasion for the teacher to perform two additional tasks. The first is to provide some degree of training for the parents so that they will be better able to carry on the school program at home. For example, the teacher may show the parents a simple way to teach their child to tell time or give correct change, or the teacher may show the parent how to make interesting word or sound games. Further, the teacher may demonstrate how to set up a contingency contract with a child so that more productivity is achieved in the home (see Chapter 9 for more details on contingency contracting).

The second task is for the teacher to set a firm plan for follow-up consultation. The follow-up plan need not be elaborate, rather the teacher should mention to the parents when they can expect it. In those instances where the teacher has demonstrated a new strategy to the parent, or where a different course of action is being engineered, it is critical that the follow-up occur soon after the conference. It might be as early as the next day. Of course, if the problems are not pressing, the follow-up could be postponed until a later time. Anecdote 5–6 shows how the last two items of the parent conference—training and follow-up—can be incorporated in the summary of the conference.

Anecdote 5–6

TEACHER: "Unfortunately, we are running short of time, but before you go let me take a minute to summarize what we have discussed so far."

PARENT: "Fine."

TEACHER: "One of the points of concern for both of us is Harry's need to learn more sight vocabulary words. While he has made progress this term, his reading recognition and comprehension might be increased if he had more knowledge of basic sight vocabulary."

PARENT: "That's right. He seems to miss many words which I feel he should know by the beginning of the third grade."

TEACHER (*about to provide a mini-training session*): "Agreed. One of the activities I've found successful with Harry was a word game. He seems to like to play this type of game. Let me take time to share with you some of the games you can play at home that will complement what I'm doing here at school." (*Teacher shows the parents how they can play word bingo, concentration, and lotto games. Then goes on to share another observation.*) "Another item which we discussed was Harry's unwillingness at times to follow instructions. While I don't consider this a chronic problem, it seems to be occurring with sufficient frequency to call attention to itself."

PARENT: "That's true. We've noticed similar behavior at home. We figured that he was imitating his friends in the neighborhood because in the past he would usually follow instructions without too much fuss."

TEACHER: "Well, why don't we just wait awhile to see what happens. If possible, let's say that we arrange a follow-up contact in two weeks. If Harry's performance with following directions has not improved we might be able to plan a joint strategy to resolve the problem. In the meantime, would you be able to count the number of times per day Harry is given an instruction and the number of times he fails to carry it out in a reasonable amount of time? I'll do the same with him in school. In two weeks I'll call you and we can compare notes to see if the trend is increasing, decreasing, or staying the same."

PARENT: "Fine, that sounds like an excellent idea. We'll do our best."

TEACHER: "Very good. Do you have any additional questions you'd like to bring up at this time?"

PARENT: "That just about covers it."

TEACHER: "O.K. If you have any questions or if you would like any additional suggestions on sight vocabulary games, please feel free to call me. If not, you can expect a telephone call from me two weeks from today. Would 7:30 p.m. be a good time to call?"

PARENT: "That would be fine."

TEACHER: "Again, I appreciate your willingness to come in for the conference. I learned a great deal. I hope you have a nice day."

PARENT: "Thank you. I learned quite a bit as well. We'll hear from you in two weeks. Goodbye."

This conference was closed in a non-threatening manner for the parents. The teacher did not tell the parents what to do, rather she suggested alternatives for the parents to consider (word bingo, lotto games, etc.).

Finally, the teacher made it clear to the parents that follow-up contact would be made in two weeks.

The parent's perception of this meeting more than likely was positive. One could speculate that the parents perceived the teacher as very interested in the development of their child, knowledgeable about instructional activities, and willing to assist them to insure that progress was made. With the positive feelings which have been generated, it is likely that, if two weeks hence a behavior management program is implemented for Harry's problem, a joint strategy can be achieved without too much difficulty.

Parent training. Numerous publications, workshops, and commercial materials are available to teach parents how to rear their children from birth to adulthood. Some references (for example, Spock, 1976) provide not only medical information, but also information about developmental milestones and behavior to be expected at each stage of maturation. More recently, a number of authors with a behavioral orientation (e.g., Cooper & Edge, 1978; Dardig & Heward, 1976; Heward, Dardig, & Rossett, 1979) have outlined specific strategies for parents to employ to solve a number of common problems which arise in the home.

Dardig and Heward (1976), for example, offer parents and children the opportunity to learn contracting strategies. The major theme of the book is that many home-based problems can be precluded or overcome if parents and children establish and implement effective contingency contracts.

Cooper and Edge (1981) offer specific suggestions to the parents for problems such as toileting, not eating food at mealtime, discipline, and a host of others. In their text is a discussion of the principles of learning, as well as case studies in which these principles were applied.

Establishing Parent-Training Programs

To establish an effective *parent-training program,* Stephens (1977, p. 425) offers the following guidelines:

1. Use a consistent theoretical model.

2. Determine parental skills to be mastered in advance.

3. Allow for varying rates of learning by parents.

4. Employ a systematic and functional approach.

5. Provide follow-up.

By using Stephens's guidelines a consultant can provide an individualized parent-training program. The program will be based on the assessed needs of each parent, and will be tailored to their individual learning styles and rates. Providing follow-up training or a refresher course is essential if the skills acquired during initial training are to be maintained. While Stephens's suggestions are consistent with a behavioral orientation, the success or failure of parent-training programs rests to a large extent on a host of other variables.

Time of meeting. Meeting times should be scheduled so that the maximum number of parents can attend consistently. Meeting times set on different days from week to week often lead to poor attendance and a lack of continuity in program. If possible, parents should have a choice of times to accommodate their particular needs. Consideration should also be given to scheduling meetings during the day so that parents who work at night or single-parent families can attend.

Length of sessions. Each instructional session should range from one to two hours. The length of individual meetings should be based on the number of parents there, and how far they have to travel to attend. If parents have to travel a considerable distance, it would be better to schedule longer meetings. Obviously, these parents would think twice about attending if the meetings were too brief to appear worthwhile.

Number of sessions. Patterson's (1975) training program is accomplished within a five- to fifteen-week period. The total number of sessions to schedule may be determined by a needs assessment, a procedure to decide the number of skills to be mastered by the parents. Keeping in mind Stephens's advice that parents will learn the skills at different rates, the consultant can establish a flexible schedule with respect to the number of sessions required. To do this the consultant can give the parents a pretest on the course syllabus at the first session. Based on the data obtained in the test, the consultant can then calculate the number of sessions she feels will be required to achieve competency. For a general guide on the number of sessions to use, the content to cover in each session, and the instructional and evaluation materials to employ, the reader is referred to Cooper and Edge (1981).

Location of sessions. To the maximum extent possible the location of the training sessions should be central, and easily accessible to the participants. School buildings, churches, or community auditoriums provide the consultant with the optimum amount of flexibility. For example, if the meetings are held in a school or community facility, there is usually access to audiovisual equipment, chalkboards, and ample space. Although the informal atmosphere in someone's home may initially be more conducive to discussion, it is generally not a good idea to use homes because of the potential distractions and the logistical problems of transporting equipment and materials.

Grouping. Although there are no clear rules on the optimum number of people in a parent-training group, experience seems to indicate that small groups, ranging from eight to twelve people, are best. Small groups offer more opportunity for each parent to participate. Further, if role playing and behavioral rehearsal are part of the training, and they should be, small groups facilitate these exercises. Frequently, individuals who are meeting to discuss problems become inhibited if the group is too large. Also larger meetings can be dominated by a few outspoken parents, and the less verbal members do not participate as much.

Finally, groups should remain intact for the length of the training program. The rationale, of course, is that personal relationships develop among the parents, and they become more willing to confide in each other.

Cost. There are a number of ways to reduce or eliminate the cost of parent-training programs to the school. These include: first, one can obtain the training through a university or college. Frequently, colleges offer course work or practicum experiences that require graduate students to actively engage in parent programming. Under the supervision of faculty members, parent training is offered at minimal cost or no cost at all. Second, apply for grant money. Many national, state, and local sources offer grant money to organizations involved in parent training. A reference list of sources can be obtained at a public library. Third, seek funds through corporations or private individuals. Many national and local corporations have funds budgeted for community projects. Guidelines are often available to help organizations apply for these sources of money, and private individuals have been known to donate funds for parent-training programs. Fourth, secure volunteer assistance. Teachers or administrators interested in establishing parent-training programs can often be enlisted to run the groups without charge.

Structure of sessions. While the topics from session to session will vary, it is important that the structure of the session remain consistent. During each session the parents should receive information that will help them at home, have the opportunity to ask questions and discuss issues related to it, as well as the chance to practice skills taught in the session, and receive feedback and reinforcement on their performance. It is one thing for the parents to gain the cognitive knowledge associated with the curriculum; it is quite another for them to gain the practical skill needed to execute the curriculum at home. Training sessions that emphasize the former at the expense of the latter only provide the parents with half of the skills they need.

The initial session should be devoted to having the parents get to know one another. Effective consultants have a battery of "icebreakers" they employ to encourage parents to meet one another.

The final session. The final session should be reserved for distributing certificates of achievement and answering any questions that parents may have. Plans for follow-up can be discussed, and individual parent concerns can be addressed (see Figure 5–6).

The team leader. To a large extent the success or failure of a parent-training program can be traced to the effectiveness of the team leader. Just as teachers are willing to accept the suggestions of supervisors they perceive as competent, so, too, will parents accept the recommendations and suggestions of a parent trainer they feel is trustworthy and expert. Parents must feel that the trainer cares about their problems and is a person in whom they can confide. Also, the parents must feel that the trainer has had experience with the types of problems they are encountering. If parents do not have confidence in the trainer's ability to help them, little progress is likely to be made.

Parents in the Classroom

Until recently, the classroom was thought to be the exclusive domain of the classroom teacher. The teacher was responsible for planning and teaching lessons and evaluating the performance of each student. Clearly, there are teacher responsibilities, but just as clearly some duties can be accomplished by parents who volunteer in the classroom.

Parent volunteers, though they require instruction and supervision by the teacher, can perform essential jobs for the teacher. For example, parent volunteers could write or explain directions to students, correct papers and provide reinforcement, or give one-to-one remedial instruction. However, without a well thought-out plan for working with parents as paraprofessionals, many of the possible benefits would be lost.

Fortunately, a number of educators have recognized the need to provide training for parents who assume the duties of a paraprofessional. Strenechy, McLoughlin, and Edge (1979), for example, identified guidelines for a *parent-tutoring program*. In general, these authors feel that potential parent-tutors should receive an in-service orientation, support

THE OHIO STATE UNIVERSITY

COLLEGE OF EDUCATION

Faculty for Exceptional Children

Hereby acknowledges that

KATHLEEN CHRISTINE LEE

Has successfully demonstrated the competencies of the

Parenting Skills Workshop

— PARENTING SKILLS ACQUIRED —

* PINPOINTING SPECIFIC CHILD
  BEHAVIORS

* OBSERVING & RECORDING CHILD
  BEHAVIOR

* GRAPHING BEHAVIORAL
  INFORMATION

* SELECTING & USING STRATEGIES
  FOR ACCELERATING APPROPRIATE
  & DECELERATING INAPPROPRIATE
  BEHAVIORS

* CONTINGENCY CONTRACTING

* EVALUATING THE EFFECTS OF
  BEHAVIORAL STRATEGIES

WORKSHOP LEADER

WILLIAM L. HEWARD
PARENT TRAINING CO-ORDINATOR

Awarded On: 1/1/82

DATE

THOMAS M. STEPHENS, CHAIRMAN
FACULTY FOR EXCEPTIONAL CHILDREN

Figure 5–6 Certificate of achievement.

from the school administration, and supervision from the teacher or consultant. Further, they recommend that parents not tutor their own children.

Many parents would be unable to participate in such a program because of family or work responsibilities, but even if a few parents were able to volunteer, the teachers, pupils, and parents would gain the following advantages:

1. Given a reduced teacher-student ratio, the teacher would be free to provide more direct remedial assistance to the students most in need.

2. Parents would become better acquainted with the problems of the mildly handicapped, and more knowledgeable about methods for remediating or coping with these problems.

3. Parent input in the Individualized Education Program (IEP) process would be enhanced.

4. If the program incorporates "foster grandparents," capable senior citizens would have the opportunity to contribute their time and talents in a worthwhile project. For them, an increased feeling of self-worth could be a valuable spin-off advantage.

SUMMARY

This chapter suggested a number of ways in which consultants can work with parents of handicapped children. A model was presented that describes the types of services professionals and parents can perform and the levels of that service. Techniques for increasing parent involvement as behavior managers and home-based educators were presented. A telephone answering service was suggested as a means by which consultants can help to increase home-school communication and student academic performance. Procedures for conducting effective parent conferences were described and several recommendations were proposed for establishing and implementing functional parent-training programs. Finally, the use of parents as in-school tutors was discussed.

Questions

---

1. Identify the four levels of parent involvement in Kroth's Mirror Model. Specify the types of activities which professionals and parents could do at each level.

2. Provide two examples which show how parents used behavior management techniques to change inappropriate child behavior.

3. List three advantages of using the telephone to enhance student academic achievement.

4. According to Stephens what are the key phases or components of an effective parent conference?

5. What guidelines does Stephens offer for establishing an effective parent-training program?

6. Name two ways to help reduce the cost of parent-training programs.

7. What advantages can be obtained from having parents participate as in-class tutors?

Discussion Points and Exercises

---

1. Argue for or against the use of parents as in-school tutors. State your reasons, and provide documentation for your position.

2. Conduct an in-service training program based on the recommendations of Cooper and Edge, Heward, Dardig, and Rossett, or Stephens. Note the effects. Rewrite in-service training components based on your experience.

3. Conduct an informal meeting with teachers, parents, and administrators. The topic of the meeting is "Managing students' behavior at school and at home." Record comments from each participant. Obtain consensus on a course of action with a current problem.

4. Discuss the special problems handicapped students have inside and outside the regular classroom environment. Identify at least three

recommendations you could offer to teachers and other support personnel for dealing more effectively with these students.

5. Present a videotape of a parent conference. Have teachers identify the four phases outlined by Stephens (rapport building, obtaining information, providing information, and summarizing). Follow up the videotape training by observing teachers during a conference. Provide appropriate praise and feedback.

REFERENCES

BARSCH, R. H. *The parent teacher partnership*. Arlington, Virginia: The Council for Exceptional Children, 1969.

BITTLE, R. G. Improving parent-teacher communication through recorded telephone messages. *Journal of Educational Research*, 1975, 69, 87–95.

CHAPMAN, J. Improving parent-teacher communication through the use of recorded messages. Unpublished thesis, The Ohio State University, 1978.

COOPER, J. O., & EDGE, D. *Parenting: Strategies and educational methods*. Louisville, Ky.: Eston Corp., 1981.

DARDIG, J., & HEWARD, W. L. *Sign here: A contracting book for children and their parents*. Bridgewater, N.J.: F. Fournies and Associates, 1976.

HALL, R. V., CRISTLER, C., CRANSTON, S. S., & TUCKER, B. Teachers and parents as researchers using multiple baseline designs. *Journal of Applied Behavior Analysis*, 1970, 3, 247–255.

HAWKINS, R. P., & SLUYTER, D. J. Modification of achievement by a simple technique involving parents and teachers. Paper presented at the AERA convention, Minneapolis, Minnesota, March 2–6, 1970.

HERON, T. E., & AXELROD, S. Effectiveness of feedback to mothers concerning their children's word recognition performance. *Reading Improvement*, 1976, *13* (2), 74–81.

HEWARD, W. L., DARDIG, J. C., & ROSSETT, A. *Working with parents of handicapped children*. Columbus, Ohio: Charles E. Merrill, 1979.

KRONICH, D. *They too can succeed: A practical guide for parents of learning disabled children*. San Rafael, California: Academic Therapy, 1969.

KROTH, R. L. *Communicating with parents of exceptional children: Improving parent-teacher relationships*. Denver, Colorado: Love, 1975.

KROTH, R. L. Personal communication, 1980.

KROTH, R. L., WHELAN, R. J. & STABLES, J. M. Teacher application of behavioral principles in home and classroom environments. *Focus on Exceptional Children*, 1970, 3, 1–10.

LERNER, J. W. *Children with learning disabilities*. (2nd ed.) Boston: Houghton Mifflin, 1976.

LICHTO, R. Communicating with parents: It begins with listening: *Teaching Exceptional Children*, 1976, 8 (2), 67–71.

McLoughlin, J. Roles and practices of parents of children with learning and behavior problems. In D. Edge, B. J. Strenechy, & S. I. Mour (Eds.), *Parenting learning problem children: The professional educator's perspective.* Columbus, Ohio: NCEMMH, The Ohio State University, 1978.

Mercer, D. C. *Children and adolescents with learning disabilities.* Columbus, Ohio: Charles E. Merrill, 1979.

Moore, B. L., & Bailey, H. Social punishment in the modification of a preschool child's "autistic-like" behavior with a mother as therapist. *Journal of Applied Behavior Analysis,* 1973, 6, 497–507.

National School Public Relations Association. *Conference time for teachers and parents.* Washington, D.C., National School Public Relations Association, 1970.

O'Dell, S. Training parents in behavior modification: A review. *Psychological Bulletin,* 1974, 81, 418–432.

Patterson, G. R. *Families: Application of social learning to family life.* Champaign, Illinois: Research Press, 1975.

Public Law 94–142. Education for All Handicapped Children Act of 1975 (5.6) 94th Congress, 1975.

Shrewsberry, R. Case study number three. In J. O. Cooper and D. Edge (Eds.), *Parenting: Strategies and educational methods.* Louisville, Ky.: Eston Corp., 1981.

Spock, B. *Baby and child care.* New York: Pocket Books, 1976.

Stephens, T. M. *Teaching skills to children with learning and behavior disorders.* Columbus, Ohio: Charles E. Merrill, 1977.

Strenecky, B., McLoughlin, J. A., & Edge, D. Parent involvement: A consumer perspective—in the schools. *Education and Training of the Mentally Retarded,* 1979, *14* (2), 54–56.

Varone, V. A., O'Brien, R., & Axelrod, S. Reinforcing parents for their children's academic performance. Paper presented at the meeting of the Council for Exceptional Children, Washington, D. C., March, 1972.

6

Individualized Instruction in Mainstreamed Elementary Classrooms

---

Individualized instruction has been the hallmark of special education since its inception. Researchers and educators in this field have consistently championed new ways to provide instruction so that the individual needs of students could be met. For example, some students with severe reading deficits have benefited from a highly structured, multi-sensory approach (Fernald, 1943). Children with severe communication handicaps have been instructed with sign language or finger spelling, and students with visual handicaps have been taught with large print readers or cassette tapes.

Since many handicapped children, who had been taught exclusively in self-contained rooms, are being integrated in the regular classes, teachers need to become resourceful about individualized instruction. Providing individualized instruction in a classroom with thirty students can be much more difficult than with ten students.

The purpose of this chapter is to describe ways in which a consultant can assist regular education teachers at the elementary level with individualizing instruction. Three areas will be explored—teaching strategies, curriculum and teaching adaptations, and technology. Consultants who are able to help teachers gain competency in these three areas will have enabled a staff to do a better job of meeting the individual needs of students.

Objectives

After reading this chapter the reader will be able to:

1. identify three strategies which regular educators can use to individualize instruction.

2. list and describe the four components of an effective classwide peer-tutoring system, and state the rationale for the so-called tutor huddle.

3. describe how a teacher can successfully manage several small instructional groups at the same time in the regular classroom.

4. provide two functional suggestions for adapting the curriculum at the elementary level to meet the individualized needs of handicapped learners.

5. list and describe two sources of technical equipment that a regular educator could use to supplement basic instruction.

Key Terms

Individualized instruction	Peer tutoring
Remedial teaching model	Cross-age tutoring
Large group instruction	Curriculum adaptations
Small group instruction	

INDIVIDUALIZED INSTRUCTION

Individualized instruction has several meanings for educators. For some teachers it means that each student has his own work folder which contains assignments designed to meet his personal needs. Other teachers consider individualized instruction in the context of a teaching method. Modes of presenting instructional tasks and expected modes of response are programmed so that the student has the maximum opportunity for success.

Like most educational concepts, individualized instruction can be conceptualized in a number of ways, and the consultant must be able to relate to the way a regular educator applies the term to the actual learning needs of the student. For example, if a regular educator's perception of individualized instruction is that each student has his own folder, yet each folder contains the same work for all students, the consultant may have to explore with the teacher other ways to meet the assessed needs of the student.

Several definitions of individualized instruction will be provided along with a model for remedial instruction that can be used to meet the individualized learning needs of all students.

Definition of Individualized Instruction

The definition of *individualized instruction* has evolved over several years. According to Good, Biddle, and Brophy (1975) individualization became a popular educational approach when school districts started to abandon their strict adherence to an age-graded curriculum. Teachers began to concentrate on teaching skills, regardless of the grade level children were assigned. For example, children in the second, third, or fourth grade who may have lacked a specific academic skill may have been grouped together in a nongraded classroom, or taught by a team of two teachers.

Since the mid-1960's, an era marked by significant legislative and litigative milestones for the handicapped, individualized instruction has come to mean that each student will progress through a specifically designed curriculum to meet goals identified for that student. Generally agreed upon educational goals for all students have been replaced by prescribed objectives to meet individually assessed needs.

To cite an example, a handicapped student in the 1950's might have been taught the same social studies curriculum in the same way as the other students. In the 1960's that curriculum still might have been taught the student, only a battery of technological hardware (taperecorders, computers, etc.) would have been used to help him learn the material. Today, the handicapped student might receive instruction in social studies only if it matched the goals and objectives specified by his Individualized Education Program (IEP).

Some authors (notably Minskoff, 1975) define individualized instruction as the teaching act which occurs between one teacher and one student for 100 percent of the time. According to Turnbull and Schulz (1977), when individual differences among students are considered along with their interest level, age, learning styles, and abilities, individualized instruction takes place. These authors contend that individualized programs can be used successfully in classrooms with large numbers of students, but teachers will need the assistance of consultants to redesign the instructional strategies.

A Model for Individualizing Instruction

Regardless of the definition one uses for individualized instruction, a *remedial teaching model* developed by Wallace and Kauffman (1978) can be employed. The model is based on a series of instructional decisions that enable a teacher to meet long-range goals (see Figure 6–1).

The model begins when the teacher collects Type I data—information from test results, observations, and records—to formulate the instructional plan. Type II data, not illustrated on the graph, is obtained as soon as the student enters the system and begins to make responses based on the presentation of instructional tasks. Type II data refers to the information a teacher uses to correct a previous teaching approach or strategy. It serves a feedback function in the system.

After long-range and immediate goals are selected, the first instructional task is presented. If the student accomplishes this task, the next task in the sequence is presented. This process continues, assuming the student meets the criterion, until all the instructional tasks and immediate goals have been achieved. At this point, the first long-term goal should have been accomplished. Another long-term goal is then selected, and the process is repeated.

If the student makes an error after the initial instructional task has been presented, the teacher's first responsibility is to analyze her own behavior. She must determine whether the presentation was appropriate, whether the student had sufficient feedback, or whether the classroom arrangement needs changing. For example, if a teacher called on a learning disabled student to answer a question during a discussion period and the student was attending to events going on elsewhere in the room, the teacher might elect to move the student's seat closer to her so that he would not be so distracted. If the student's future responses were appro-

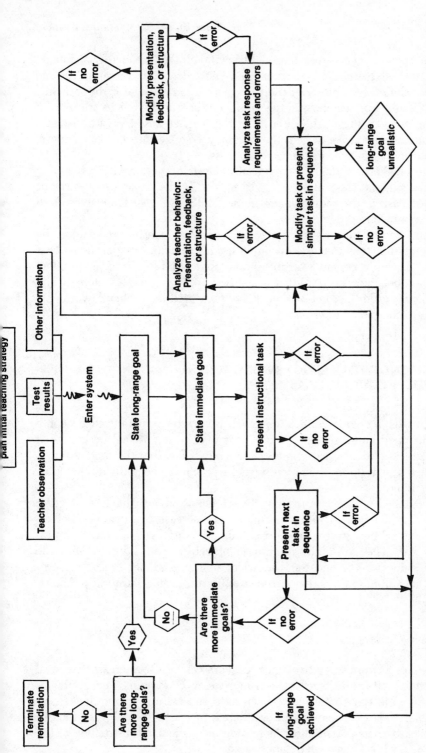

Figure 6–1 Schematic representation of a remedial teaching system. SOURCE: From Wallace, G., & Kauffman, J. M. Teaching children with learning problems (2nd ed.). Columbus, Ohio: Charles E. Merrill, 1978. P. 96. Reprinted with permission.

137

priate, the teacher could be reasonably confident that the change she made was effective. If student errors persisted, regardless of seat assignment, the teacher should look closer at the student's response to see if the task was appropriate. For instance, if the student was still unable to supply the correct answer during the discussion, the teacher might give him clues. The clues might serve to help the student recognize the correct response, thereby increasing the likelihood of success.

The teacher decides, based on an analysis of her teaching behavior and the student's responses, whether to modify the present task, present the next task in the sequence, or, if the long-range goal is unrealistic, to write a new long-range goal.

The present authors take the position that consultants should be aware of the steps that are available in this remedial model, because it serves as an excellent starting point for individualizing instruction. Teacher behavior and student responses are considered systematically and higher order instructional goals are presented only when lower order tasks are completed to criterion.

USING INDIVIDUALIZED PROCEDURES IN THE REGULAR CLASSROOM

One reason a regular education teacher may be reluctant to accept a handicapped child into his classroom is that he might feel he is unable to meet the student's learning needs. He might feel that the time required to teach thirty or more students would preclude the individualizing of instruction.

A teacher who expresses negative feelings about "having to go it alone" can be helped. The consultant can increase his awareness of effective teaching strategies, curriculum adaptations, and technological hardware. The consultant's ultimate objective would be to help the teacher develop the necessary knowledge and confidence to direct a program so well-organized that it appeared to run itself (Turnbull & Schulz, 1977).

Teaching Strategies

There are a number of strategies teachers can use to increase the level of individualized instruction in the regular classroom. The strategies mentioned in this section have been used successfully in regular education classrooms, or have been validated by experimental research. In either case, their potential for increasing individualized instruction at the elementary level has been demonstrated.

Large group instruction. Many regular educators may feel that it is impossible to individualize using *large group instruction*, where one teacher is directing a lesson with thirty or more students. Individualized instruction, however, can be provided if the modes of presentation and expected student response modes are matched. For instance, suppose that a teacher in an elementary school class was introducing a geography unit on the Nile Valley. Some students in the class might be required to give oral responses to the teacher's question. Other students (for example, a cerebral-palsied student with articulation problems) might be required to demonstrate or point. Anecdote 6–1 illustrates how this geography lesson might take place.

Anecdote 6–1

TEACHER (*calling on April*): "April, tell the class why the Nile River is so important to the economy and well-being of Egypt."

APRIL: "The river is important because it serves as a source of water for irrigation and transportation for people up and down the valley."

TEACHER: "Very good. Since much of Egypt is arid, the Nile provides the necessary water to raise crops and livestock."

TEACHER (*calling on Richard, the cerebral-palsied student*): "Richard, please turn on the overhead projector. You'll notice that an outline map of Egypt and a grease pencil are on the stage. I'd like you to do the following: first, draw the location of the Nile; second, shade the area around the Nile that was once known as the floodplain; and last, locate the series of dams which have been constructed along the river to prevent flooding and provide hydroelectric power."

RICHARD: (*takes the grease pencil in his hand and performs the tasks*)

TEACHER: "Excellent! Class, notice that Richard has shaded a large area of the river valley. Prior to dam construction projects, this shaded area represented the land that was flooded annually by the Nile." (*Teacher continues with the rest of the lesson.*)

The teacher in this anecdote provided individualized instruction to a handicapped student in a large group setting. She knew the content she wanted to teach and the expected student responses. April had to supply an answer orally, while Richard's participation in the same activity was tailored so that he could be successful. He did not say a word, yet he performed exactly what was required. The teacher's verbal praise not only reinforced Richard's performance, but also publicly announced his success to the class. For handicapped students, public recognition for acceptable performance can be a definite boost to confidence.

Small group instruction. In graded classrooms it is not surprising to find a wide range of student abilities, interests, and rates of learning. When faced with such heterogeneity teachers usually divide the students for *small group instruction.* While the teacher is working with one group, the other students may be assigned seat work, board work, or independent activities. To provide individualized instruction to all students, including the handicapped, the teacher must be able to manage each group simultaneously. As Mercer (1979) states, "small group instruction is essential in mainstreamed classrooms" (p. 320). Anecdote 6–2 describes a conversation between a consultant and a teacher who was having difficulty with her classroom, which contained two educable mentally retarded students.

Anecdote 6–2

TEACHER (*talking to consultant*): "Mr. Krebs, I'm having trouble with my reading groups, and I'm really lost for ideas on what to do with Dale and Joe while I'm with a reading group. They seem to demand so much attention."

CONSULTANT: "Tell me about it."

TEACHER: "Right after morning exercises and announcements I explain all the board work to the class and I try to take extra time with Dale and Joe. I go over each assignment, and ask if there are any questions."

CONSULTANT: "Do many students ask questions?"

TEACHER: "A few do, but most wait until I take my first reading group. Then they'll raise their hand or come back to my desk to ask for help with a problem I just explained."

CONSULTANT: "I know what you mean. I used to have the same problem, and it wasn't just the handicapped students who would interrupt."

TEACHER: "What did you do?"

CONSULTANT: "Well, I started the morning the same way you do. But I told the students that I wasn't to be interrupted while I was with a reading group. If they had questions they were to put their names on the board, and continue with the work they could do. I made quick trips to a student who needed help when I thought it necessary."

TEACHER: "How do you do that without interrupting the flow of instruction?"

CONSULTANT: "Suppose the first group you had was reading a story. One thing you could do is have the students read the next paragraph of the story to themselves. Tell them to read to find out why something happened, or read to find what the paragraph was about. While they were reading silently, slip off to the student whose name appears first on the board to provide individual help. While you are at the student's desk, praise her for her work. The system should reduce the number of interruptions you have, and the student's on-task behavior should improve because you will be praising their effort and achievement."

TEACHER: "That sounds like a great idea. I think I'll try it."

CONSULTANT: "It worked for me when I taught. I'm sure it will work for you. You may have to make extra trips to Dale's and Joe's desks to help them, but as you gain experience you'll find ways to cut down the number of times you have to visit their desks during the reading period."

In this case the consultant provided a functional suggestion on how individualized instruction could be handled in a classroom where students were having difficulty with their daily assignments. Further, the consultant indicated that Dale and Joe may need more assistance initially, but that later this direct help with seat work assignments could probably be reduced.

Peer tutoring. An often forgotten resource for providing direct instruction is the students themselves. Research on *peer tutoring*, defined as same-age students teaching one another, has demonstrated that it is an effective strategy for increasing academic skills of both students (Conlon, Hall, & Hanley, 1972; Harris, Sherman, Henderson, & Harris, 1972; Allen & Boraks, 1978) and tutors (Dineen, Clark, & Risley, 1977; Parson & Heward, 1979).

Clearly, peer tutoring has several distinct advantages over other techniques. First, tutors are available. Teachers do not have to rely on volunteers, parent-aides, or paraprofessionals. Second, when tutors and students switch roles both benefit. According to Lovitt (1977) the tutor learns because he has additional practice with the skill, may have to look up answers for questions, or defend his reasoning if challenged by the student. Finally, academic achievement is enhanced.

Although peer tutoring is used in regular education classrooms, it is usually done on a limited and impromptu basis. Typically the teacher assigns a proficient pupil to tutor a student who has yet to master a skill or concept, and the tutor-student pair work together without direct teacher supervision (Deterline, 1970).

To use peer tutoring on a classwide basis, however, a different procedure needs to be employed that will enable the tutor to learn the new skill and simultaneously to teach it to his student. To achieve this objective, Heward, Heron, and Cooke (1980) devised a procedure known as *tutor huddle*.

To form a tutor huddle, a class is divided into tutor-student pairs. The division can be based on achievement scores or compatibility. A handicapped student may serve as either tutor or student depending upon the goals of the tutoring program. Once the tutor-student pairs are formed, they are combined in groups of three to five pairs. For example, if there were thirty-two students in the class, sixteen tutor-student pairs might be arranged in four tutor huddles.

At the beginning of each tutoring session, the tutors from each huddle meet for five minutes to review the material they are to present to their respective students. As Figure 6–2 illustrates, the tutors are presenting sight-word vocabulary to one another; the same sight words that they will present to their students during the five-minute practice session which follows.

During tutor huddle, the tutors confirm each other's responses to the sight vocabulary words by saying "yes." If a tutor makes a mistake, the other tutors provide corrective feedback. If none of the tutors is able to provide the word, a tutor raises his hand to obtain teacher assistance. While the tutors are reviewing in the huddle, their students are engaged in seat work at their desks.

At the teacher's signal, a five-minute practice session begins. Each tutor is joined by his student for flash card drill (see Figure 6–3). The tutor presents the cards to the student as quickly as possible. If a student is not able to identify a word, or says a word incorrectly, the tutor uses a two-step prompting procedure to help. At the end of the five-minute practice session, the student is tested by the tutor and the result is graphed. During practice and testing, the student receives verbal reinforcement from the teacher for looking at the flash cards and following the tutor's directions.[1]

---

[1] A complete description of the classwide peer-tutoring training package can be obtained by writing Timothy E. Heron, Faculty for Exceptional Children, The Ohio State University, 1945 N. High Street, Columbus, Ohio 43210.

Figure 6–2 Four first-grade children participating in a tutor huddle.

In a tutor-huddle procedure "a tutoring system within a tutoring system" is arranged (Heward et al. 1980, p. 9). Tutors learn from one another, and the consequence of having to teach their students the assignment within a matter of minutes may add an extra incentive to learn.

Cross-age tutoring. Some regular education teachers, especially those at earlier grade levels, may feel that the students within their classroom are not ready to teach one another, yet they still want a tutoring program to individualize instruction. *Cross-age tutoring*—older students helping younger ones—can effectively solve the teacher's problem if some logistical hurdles can be overcome. For example, if a sixth grader were to tutor a second grader in math on Monday from 9:00 a.m. to 9:30 a.m., the teacher would have to resolve any scheduling conflicts for the sixth grader. According to Dineen et al. (1977) special arrangements may have to be made for missed class time. Also, it is highly unlikely that more than several older students could be used at once. So, the chances of having a classwide program using cross-age tutors are slim. However,

Figure 6–3 A first-grade tutor presenting sight-word vocabulary to her student.

if the teacher is interested in cross-age tutoring for a few students, the technique can be effective (Cloward, 1967; Frager & Stern, 1970; Johnson & Bailey, 1974).

AIDES, PARAPROFESSIONALS, VOLUNTEERS AND PARENTS

Ancillary personnel, such as classroom aides, paraprofessionals, volunteers, and parents, can help the teachers in mainstreamed classrooms to individualize instruction. Generally speaking, these individuals work with one student or a small group of students while the teacher handles the rest of the class. Typically the assistant helps students with review work, provides the opportunity for supervised practice, or gives exams. Such assistants can provide the personalized help that many students need.

Recommending the various teaching strategies that have been mentioned is one way which consultants can help teachers individualize instruction. It is not the only way, however. By adopting existing curriculum materials and alternating their basic instructional approach, teachers can individualize instruction across a number of skill and content areas.

CURRICULUM ADAPTATIONS

While the school curriculum may be outlined by the district, the choice of instructional materials and methods is usually left to the teacher (Turnbull and Schulz, 1979). The teacher selects materials based on several criteria, including the publisher's guidelines, previous experience teaching the skill, availability, and the student's individual needs. *Curriculum adaptations* refer to changes in instructional methodology or materials made to meet the unique learning needs of students.

Unfortunately, the match between the first three variables and student need is often imprecise (Lovitt, 1977), or there are units of instruction for which materials do not currently exist. Sometimes the teacher must make the materials himself or forego teaching the unit. For a teacher to adapt existing curriculum materials that meet the predetermined needs of handicapped students, it is essential that he have a clear idea of the content to be taught, and the best method for teaching it to an individual student. There are several strategies a teacher can use to do this.

Reducing distractions. A number of special educators have indicated that some handicapped children (for example, the learning disabled, behaviorally disordered) are distracted by stimulation in their environment (Stephens, 1977; Wallace & McLoughlin, 1979). By adapting the method by which the handicapped student is required to complete an assignment, the teacher might reduce or eliminate the distractibility. For example, a learning disabled student might be repeatedly off-task during a class session where a written response is required. However, if the teacher adapted the task to an oral response, the student's level of distractibility might lessen. If written responses are necessary, the teacher might use *shaping*—a procedure whereby successive approximations to an objective are rewarded. In the case where an LD student was required to write a full page of composition, the teacher might begin by having him write one sentence, then one paragraph, and gradually increase the requirement to the full page.

Also, some handicapped students who perform poorly with paper and pencil do much better when they can write their response on acetate and show it on an overhead projector.

Another way to reduce distractions is to have the student complete assignments in a study carrel. As Haubrich and Shores (1976) found, LD students who worked in enclosed carrels had higher attention spans, though not necessarily higher achievement scores, than when they worked at conventional desks. The carrels effectively screen distracting visual stimuli.

Pacing lessons. Another way that the existing curriculum can be modified for the handicapped is to pace the activities or tasks the students are required to complete. Instead of issuing one major assignment (for example, completing five pages of math), the teacher might assign three shorter tasks which involve the same skill, but do not require the same sustained concentration. Further, the teacher might modify an assignment so that the student is not penalized for his disability. For example, suppose that a cerebral-palsied student, integrated in the regular classroom for math, had to complete twenty-five math problems which were written on the board. While the other students in the class might be required to copy the problems and solve them without a manipulative device or a calculator, the cerebral-palsied child could work directly from the board, using a calculator or an abacus. In this way, he is not penalized for his inability to copy the problems. To the contrary, he would be demonstrating to the teacher that he had mastered the mathematical operation required.

Promoting overlearning. Generally, skill instruction in the regular classroom proceeds in a vertical fashion. That is, once a student has mastered a lower-order skill, instruction begins on the next higher-order skill. With many handicapped students, however, it is necessary to overlearn a skill, so that proficiency and long-term retention is enhanced. Teachers can adapt the existing scope and sequence of a curriculum and promote overlearning by giving handicapped students additional practice and review with previously learned skills.

Modifying delivery of content. Unquestionably, most of the goals established by a teacher for her students are achieved through some type of verbal behavior (Popham & Baker, 1970). While lecturing to students can be an effective technique for presenting new ideas, it does not usually provide the students with the opportunity to practice the skills the teacher is attempting to teach. Further, if the teacher gives a lecture to her class, and fails to ask the students pertinent questions after the talk, it is unlikely that they will remember much of what was said.

On the other hand, a class discussion can be a valuable learning experience for the handicapped student as well as the rest of the class. If the students have sufficient background on the topic and the teacher has the ability to lead the group, a discussion can lead to affective changes in learners (Popham & Baker, 1970). For example, suppose that a teacher were leading a discussion on the effects of poverty on individuals. During the discussion the teacher could raise additional questions about how the lack of resources—monetary, physical, or social—reduces a person's ability to participate in the mainstream of the society. If the teacher is skillful, students might begin to gain an understanding of how the handicapped, for example, must make use of all the resources at their disposal to succeed. Normal students might come to sense that the problems that face sensorially, physically, and emotionally handicapped individuals are not so different from those which affect the poverty-stricken. Both groups suffer social alienation and rejection.

Finally, according to Popham and Baker (1970), lectures and discussions need to be supplemented with demonstrations that show students the tasks that the teacher wants them to learn. Consultants need to remind teachers that the criteria for using demonstration as an instructional method are: 1) make sure the teacher can perform the demonstration; 2) have all necessary apparatus available; 3) schedule practice sessions after the demonstration so that students can imitate the behavior, and 4) provide feedback to the students on their ability to imitate the demonstrated task.

Technology

Each year computers and related hardware are produced that are smaller, more efficient, and less expensive, and educational publishers are using highly sophisticated computer systems to program educational lessons on a wide range of topics. This section of the chapter will discuss several types of technological hardware and audiovisual equipment that teachers can use, and present the advantages and disadvantages of each for the teacher.

Tape recorders. The cassette tape recorder is an excellent device for individualizing instruction in any classroom. It has several uses. For example, the teacher can record review lessons, stories, tests, and directions for completing assignments. Students who have difficulty comprehending oral instructions are able to use the tape recorder effectively because they can replay the instructions several times. Further, the teacher can pace an exercise with the recorder so that students with lower rates of learning can be challenged while faster students can be moved ahead. Sample teacher directions to a handicapped student are found in Anecdote 6–3.

Anecdote 6–3

(*Student turns tape recorder on.*)

TEACHER: "Good morning. Today we are going to take our practice spelling exam. I'll say one word at a time, use the word in a sentence, and then say the word again. After I have pronounced each word the second time, turn off the recorder and write the correct spelling. When you are finished, turn the recorder back on and I'll spell the word. You can correct your own paper. The first word is *typhoon*. A typhoon is a fierce storm. *Typhoon*."

(*Student turns off tape recorder and writes the response; then turns on tape recorder to hear teacher spell the word.*)

TEACHER: "Typhoon, *t-y-p-h-o-o-n*."

In this anecdote the teacher programmed a written response for the student. Perhaps for another student, she may have programmed an oral response and the student would have spelled the word directly onto the tape.

The tape recorder, when used with supplemental materials such as paper and pencil exercises, can be the cornerstone of a self-instructional package. These packages, which contain the student's assignment, mode of response, and self-checking component, can be of great value in helping the handicapped student remain within the mainstream (deGrandpré & Messler, 1979).

One potential disadvantage of the tape recorder is that it takes time to produce the tapes. The teacher may be able to ask students, assistants, paraprofessionals, or volunteers to help make the tapes.

Overhead projector. Next to the tape recorder the piece of instructional hardware most common to individual instruction is the overhead projector. It can be used in a group lesson as we noted in Anecdote 6–1. Also, the overhead can be used to introduce new lessons, review key points prior to an exam, or as a way to observe an individual student's response.

One advantage of the overhead is its low cost. By using write-on transparencies and washable pens, teachers can reuse transparencies almost indefinitely. Like audiotapes, transparencies can be catalogued and filed according to the skill or content they are designed to teach.

Computers. Some school districts have purchased on-line computers with telephone couplers which are linked to a master computer. The teacher dials a code number to enter the system and request a specific lesson. Once the lesson has been requested, the student uses the keys on his computer console to type his response. The computer, based on the student's accomplishment, automatically presents appropriate trials to the student. Some computers provide a tally at the end of the exercise of the number and rate of correct and incorrect student responses.

One disadvantage of the computer is that it is costly. With the increasing cost of education it is unlikely that computer-assisted instruction will achieve nationwide use. A second disadvantage of this approach is that only one student at a time can use the computer console.

Filmstrips and recorders. For students who have poor reading skills, filmstrip-tape packages offer the opportunity to participate in an individualized program. Students listen to a tape of a story or lesson while simultaneously viewing the filmstrip. Students enjoy using the filmstrip projector with the tape recorder. The teacher can use this approach to review lessons or as an independent seat-work assignment. If deaf or hard-of-hearing students are integrated in the regular classroom, the consultant might recommend that captioned films or filmstrips be used so that these students will be able to participate as well.

SUMMARY

A regular education teacher with a handicapped student enrolled in her classroom must be able to provide individualized instruction so that the assessed needs of the student can be met. The success of the child's program will be determined in large part by the ability of the teacher to use functional teaching strategies, adapt the existing curriculum and instructional methods, and use technological hardware. Consultants should be ready to recommend alternatives to regular class teachers in each of these areas.

Questions

1. Define individualized instruction.

2. Describe the purpose of a tutor huddle.

3. Provide one suggestion for a teacher that would help her manage several small group activities simultaneously.

4. List two ways a regular education teacher could adapt her existing curriculum.

5. State how the following pieces of equipment could be used to individualize instruction for handicapped students: tape recorder, overhead projector, computer, filmstrips.

Discussion Points and Exercises

1. Conduct a meeting with the special and regular education teachers to determine how existing curriculum materials in both classrooms could be adapted to meet the needs of a specific handicapped student.

2. Conduct a pilot study with a group of regular education teachers to determine the efficacy of various pieces of instructional hardware (for example, tape recorder, overhead). Include in the study a complete evaluation of how individualization was enhanced.

3. Show a videotape of a teacher instructing her class in social studies, science, or math. Obtain the views of the audience of regular and special teachers on how the lesson could have been better individualized.

REFERENCES

ALLEN, A. R., & BORAKS, N. Peer tutoring: Putting it to the test. *The Reading Teacher*, 1978, 31, 274–278.

CLOWARD, R. D. Studies in tutoring. *Journal of Experimental Education*, 1967, 36, 14–25.

CONLON, M. F., HALL, C., & HANLEY, E. The effects of a peer correction procedure on the arithmetic accuracy for two elementary school children. In G. Semb (Ed.), *Behavior analysis and education*. Lawrence, Kansas: The University of Kansas Support and Development Center for Follow Through, 1972, 205–210.

DETERLINE, W. C. *Training and management of student-tutors: Final report*. Palo Alto, California: General Programmed Teaching, 1970. (ERIC Document Reproduction No. 048–133).

DINEEN, J. P., CLARK, H. B., & RISLEY, T. R. Peer tutoring among elementary students: Educational benefits to the tutor. *Journal of Applied Behavior Analysis*, 1977, 10, 231–238.

FERNALD, G. *Remedial techniques in basic school subjects*. New York: McGraw-Hill, 1943.

FRAGER, S., & STERN, C. Learning by teaching. *The Reading Teacher*, 1970, 23, 403–417.

GOOD, T. L., BIDDLE, B. J., & BROPHY, J. E. *Teachers make a difference.* New York: Holt, Rinehart and Winston, 1975.

DEGRANDPRÉ, B. B., & MESSIER, J. M. Helping mainstreamed students stay in the mainstream. *The Directive Teacher,* 1979, *2* (2), 12, 15.

HARRIS, V. W., SHERMAN, J. A., HENDERSON, D. G., & HARRIS, M. S. Effects of peer tutoring on the spelling performance of elementary classroom students. In G. Semb (Ed.), *Behavior Analysis and Education.* Lawrence, Kansas: The University of Kansas Support and Development Center for Follow Through, 1972, 222–231.

HAUBRICH, P. A., & SHORES, R. Attending behavior and academic performance of emotionally disturbed children. *Exceptional Children,* 1976, *42,* (6), 337–339.

HEWARD, W. L., HERON, T. E., & COOKE, N. L. Tutor huddle: Key element in a classwide peer tutoring system. *The Elementary School Journal,* 1981, (in press).

JOHNSON, M., & BAILEY, J. S. Cross-age tutoring: Fifth graders as arithmetic tutors for kindergarten children. *Journal of Applied Behavior Analysis,* 1974, 7, 223–232.

LOVITT, T. C. *In spite of my resistance . . . I've learned from children.* Columbus, Ohio: Charles E. Merrill, 1977.

MERCER, C. D. *Children and adolescents with learning disabilities.* Columbus, Ohio: Charles E. Merrill, 1979.

MINSKOFF, E. Research on psycholinguistic training: Critique and guidelines. *Exceptional Children,* 1975, 42, 136–144.

PARSON, L., & HEWARD, W. L. Training peers to tutor: Evaluation of a tutor training package for primary learning disabled students. *Journal of Applied Behavior Analysis,* 1979, 12, 309–310.

POPHAM, W. J., & BAKER, E. L. *Systematic instruction.* Englewood Cliffs, New Jersey: Prentice-Hall, 1970.

STEPHENS, T. M. *Teaching skills to children with learning and behavior disorders.* Columbus, Ohio: Charles E. Merrill, 1977.

TURNBULL, A., & SCHULZ, J. B. *Mainstreaming handicapped students: A guide for the classroom teacher.* Boston: Allyn and Bacon, 1979.

WALLACE, G., & KAUFFMAN, J. M. *Teaching children with learning problems* (2nd ed). Columbus, Ohio: Charles E. Merrill, 1978.

WALLACE, G., & MCLOUGHLIN, J. A. *Learning disabilities: Concepts and characteristics,* (2nd ed.). Columbus, Ohio: Charles E. Merrill, 1979.

7

Individualized Instruction in the Mainstreamed Junior and Senior High School Classroom

---

To provide individualized instruction for secondary-level handicapped students can be a challenging task for regular education teachers. Unlike their elementary colleagues who are responsible for thirty students per day, teachers at the secondary level are usually responsible for up to 180 students per day. To assist them with effective teaching programs for handicapped students the consultant needs a thorough understanding of the secondary-level classroom and how it works.

Many handicapped students, even those who may have had specialized instruction at the elementary level, enter the upper divisions still hampered by their disabilities (Deshler, 1978). Consequently, the regular teacher may be faced with students who lack basic skills. As the number of handicapped students increases, the more difficult the task can become.

The purpose of this chapter is to examine ways in which a consultant can assist the regular education teachers at the secondary level with the individualizing of instruction. The chapter presents five models of instruction that represent current instructional approaches at the secondary level (Deshler, Lowery, & Alley, 1979). Each model is discussed separately, but the reader should be aware that in actuality the models do not function in isolation. Districts use combinations of them to serve students.

A teaching strategy for each model will illustrate how individualization can be achieved. Some strategies show how a model is used alone; others show how the models can be combined. All will focus on ways in which the consultant can help the regular educator at the secondary level, despite the problems of large enrollment and the heavy emphasis on content acquisition.

Objectives

After reading this chapter the reader will be able to:

1. identify five models for individualizing instruction at the secondary level.

2. discuss a teaching strategy within each model which can be employed by special and regular educators to individualize instruction.

3. compare and contrast the five models citing their advantages and disadvantages.

Key Terms

Remedial model	Tutorial model
Shaping	Work-study model
Functional curriculum model	Learning strategies model

MODELS OF INSTRUCTION

According to Alley and Deshler (1979), five models of instruction represent the basic approaches by which many handicapped students are taught at the secondary level. These include the remedial, functional curriculum, tutorial, work-study, and learning strategies models. Before a consultant can effectively help any educator at the secondary level with individualizing instruction, it is necessary to know the strengths and shortcomings of each approach. Only then will the consultant be able to provide concrete suggestions for individualizing within each model.

The authors do not endorse any one model over another. Rather, the intent here is to present the models and teaching strategies so that the consultant will have the necessary information when working with teachers or districts who are mainstreaming students using these models.

The Remedial Model

The *remedial model* is concerned with having the student acquire skills in basic subjects, such as reading and math. The teacher uses activities, similar to those used in special education classrooms at the elementary level, to eliminate, or reduce, the deficiency (Marsh & Price, 1980). For example, if a junior in high school spelled on a fifth-grade level, a remedial program would be designed to systematically improve his spelling ability.

According to Alley and Deshler (1979) several assumptions underline the use of the remedial model. First, the consultant assumes that the skills which the student lacks can be identified through assessment. Second, it is assumed that the student will benefit from instruction despite a past history of poor performance. Further, it is agreed that the missing skills are necessary for success in secondary school and later in life.

Despite the inherent strengths in the remedial approach—that is, providing increased competence with skills which may, in turn, increase the student's ability to learn content-related material—there are several shortcomings. First, limited instructional time in both the regular and special education classrooms precludes closing the gap to any significant extent between the present levels of performance and the hoped-for grade level placement. Teachers in content areas like science, math, or social studies simply do not have the time to do this. Second, students may become bored with rehashing the same old skills, even with the use of high-interest, low-level materials. Third, since lower-order skills have yet to be mastered, little time is spent on the more advanced skills that the student's peers are acquiring, and the student falls farther behind.

Finally, since skills are usually taught in the special education classroom, minimal effort is made by the special or regular education teacher to demonstrate to the student how to incorporate skills learned through the remedial model in the regular classroom or in real-life experiences (Alley & Deshler, 1979).

Teaching Strategies for the Special Educator

The consultant, working with a special educator at the secondary level who uses the remedial model, is faced with two important considerations. The first concern is what skills or competencies the teacher should teach. As stated previously, many handicapped students at the junior and senior high level have gaps in their academic and social repertoires. The difference between what they might be expected to perform and what they actually perform is large, and the gap grows larger with each passing year. The question which the consultant and the special educator need to answer is "Where should instruction begin?" The second concern deals with the most appropriate teaching strategies to use. Positive reinforcement, modeling, contingency contracting are examples of the techniques that could be used to help close the gap. The strategy that the consultant and special educator elect depends on several variables including the degree of handicap exhibited by the student, the amount of time the teacher has available for instruction, and the resources the consultant and teacher can muster to provide supportive services for other environments, such as the regular classroom or the home.

Jerry, an LD adolescent mainstreamed in a secondary-level English class, illustrates a case which consultants and remedial-model teachers frequently encounter. Jerry's listening comprehension is adequate. His verbal skills are above average, but his written expression is poor. He has difficulty writing essays, themes, book reports, and narratives. He has trouble organizing his thoughts on paper, and he has little knowledge of punctuation and grammar. Consequently, he is at a severe disadvantage compared to the other students in the class. He does, however, maintain a *C* or better average in other assignments, such as oral reports and group projects.

To assist Jerry, the consultant and special education teacher worked out a program where he wrote several essays and stories each week similar to the ones required of him in the English class. The stories were assigned to assess the magnitude of Jerry's problem. Not only did the data confirm that Jerry's writing ability was poor, but also that Jerry's attitude toward writing was extremely negative—a factor which Irmscher (1972) indicates must be addressed before formal instruction can begin on the writing skills themselves.

Given Jerry's poor attitude toward writing assignments, the teacher began a four-step plan, recommended by Alley and Deshler (1979), to improve his attitude.

Step one. Daily writing assignments were issued with the instructions to write as quickly as possible about any ideas on the topic at hand. Jerry was told not to worry about punctuation, grammar, and spelling. He was reinforced (praised) for generating ideas and expressing his ideas as best he could.

Step two. To assist Jerry with generating ideas, the teacher planned a five-minute, small group meeting with two other students. The purpose was to talk about ideas. The ideas could be related to family, sports, work, future goals, etc. Once the students had the opportunity to discuss their ideas, they were directed to write them on paper. Step two provided the pool of ideas on which the writing assignment could be based.

Step three. The teacher gave Jerry a tape recorder. He was told to express his ideas on tape, and later to transcribe these ideas on paper. Initially, step three only required that Jerry copy his thoughts onto the paper from the tape. Later, he would be asked to generate an outline of his ideas from the tape, and edit his outline to improve its organization.

Step four. Jerry kept a journal. The journal contained a brief synopsis of his daily activities. Elbow (cited in Alley & Deshler, 1979) states that daily writing activity in a journal can be an important aspect of a writing program because it provides another opportunity for self-expression.

The special education teacher and the consultant also worked on two other deficiencies in Jerry's writing. These were his inability to organize sentences and paragraphs, and his poor skills in grammar, punctuation, and spelling. Of course, intensive work on these skills did not begin until Jerry had experienced success with the four-step program just mentioned.

One strategy that the teacher and the consultant found most useful was a prompting plus differential reinforcement procedure. Jerry received points for those sentences (or paragraphs) that logically followed one another and expanded upon the topic sentence. If consecutive sentences were not related, Jerry received no points. When teaching grammar and punctuation the teacher would initially indicate the number of punctuation marks or capitals required in the sentence. For example, in the sentence, "the boy said i am hungry (6)," the number six in the parenthesis served as a cue to Jerry that there were six punctuation marks or capitals to be identified. As Jerry's skill improved, the numerical cue was eliminated.

The consultant and teacher agreed that the instructional sequence should begin with an improvement in Jerry's attitude toward writing, hence the four-step program. Both realized that there was little hope of improving Jerry's writing ability as long as he was so negative. They felt that a plan was needed which progressively reinforced Jerry for writing anything—even sketchy ideas—if, over time, those ideas could be structured and used as a way to teach organizational and mechanical skills. In behavioral terms, the plan called for the reinforcement of successive approximations to a terminal goal, a process referred to as *shaping*.

Teaching Strategies for the Regular Educator

Because of the nature of a handicapped student's problem, the consultant must be prepared to use the remedial model with regular education teachers. To do so, the first objective the consultant might set would be to inform the regular education teacher of the scope and sequence of the handicapped student's program in the special education classroom. After doing so, the consultant could discuss with the teacher how the problem might be addressed within the regular class. Anecdote 7–1 continues our example with Jerry and illustrates what might be said.

Anecdote 7–1

CONSULTANT (*just finishing a description of Jerry's program in the special education classroom*): "Mr. Holbrook, do you have any questions about the program the resource room teacher and I established?"

MR. HOLBROOK: "No. It seems like a good idea. I just hope there's enough time left in the school year to see an improvement."

CONSULTANT: "I do, too. The year is going very fast which brings up my reason to meet with you. As Jerry's English teacher, you can play an important part in his program."

MR. HOLBROOK: "Me! I'm responsible for teaching junior English to 180 students. I don't have the time to teach Jerry the proper use of commas and periods. Besides, he can hardly write anyway."

CONSULTANT (*resolutely*): "I am well aware of the limitations on your time, Mr. Holbrook. You have a difficult job, and I don't mean to imply that you should take primary responsibility for Jerry's instruction."

MR. HOLBROOK (*straightforwardly*): "Then what are you asking?"

CONSULTANT: "I'd like to discuss some ways that you might individualize Jerry's instruction and at the same time reinforce the program we've established in the special education class."

MR. HOLBROOK: "Sounds like I am going to have to do more work."

CONSULTANT: "Maybe. But try to think in terms of helping Jerry."

MR. HOLBROOK: "I'm listening."

CONSULTANT: "I understand that Jerry, along with other students in the class, has written and oral assignments to complete each marking period."

MR. HOLBROOK: "That's right."

CONSULTANT: "One way to individualize Jerry's program would be to issue all, or most, of his writing assignments at one time. He could work on them in the resource room. Not only would he be able to schedule his work over the marking period, but also the smaller group in the resource room would serve as a source of ideas for writing. The resource teacher could use your assignments as a base for offering remedial help."

MR. HOLBROOK: "That doesn't sound too difficult. Anything else?"

CONSULTANT (*feeling more confident*): "Yes. I understand students in your class earn extra points for additional work."

MR. HOLBROOK: "That's right. I frequently give bonus points for extra assignments."

CONSULTANT: "Good. I'd like you to think about doing that in Jerry's case so that he could earn extra points when consecutive writing assignments show improvement."

MR. HOLBROOK: "You mean he wouldn't have to do extra work, just show improvement from assignment to assignment?"

CONSULTANT: "That's right."

MR. HOLBROOK (*hesitating*): "Well, that's a bit different than my normal procedure, but I guess I could work it out."

CONSULTANT: "The last two items refer to testing and evaluation. Until Jerry's writing begins to show improvement, I'd like to reduce the number of written tests he has to take. I realize it's not possible to eliminate all of them. But I think Jerry's attitude toward writing, evidenced by his procrastination, doodling, and poor performance, suggests that we should ease off on the number of writing tasks he has to complete—at least right now."

MR. HOLBROOK: "Maybe the resource teacher can help with some of the tasks?"

CONSULTANT: "That's a good idea. I'll ask Mrs. Graham. I'm sure she'd be willing. Finally, is there any way that Jerry could be assigned to a discussion group for his writing tasks the same way he is in the special education room?"

MR. HOLBROOK: "I haven't used discussion groups lately. But come to think of it, it might be a good idea for all the students. The group might help to clarify the topics."

CONSULTANT: "Precisely."

MR. HOLBROOK: "I'll do what I can with the suggestions you've made."

CONSULTANT: "I couldn't ask more. I'll stop around next week to see how it's going. In the meantime, maybe you can meet informally with Mrs. Graham so that you get a better idea of Jerry's whole program."

MR. HOLBROOK: "I'll try to meet her this week."

CONSULTANT: "Thank you. Good luck."

To begin to individualize Jerry's instruction in the regular classroom, the consultant met with the English teacher to explain the program in the resource room. He wanted the English teacher to know that a plan was already in effect to improve Jerry's writing skills. The consultant knew if Jerry's program was to succeed he needed the English teacher's help. The tasks he asked the teacher to assign were designed not only to individualize the English class, but also to reinforce Jerry's program in the resource room. To accomplish one of his objectives (having Jerry earn bonus points), the consultant suggested an extension of the teacher's plan to give bonus points for extra work. Because the consultant was aware of this plan, he was able to secure the teacher's cooperation. As

Heron and Catera (1980) indicate, consultants who are able to match proposed interventions with class strategies already in effect are more likely to be successful. Finally, the consultant was able to convince the English teacher that testing and evaluation procedures needed to be adjusted if individualization was going to work in this case.

The four parties to Jerry's program—the consultant, the special educator, the English teacher, and Jerry himself—recognize that there is a long way to go before the goals for the writing skills are met. The consultant may even realize that they may never all be fully met. In a remedial model, teaching follows assessment, and a systematic program is designed to increase the probability of skill acquisition.

The Functional Curriculum Model

According to Alley and Deshler (1979) the *functional curriculum model* is designed to help students acquire independent-living skills. These skills may include consumerism, banking and finance, or job-related competencies. The functional curriculum model assumes that the scope and sequence of the regular curriculum is inappropriate. So a new curriculum is generated which attempts to provide students with the skills necessary to obtain a job, find a place to live, and the means to function independently. It attempts to blend specific content that students have to acquire (e.g., knowledge of basic math facts) with a career orientation (e.g., balancing a checkbook or paying bills). In many ways this approach resembles the career education orientation which will be described later in chapter 10.

According to Alley and Deshler (1979) there are two potential disadvantages to the functional curriculum. The survival skills, which allegedly should sustain the students for life, may fall victim to technological advances. What is thought essential today may be considered irrelevant tomorrow. Also, since the functional curriculum is taught almost exclusively in self-contained classrooms, there is little potential for interaction with regular education students.

Teaching Strategies for the Special Educator

Consultants working with special educators using the functional curriculum model need a thorough understanding of the skills the teachers are trying to develop. Different teachers may wish to stress different skills. Unfortunately, there is no generally agreed-upon corpus of survival skills and the consultant must be sensitive to this, as well as to large-scale changes in society and the environment, which must be translated into a functional curriculum.

Ernie is a sixteen-year-old educable mentally retarded (EMR) student enrolled in a suburban high school. His academic skills have developed slowly but steadily throughout his elementary and junior high years, but his achievement has reached a plateau. Socially, Ernie is very immature. He has difficulty making and keeping friends, and his interactions with peers are tentative and awkward. His special education teacher used a functional curriculum model to try to teach essential vocabulary words (for example, danger, poison, flammable), the bases of banking (using a checkbook and savings account), and how to complete necessary forms and applications (such as job and driver applications, apartment leases, and credit applications). The teacher requested help from the district's consultant because Ernie was having trouble learning these skills. Anecdote 7–2 describes a conversation the special education teacher had with the consultant about Ernie.

Anecdote 7–2

TEACHER (*expressing frustration*): "I'm not making much headway with Ernie on his survival skills."

CONSULTANT: "What skills do you consider survival skills?"

TEACHER: "Basically four skills—essential sight vocabulary, banking and finance, completing forms, and consumerism."

CONSULTANT: "That's an ambitious plan. But since Ernie will be graduating soon, I can understand your reasoning. Tell me how you've been teaching finance and banking. Maybe we can start with these skills."

TEACHER: "Well, I got sample checkbooks from the local bank. I use the checkbooks in class to teach the unit. Ernie has learned the location of his account number, and how to write a check. Also, I taught him how to make deposits and withdrawals, and how to balance his checkbook."

CONSULTANT: "Is Ernie able to use calculators to do the math that's required?"

TEACHER: "No. Since his skills are so poor in basic addition and subtraction, I try to give him as much practice as I can. I have him check the balance using paper and pencil."

CONSULTANT (*recognizing that the teacher has mixed the remedial model —teaching basic skills—with the functional curriculum model*): "Does it take a long time for Ernie to balance his book using paper and pencil?"

TEACHER: "It sure does."

CONSULTANT: "Maybe letting him use a small calculator would reduce the time it takes to do the addition and subtraction."

TEACHER: "Maybe so. But how's he to learn the basic skills if he doesn't practice them?"

CONSULTANT: "Chances are if he hasn't mastered them by now it's unlikely that he's going to. Besides, calculators are so small these days he could carry one with him to use whenever he needed it."

TEACHER: "I see your point."

CONSULTANT: "Also you might plan a field trip to the bank. Students, including Ernie, could set up an account and make an actual deposit. Before the field trip they could role play the behaviors that would be required in the bank."

TEACHER: "Sounds like a good idea."

CONSULTANT: "Also, if you can get the form the bank uses to open an account, you could build a lesson around completing the form."

TEACHER: "That's a great idea."

CONSULTANT: "You might let the bank know before the visit that several of your students are planning to open accounts. With advance notice, they might be able to offer help when you arrive."

TEACHER: "Sounds ideal. What's the first step?"

(*The consultant spends the rest of the time explaining how to set up the lesson on completing the bank forms. Also, she carefully describes how a role-playing—behavioral rehearsal—situation could be structured so that each student, including Ernie, has the opportunity to practice and receive feedback on his performance.*)

The consultant made two notable suggestions to the teacher. First, she recommended the hand-held calculator because its use is consistent with the functional skills curriculum. At this point in Ernie's life, it is probably more practical for him to learn to use a calculator effectively than it is for him to struggle with math calculations.

Second, the consultant recommended the role playing to give students the opportunity to practice the skills required in a new setting (Stephens, 1977). Students can learn what to expect from the tellers prior to interacting with them. Finally, asking the students to complete the same forms in class and at the bank promotes generalization of skills (Sulzer-Azaroff & Mayer, 1977).

Teaching Strategies with the Regular Educator

According to Alley and Deshler (1979) the functional curriculum model is used by less than one-in-five secondary programs, and then almost exclusively in self-contained classrooms. In short, this approach is not often used with regular education teachers. Some suggested approaches which employ a career education orientation with secondary level regular educators will be presented in Chapter 10.

The Tutorial Model

In the *tutorial model* the emphasis of instruction shifts from teaching basic skills, such as decoding words, to teaching content, such as identifying the factors which led to the Civil War. Specifically, the students are taught the content they may not have been able to learn in the regular classroom by a special education teacher or tutor. The goal of this approach is to keep the student in the regular class with his peers (Alley & Deshler, 1979). It has two advantages. First, it addresses the student's immediate needs, and second, it allows him to remain in the regular classroom with his peers. For handicapped adolescents, the opportunity to interact with peers can enhance feelings of self-esteem.

The consultant should realize that the tutorial approach offers the regular and special educator only a limited solution to the problems of the handicapped student. The student's skill deficit is not addressed, rather he receives instruction in the courses in which he is enrolled. If enough credits are generated, the student is promoted, and eventually graduates from high school. Unfortunately, although the student may have graduated, he probably still lacks the skills. The handicapped student was simply given "a fish for the day" rather than learning "how to fish for himself."

Clearly, the tutorial model fails to look at the long-range goals for the student. A short-term compromise is offered, which is intended to help the regular teacher keep the student in class.

The shortcomings of the tutorial model are several. This model may inadvertently reinforce the regular education teacher's failure to provide an individualized approach for the student. The regular teacher may feel that the tutor will review the requisite material in his session with the student, and so more individualized assistance will not be necessary. Nor may the tutor have the skills needed to teach all subject areas (Alley & Deshler, 1979). Therefore, a situation could arise where the regular educator, who is able to teach content, does not do so, and the tutor, who is skilled at individualizing instruction, lacks the background in certain areas to put his skill to work. Under these circumstances the student loses—twice.

Teaching Strategies for Special Educators

One of the most useful recommendations a consultant can make to a special educator using the tutorial model is to determine the scope and sequence of the content which the regular classroom teacher is using. Once the tutor identifies this, he can begin to make decisions on how that content might be handled in the tutorial session. For example, if a handicapped student integrated in a junior high school geography class was required to learn map reading, the tutor might concentrate her instruction of key skills on reading the legend, orientation and direction, and distance. Overhead transparencies, prepared with a series of overlays, might be used to teach the use of scale and measurement. After basic map-reading skills were acquired, more complex skills could be introduced.

The consultant might recommend that the tutor and regular educator work together to prepare short tape recordings which could be used to introduce or review key concepts in map skills or vocabulary. Of course, if the student had a hearing impairment, visual materials could be substituted.

Consultants can also help the tutor guide the student's program in the area of testing. The tutor should know how the handicapped student is going to be tested in class before directive instruction begins. Will the student have to supply answers to questions in writing or orally? Will the student have to recognize the correct answers from among alternatives? Is the exam a true/false test? Answers to these questions are important because they will help the tutor determine how to prepare the student.

Teaching Strategies for the Regular Educator

Several teaching strategies can be recommended to the regular classroom teacher to improve knowledge acquisition by handicapped students in content-related subject areas.

Summaries. Providing handicapped students with written or taped summaries of key concepts or definitions of vocabulary is an excellent way to facilitate learning. Students can read the summary or listen to the tape to learn the required material.

Multisensory approach. The use of visual, audio, or kinesthetic modalities can provide handicapped students with a variety of response opportunities. For example, the handicapped student in a physical science class might hear a lecture or audiotape titled "Forces of the Earth." The lecture or tape might be followed by a film, filmstrip, or slide presentation on volcanoes, earthquakes, or storms. Finally, the student might have the opportunity to demonstrate via experiments or simulations some common physical forces which affect our lives.

Involving peers. Small discussion groups can serve as an excellent way to individualize instruction at the secondary level. The goals of the small groups may vary, and the handicapped student's participation would be limited to those areas in which he or she could succeed.

The Work-Study Model

In the *work-study model* students spend a portion of their day (or week) on a job, and the remainder of the day (or week) is spent in the special or regular education classroom (Alley & Deshler, 1979). Like the functional curriculum approach, this model assumes that the regular curriculum is inappropriate, a view shared by several educators (e.g., Clark, Klein, & Burke, 1972; VanTil, 1971). However, it goes a step farther by reordering the school and work experiences of the student. Students attend school, yet they also work at a business or trade, an option not usually available to their nonhandicapped peers.

The work-study model has the advantage of providing the student with the opportunity to obtain on-the-job experience while he is still under the sponsorship of the educational system. The curriculum in the work-study model is geared toward increasing skills that are likely to be needed in the students' working careers. Also, it provides the opportunity for the handicapped students to earn money to buy reinforcers (for example, clothes, gasoline for their automobiles, consumables) at a time when their nonhandicapped peers are probably doing the same. It is difficult to assess the impact that earning money has on the handicapped adolescent, but presumably it benefits his social position with his nonhandicapped, secondary-level peers.

The obvious disadvantages to the work-study model relate to the type of jobs which are available to handicapped students. According to Alley and Deshler (1979) handicapped students are typically hired for menial jobs in the food and restaurant industry. They are, therefore, exposed to a limited repertoire of job possibilities, and the likelihood of promotion is also limited. The chance for students to find positions with better career potential is usually related to the personal initiative and community contacts of the work-study coordinator.

Teaching Strategies for the Special Educator or Work-Study Coordinator

Probably one of the most important skills for handicapped students in high school to have is the ability to act appropriately in social situations. According to Brolin and Kokaska (1979) one of the major reasons why handicapped students are dismissed from work-study positions is that their social interactions with their employers or colleagues are inappropriate. Stephens (1978) indicates that social-skills training should be an integral component of the curriculum so that students will be better prepared to function within a variety of social settings.

Stephens (1978) uses a directive teaching approach to social skills. He recommends techniques such as modeling, role-playing, contingency contracting, and positive reinforcement to help the educator with social skills instruction. Each approach has been discussed elsewhere in the text and will not be repeated here.

Teaching Strategies for the Regular Educator

Few handicapped students enrolled in work-study programs are integrated in regular class settings. For those who are, the consultant can assist the regular teacher by determining the on-the-job behaviors that the student must have if he is to stay employed. These include being on time, appropriate social interactions, and coping behaviors.

On time. Regular educators can use a variety of techniques to improve on-time behaviors. The easiest approach is social praise. If the teacher's praise or attention is a reinforcer for the student, on-time behavior should be acquired and maintained. Conversely, a punishment approach may be used whereby the student loses a privilege (for example, use of the hall pass, or free time).

Social interactions. Appropriate social interactions can be encouraged in several ways. While it is beyond the scope of this text to discuss all possible techniques, modeling and contingent reinforcement are two approaches that regular educators can use without difficulty.

Coping behavior. Stressful or unanticipated events are harrowing for any individual. For some handicapped students an unexpected change in routine can be devastating. The regular educator needs to be aware of the tolerance level for change in his handicapped students and should introduce change only under controlled conditions. The teacher might attempt to use a reinforcement procedure to reward the student for managing stressful situations successfully.

The Learning Strategies Model

The *learning strategies model* is used to teach handicapped students how to learn rather than what to learn (Alley & Deshler, 1979). This approach focuses on procedures and rules that students can apply across skill areas. The main advantage of this model is that the students are taught how to access and process information in ways they may put to use later in life as well.

The model basically assumes that: 1) knowledge is transitory; 2) current educational practice fails to teach students how to relate what they know to real-life problems; 3) learning strategies can be taught directly; and 4) that these skills can be demonstrated in the regular classroom.

The learning strategies model has two inherent shortcomings. First, limited data are available on the efficacy of the approach, especially with regard to generalization and maintenance. Second, the approach seems to work best for those students within the normal range of intelligence who are able to read independently on a third-grade level or better, and who are able to deal with symbols (Alley & Deshler, 1979).

Teaching Strategies for the Special and Regular Educator

According to Alley and Deshler (1979) cooperative planning between the regular and special education teacher is a critical factor in the success of the learning strategies approach. Because the roles of these two professionals are so closely meshed in this instance, both are included in this section.

The strategies in the model proceed through five steps. These include:

1. Pointing out to student the ineffective strategy that is currently in use.

2. Demonstrating the new strategy.

3. Applying the strategy in controlled settings or situations.

4. Transferring the new strategy to the regular classroom.

5. Grouping for practice and reinforcement.

Pointing out the ineffective strategy. Suppose, for example, that a college-bound, learning disabled student in the special education class was asked to identify three articles in popular magazines that were related to the topic of ecology and write a brief synopsis of them. To start his assignment, the student began to thumb through magazines in the library. The special educator might intervene and point out that this method was time-consuming, laborious, and potentially ineffective. He could tell the student that only by chance would he find the articles he needed using this approach.

Demonstrating the new strategy. The special education teacher could then show the LD student where to find the cumulative index for the magazine or journal and explain that the index lists all of the articles by subject and author for a given year. Next, the teacher might obtain an index, open it to the subject section and check for the term *ecology*. She would point out that ecology is a broad term that describes the relationship between many environmental factors. The student could be taught to use the thesaurus to find synonyms for the main term. Next, the student would be shown how to locate the articles he identified through the index. Once he found the periodicals in the library, he could learn how to use a table of contents to locate the pages he needed. Of course, if the school library had a computerized system, the student would be shown how to use the terminal.

Applying the strategy in controlled settings. The special teacher, assisted by the consultant, should plan on having the student practice his newly acquired skill in a controlled way. This means that the student should be given additional assignments, within a restricted range, so that the likelihood of success is increased. Returning to our previous example, the LD student could research articles but now the topic would be more specific—say air pollution—and he would be told to use only the 1981 index to *Time* magazine. Thus, potentially confusing variables (multiple indexes and years) are eliminated. The student has the opportunity for intensive practice on his own within a well-structured area.

Transferring the new strategy to the regular classroom. As Alley and Deshler (1979) indicate, students need to demonstrate skills learned in the special classroom in the regular setting. If an LD student has received sufficient practice and reinforcement within the special class, he should now be ready to apply his knowledge to curriculum-related tasks in the regular class. Again, it is important for the student to practice in the regular class because potentially more topics and more research will be expected of him with less time to complete them. If the special and regular education teachers worked together on the way in which the tasks were presented, the student should be able to respond to the new tasks without much difficulty.

Grouping for practice and reinforcement. The regular teacher would be advised to establish groups for the purpose of practicing and reinforcing the newly acquired skill. Students could learn from one another how to expand their skills.

SUMMARY

Five models of instruction for secondary-level students have been presented. These models were chosen because they represent the basic approaches to most upper division, handicapped students. Consultants need to be knowledgeable about these models so that appropriate recommendations can be made to special and regular education teachers. The consultant also needs to know when these approaches can be combined, and the extent to which the programs are successful.

Strategies for the special and regular educator were presented within each model. These strategies indicate ways in which a consultant can work with professionals to assist handicapped students.

Questions

---

1. Describe the remedial model. Identify the underlying assumptions, and indicate its strengths and weaknesses.

2. Describe the functional curriculum model. Identify the underlying assumptions, and indicate its strengths and weaknesses.

3. Describe the tutorial model. Identify the underlying assumptions, and indicate its strengths and weaknesses.

4. Describe the work-study model. Identify the underlying assumptions, and indicate its strengths and weaknesses.

5. Describe the learning strategies model. Identify the underlying assumptions, and indicate its strengths and weaknesses.

6. For each model provide a school-related strategy which a consultant could recommend to a special or regular educator.

Discussion Points and Exercises

1. Visit a junior or senior high school to determine the models which are used to accommodate handicapped students. Discuss with the principal, special educators, and regular teachers their perceptions of the efficacy of the models in use.

2. Attend an IEP meeting for a handicapped junior or senior high school student. Based on the student's current levels of achievement and future potential, discuss with team members the most appropriate model(s) to use with the student.

3. Conduct an interview with an upper division, mainstreamed handicapped student. Determine from the student the type of academic program he is receiving and obtain his evaluation of the educational approach the school has used with him.

REFERENCES

ALLEY, G., & DESHLER, D. *Teaching the learning disabled adolescent strategies and methods.* Denver: Love, 1979.

BROLIN, D. E., & KOKASKA, C. J. *Career education for handicapped children and youth.* Columbus, Ohio: Charles E. Merrill, 1979.

CLARK, L. H., KLEIN, R. L., & BURKS, J. B. *The American secondary school curriculum.* New York: Macmillan, 1972.

DESHLER, D. Issues related to the education of learning disabled adolescents. *Learning Disability Quarterly*, 1978, *1* (4), 2–10.

DESHLER, D., LOWEREY, N., & ALLEY, G. R. Programming alternatives for learning disabled adolescents: A nationwide survey. *Academic Therapy*, 1979, 14 (4).

ELBOW, P. Writing without teachers. In G. Alley and D. Deshler (Eds.), *Teaching the learning disabled adolescent: Strategies and methods.* Denver: Love, 1979.

HERON, T. E., & CATERA, R. Teacher consultation: A functional approach. *School Psychology Review*, 1980, 9 (3), 283–289.

IRMSCHER, W. F., *The Holt guide to English.* New York: Holt, Rinehart and Winston, 1972.

MARSH, G. E., & PRICE, B. J. *Methods for teaching the mildly handicapped adolescent.* Columbus, Ohio: Charles E. Merrill, 1980.

Stephens, T. M. *Social skills in the classroom.* Columbus, Ohio: Cedars Press, 1978.

STEPHENS, T. M. *Teaching skills to children with learning and behavior disorders.* Columbus, Ohio: Charles E. Merrill, 1977.

SULZER-AZAROFF, B., & MAYER, R. *Applying behavioral analysis procedures with children and youth.* New York: Holt, Rinehart and Winston, 1977.

VANTIL, W. *Curriculum: Quest for relevance.* Boston: Houghton Mifflin, 1971.

8

Conducting Observations in Applied Settings

Consultants are frequently called upon to conduct observations in applied settings. Such observations are usually conducted for one of two purposes: to assist with the identification of a student problem, or to evaluate an ongoing program or intervention. Direct observation, if skillfully executed, can provide valuable information that cannot be obtained readily from any other source. For example, it would be difficult for the classroom teacher to observe the ongoing behaviors of several students in the room, while simultaneously teaching a lesson. Further, the consultant, as a third-party observer, would be able to note the pattern of teacher-student interactions, an important variable that most teachers are unable to estimate on their own (Martin & Keller, 1974; Brophy & Good, 1974).

This chapter briefly discusses the purposes of direct observation for the consultant and provides an overview of eight observation techniques that can be used to measure classroom-related behavior.

Objectives

After reading this chapter, the reader will be able to:

1. describe the general purposes of observation.

2. identify at least two issues of concern to educators regarding educational evaluation.

3. distinguish between the terms *formative* and *summative evaluation*.

4. describe the two traditions of observational methodology in use in this country.

5. state the purpose of each of the eight observational approaches presented.

6. describe the procedures basic to each of the eight observational approaches.

7. list Zelditch's "Criteria for Goodness" and apply these criteria to an observation technique.

Key Terms

Identification

Survey level

Specific level

Evaluation

Formative evaluation

Summative evaluation

Secondary effects

Psychometric approach

Ethnographic approach

Applied behavior analysis

Event recording

Reliability check

Interaction analysis

Brophy-Good Dyadic Interaction System

Flanders Interaction Analysis

Sociometric analysis

Sociogram

Ecological assessment

Information processing

Permanent product measure	Ecological context
Frequency	Psychological context
Percentage	Field study
Rate	Multi-modal data
Interval sampling	Narrative recording
Time sampling	Rating scale
Duration recording	Checklist

PURPOSES AND ADVANTAGES OF DIRECT OBSERVATION BY THE CONSULTANT

Within an educational setting, the consultant will have occasion to observe a variety of individuals and situations. For example, if a student is experiencing difficulty in a particular educational placement, the consultant might observe his behavior to help determine the nature of the problem and, thereby, play a role in solving it.

On the other hand, the consultant may be required to observe groups rather than individuals. For example, the school administration may be interested in the effect of placement of the mainstreamed handicapped on their nonhandicapped peers. The consultant might conduct observations in several representative classrooms to note peer acceptance and interaction.

In addition to observing individuals and groups, the consultant may be asked to focus on programs. Perhaps the consultant may have to evaluate an in-service teacher program. One criterion for evaluation might be the number of times the teachers employ in class the behaviors learned during the in-service program.

Several advantages are derived by the consultant who observes behaviors in applied settings. First, direct observations serve as a reliability check on teacher estimates of student behavior. A reliability check is conducted by an independent observer (the consultant) to obtain an index of agreement between the consultant and the teacher. Second, observations provide data which can be used for comparison purposes. Finally, an observation conducted by the consultant may indicate that other problems, not initially noticed by the teacher, are more deserving of attention than the one specified in a referral.

In this chapter observation will be considered under two broad headings: identification and evaluation.

Identification

Two levels of *identification* can be defined: survey and specific. At the *survey level*, the consultant attempts to diagnose the problem. Its focus can be an individual, a classroom, or the whole school. Sometimes the referral a consultant receives about a problem situation is vaguely worded. For example, "Sally misbehaves." Here it is necessary to observe the situation before the consultant can specify the exact nature of the misbehavior. Only after the problem has been accurately identified can it be assessed and then procedures begun to remedy the situation. To cite another example, a teacher may complain that the students in her classroom are always fighting, and she feels frustrated in her attempts to teach them. The consultant, in this case, would need to identify the factors which contribute to the fighting. Through direct observation, the consultant may discover that a few students instigate most of the fights, and that the problem is not as widespread as the teacher believes. It is also possible that some ingredient that should be present in a successful classroom situation is missing. The consultant, after observing the classroom of our frustrated teacher, may find that the teacher attends to the few students who misbehave far more frequently than to the appropriate behavior of the rest of the class.

It is at the *specific level* that the consultant tries to assess the factors contributing to the problem. A necessary consequence of this assessment is the development of a program designed to remedy the situation. Today the strengths and weaknesses of handicapped students are routinely assessed to develop appropriate individual educational programs for them. If a handicapped student shows maladjusted behavior in class, the consultant may observe the student to determine the nature and degree of inappropriate behavior. For example, a handicapped secondary student may be described by his algebra teacher as having a "poor attitude." During observation the consultant may note that the teacher provides few initiations to the student, waits only a short period of time for oral responses, and does not use prompting procedures effectively.

The consultant might then observe the frequency of both teacher and student behaviors in the algebra class. After obtaining the results, a program could be developed and implemented to improve the student's attitude. Subsequent observation of both student and teacher would reveal whether the attitude had indeed been changed and whether there was any change in the teacher's reaction to the student. Thus, the systematic use of an observation technique could help a consultant assess the success of an intervention program.

Evaluation

In addition to specifying and assessing problems, the consultant may also be asked to evaluate students and programs in the school. *Evaluation* provides the means to determine effectiveness of a given course of action. Program evaluation can provide valuable information for decision making (Angrist, 1975). Traditionally, program evaluation has relied on the use of standardized measures of student achievement, such as test scores. Usually, a pretest of either the children or the teachers is made, the innovative program is implemented, and a posttest is administered at the conclusion. However, there has been a growing dissatisfaction among educators with this approach. Perhaps one of the most vocal protests was made by parents, teachers, and evaluation researchers during the First Annual Conference on Educational Evaluation and Public Policy (North Dakota Study Group on Evaluation, 1977). An opinion frequently expressed at this conference was that the current trend in evaluative practices tends to discount educational outcomes that are not easily quantified through standardized testing. A plea was made for the use of evaluation measures that are sensitive to the goals of each program. Therefore, a need for a wide variety of evaluation methods to match the wide variety of program goals is apparent. Many programs attempt to affect the process of teaching (interaction between teachers and students), and not just the products (test scores). Therefore, the precise measurement of process variables becomes as important as the measurement of product variables. Observation techniques can be employed to measure a host of process variables, which, in turn, may lead to a more refined picture of the teaching act.

Evaluation involves judgment. Other than appraising the success or failure of a program, decisions as to the nature of the program evaluation itself must be made. Deciding what is of value in a particular situation is at the core of evaluation, and often the responsibility of the educational consultant. Therefore, a discussion of a few issues in program evaluation will be made. The consultant should be aware of these issues because they may greatly affect the objectivity, accuracy, and interpretation of the program evaluation.

As stated, both process and product measures should be considered in evaluating the success of a given educational program (Bussis, Chittenden, & Amarel, 1976; Carini, 1975; Parlett & Hamilton, 1977). Evaluation, therefore, can be conceptualized as part of an ongoing feedback loop in which program outcomes are judged against both process and product program goals (Angrist, 1975).

Formative evaluation. *Formative evaluation* is conducted during the actual implementation of the program (the intervention mutually agreed upon by the teacher and the consultant). In formative evaluation the consultant determines whether the plan is being implemented as intended, and the effectiveness of the plan for changing behavior. Formative evaluation allows for "midcourse correction." If the plan is implemented as intended, yet no functional effect on the targeted behavior is noted, another strategy can be initiated immediately.

Summative evaluation. Summative evaluation is conducted at the end of the intervention. The question the consultant seeks to answer then is, "Did the plan have a functional effect?" If the teacher's (or students') behavior changed a significant amount in the desired direction and adequate controls were used to eliminate competing explanations for the change, then the consultant can be reasonably confident that the plan accounted for the change.

This combination of formative and summative evaluation can be used for groups and individuals. For example, the IEP process demands a yearly or summative evaluation. However, short-term objectives for each annual goal and methods for evaluating those objectives are also written into an IEP. If during implementation it is found that these short-term objectives are not being met, steps can be taken to modify the educational program. The appropriateness of the instructional methodology or the assessment instrument itself may be examined. Rather than waiting a year to determine whether the IEP has been successful for the student, a formative evaluation of short-term objectives can indicate program success (or failure) and suggest alterations in the IEP that could increase the probability of overall success.

Another methodological concern to evaluators is the measurement of *secondary effects*, the unplanned effects that were not designed as program outcomes (Angrist, 1975). Should evaluators be concerned with potentially harmful or beneficial secondary effects of program implementation? If so, there are observation techniques that are useful for describing and identifying these factors. For example, one goal of a new mathematics program may be to increase the rate of arithmetic skill mastery of a third-grade class by 20 percent. Formative evaluation (that is, evaluation that examines not only the rate of skill mastery but also the process by which the instruction was delivered) may use product measures, the student's daily worksheets, and in-class observations. If an open-ended method of observation were used, such as a field study, the evaluator would be able to describe the actual educational process that occurred when the program was implemented. The evaluator may discover that while the program goal of a 20 percent increase in the rate of skill mastery was achieved, a side effect of the program was that student-student interaction seemed to decrease. The evaluator may then decide to use a structured observation technique to assess the level of student-student interaction to see whether this secondary effect has any appreciable bearing upon the overall goals of the students' educational program.

Whether to use formative or summative evaluation procedures and the measurement of secondary effects are only two issues facing consultants who observe behaviors in applied settings. There are many ethical and methodological concerns in program evaluation; for example, the influence of professional and personal viewpoints in deciding what is of value in a program (Caro, 1971), the match of evaluator with program clients and implementors (North Dakota Student Group, 1977), and the effect of evaluation at both individual and program levels (Angrist, 1975). Our concern here is primarily with the methodological issues of importance to the educational consultant.

The rest of this chapter is devoted to a description of observation techniques. These techniques can be used by themselves or with other assessment devices to generate information for identification and evaluation.

OBSERVATION TECHNIQUES

More than a hundred protocols for observing classroom behavior have been developed (cf. Simon & Boyer, 1974). It is beyond the scope of this chapter to present all of them here. Instead, eight observational approaches have been selected for discussion. In our opinion these techniques represent not only the traditional methods for conducting observations in applied settings, but the emerging methods as well. Further, these approaches can be used to observe process variables (such as teacher-student interactions) as well as product variables (such as achievement scores).

Essentially there are two major traditions in the observation field. One tradition is based upon the techniques of psychometry; the other is based on ethnography. (See Table 8–1.)

The Psychometric Approach

The *psychometric approach,* conducting observations to obtain numerical data suitable for statistical or graphical analysis, has been the dominant system used in this country (Hamilton & Delamont, 1974). According to Hamilton and Delamont, this tradition has the advantages of simplicity and reliability, and is flexible enough so that it can be used in large

Table 8–1 A Comparison of the Characteristics, Purpose, and Observation Techniques of Psychometry and Ethnography.

OBSERVATION SYSTEMS

PSYCHOMETRY	ETHNOGRAPHY
Characteristics:	*Characteristics:*
Focus upon specified, exhibited behaviors, objectivity achieved through separation of observer and observed	Focus open-ended, not prespecified behaviors, though will focus upon individual, group, program, institution, etc.
Assessment tabulation and/or computation	Data multi-model
Focus can be upon behavior of individual and/or group	
Purpose:	*Purpose:*
Reduce behavior to small-scale units for assessment.	Identification/understanding as well as behavioral description
Sample Observation Techniques:	*Sample Observation Techniques:*
Direct and Daily Measurement	Ecological assessment
Brophy-Good Dyadic Interaction System	Information processing
Flanders Interaction Analysis	Field study/case study
Sociometric analysis	
Checklists and rating scales	

180

scale studies. It has, however, several distinct disadvantages. First, the context in which the data are collected is sometimes ignored. The observer may not be interested in knowing whether the observation occurred during reading, spelling, or math. Second, data are usually gathered over short periods of time (for example, minutes or hours versus days). Third, many observation methods are only concerned with recording overt behavior like verbal comments or task performance. Nonverbal behaviors (gestures) are not observed. Fourth, a focus on predetermined behaviors may preclude the examination of secondary effects, which originally may have been unforeseen. Finally, focusing on preestablished behaviors often needlessly binds the observer to a specific theoretical position.

The psychometric approach is represented in this chapter by the following techniques: Applied Behavior Analysis, Brophy-Good Dyadic Interaction System, and Flanders Interaction Analysis.

The Ethnographic Approach

The *ethnographic approach*, which is based in a social-anthropological tradition, is designed to provide the observer with a means to understand and describe a given situation rather than merely quantifying it. By using a so-called holistic approach, the ethnographic observer attempts to analyze the context in which behavior occurs. Also the ethnographic approach attempts to minimize some of the disadvantages of the psychometric measurement. Clark (1978–1979), for example, indicates that the face validity of an instrument—the notion that the instrument appears to measure what it is supposed to measure—is important as a criterion for acceptability as a research tool. Ethnographic approaches have face validity.

Examples of ethnographic approaches to observation and measurement can be found in the sections on Ecological Assessment, Information Processing, and Field Study in this chapter.

All observational approaches discussed in the chapter can be used by the consultant to observe and record classroom behavior. Some techniques are more appropriate in certain situations than others. Basic procedures for each of eight observation techniques are presented as well as suggestions for their appropriate uses in applied settings.

When making suggestions about the use of a given technique, the authors refer to Zelditch's (1969) "Criteria of Goodness." Zelditch's two basic criteria for effective observation are: 1) informational adequacy (are the data accurate and complete); and 2) efficiency (are the data collected with a minimum amount of cost and effort).

APPLIED BEHAVIOR ANALYSIS TECHNIQUES

According to Cooper (1981), most academic and social behavior can be observed using either permanent product or observation measures. A permanent product measure is defined as any teacher or student behavior that can be repeatedly observed (for example, student written responses on tests or homework). Observation measures, on the other hand, are used to record transitory behaviors that cannot be repeatedly observed (hand raising, call-outs, or out-of-seat behavior). The distinguishing features of *applied behavior analysis* (ABA) are the emphasis on the repeated and precise observation of the behavior, systematic intervention to determine treatment effects, and determination of the reliability of observation.

An obvious advantage of ABA techniques is that the observer can record any behavior of interest wherever it occurs as well as the conditions before and after its occurrence. ABA techniques are flexible, highly reliable, and can be used by most teachers after training and practice.

However, unless the behavior under evaluation is sampled systematically, an erroneous estimate of its "true" level might be obtained. Instructional decisions made on sketchy or incomplete data could affect program decisions for handicapped students.

Procedure

Permanent product measures. These measures can be obtained on any student behavior that is written, tape-recorded, or videotaped. In effect, a *permanent product measure* is a performance result that can be reviewed repeatedly. Also, a helpful feature is that the observer does not have to witness the behavior as it occurs. Measures can be taken after the fact. Common examples of permanent product measures include: student math papers; number of sentences that were recorded on an audiotape; or the number of correct spelling words written on a weekly spelling test. Typically permanent product measures are collected in one of three ways: frequency, percentage, and rate.

Frequency is simply a tally of the number of responses emitted by the student in a unit of time. Frequency data could be obtained on the number of math problems or workbook pages a handicapped student completed. While frequency data may yield important information on the number of items the student completes, other types of data can, and should, be used to give the teacher an accurate index of the student's achievement. Frequency counts can be plotted on both cumulative and noncumulative graphs. (See Figures 8–1 and 8–2.)

Percentage correct is the ratio of the number of correct responses

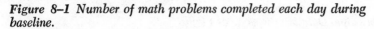

Figure 8–1 Number of math problems completed each day during baseline.

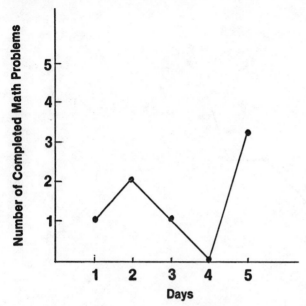

emitted divided by the number of items attempted. For example, if a learning disabled student were issued twenty math problems and he completed ten of them correctly, his percentage correct would be fifty percent. Percentage is usually considered an index of accuracy, that is, how well a student responds to given stimulus items. If a student were given fifty math problems and he attempted twenty, and answered fifteen out of the twenty correctly, his percentage correct would be 75 percent, not 30 percent. If the percentage is calculated on number issued rather than number attempted, a child's ability might be underestimated. Figure 8–3 provides an example of percentage correct for a student during a daily reading period.

Whereas percentage is an index of accuracy, *rate* is an index of proficiency. The question that rate data answers is how well does a student perform per unit of time. Many handicapped students are able to successfully complete an assigned task in the regular classroom. Their problem, however, is that it takes an inordinate amount of time to do it.

Lovitt, Kunzelman, Nolen, and Hulten (1968) state that rate correct and rate incorrect data are essential for deciding on the functional value of an intervention program. As rate correct increases, rate incorrect should remain stable or decrease, depending on the number of problems given. Figure 8–4 shows rate correct and incorrect per minute for math.

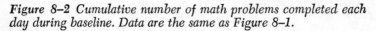

Figure 8–2 Cumulative number of math problems completed each day during baseline. Data are the same as Figure 8–1.

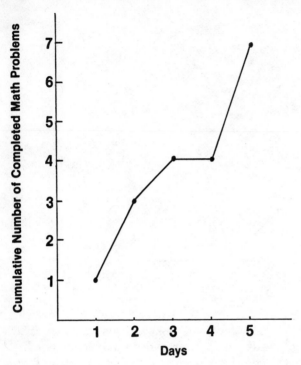

Applied Examples

Data obtained through permanent product measurement can be useful to the consultant who is helping teachers program instruction. For example, suppose that the consultant checked a student's math paper each day for a one-week period and noted that an average of eight errors was made daily. By counting the number and type of mistakes, the consultant could determine a pattern of errors and recommend to the teacher a method of instruction that would benefit the student. Also, the consultant would be able to help the teacher program more efficiently for generalization.

Not all behaviors that occur in the classroom result in permanent products. In fact, many behaviors that have a direct bearing on the success or failure of a mainstreaming program are transitory in nature. Given the rapid pace of both teacher and student behaviors, another form of data collection, the observation system, has been developed. The

Figure 8–3 Percentage correct on daily reading comprehension questions.

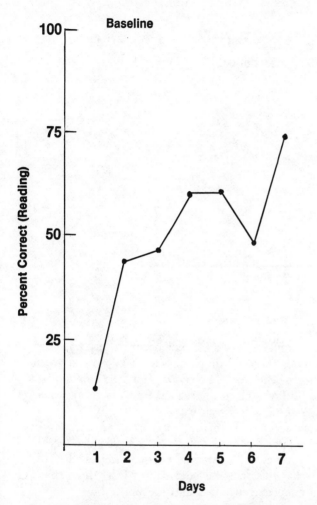

principal techniques in the observation system are interval recording, time sampling, duration recording, and event recording.

Interval recording. Interval recording refers to an observational system where the occurrence of the target behavior at *any* time during a prescribed interval of time (for example, 5 or 10 seconds) is scored. For example, if one were measuring the on-task performance of a student for one minute using ten-second intervals, only one occurrence of the behavior within any interval would be required to score that interval

Figure 8–4 Rate correct and rate incorrect performance (math) per minute during baseline.

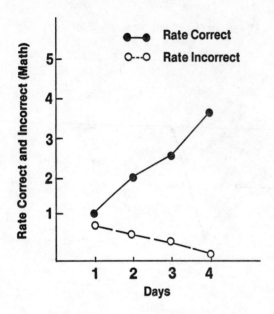

as an occurrence. If the target behavior did not occur at any time during the prescribed interval, then the interval would be scored as an interval of nonoccurrence of the target behavior. Hence, if the student was on-task at any time during each of ten-second intervals, a maximum of six intervals would be scored as occurrences.

Interval sampling is sensitive to both the frequency and duration of behavior (Cooper, 1981). Specifically, if out of six ten-second intervals, three were scored as occurrences and three as nonoccurrences, the consultant could determine that the behavior occurred at least three times, and the total duration of nonoccurrence was thirty seconds.

Time sampling. When behaviors are recorded at the conclusion of every *n*th interval, the procedure is called *time sampling.* For example, if a behavior is recorded using a thirty-second, time-sampling technique, it is recorded twice each minute, at the thirtieth second and the sixtieth second. The observer need not pay attention to what goes on between intervals because it is irrelevant in this observation system.

The determination of interval length is a primary factor in the success of this approach in the classroom. If the intervals are too short, the teacher will not be able to instruct the students and observe simultaneously; if the intervals are too long, the data may not accurately reflect the "true" level of the behavior (Cooper, 1981).

Axelrod (1977) offers one variation of the time-sampling approach. He suggests that x number of observations take place during a given time period. A timer is set at a random interval, and when it goes off, the target behavior is recorded. The teacher then resets the timer for the next interval and so on until all the observations are made. Two advantages of this variation are: (1) the students are not likely to predict the end of interval since it is random; and (2) the teacher will have a cue—the sound of the timer—to remind her to record the behavior.

Duration recording. Typically *duration recordings,* made by an observer using a stopwatch, yield data on the total amount of a given behavior. When the desired behavior is emitted, the stopwatch is activated. When the behavior ceases, the watch is stopped. The elapsed time shown on the stopwatch is the duration of the behavior.

So, if a teacher were interested in the actual time that an educable mentally retarded student worked each day from 9:00 a.m.–9:30 a.m., she would press the stopwatch button when the student worked, and stop it when the student paused or finished. Since the stopwatch would show cumulative working time, the teacher would be able to determine the total number of minutes the student was on-task during the half-hour time frame.

Event recording. *Event recording* is a tally of the number of times a given behavior occurs. For example, the number of times a student talks back or interacts appropriately with his peers might be tallied this way. Some behaviors, however, may not lend themselves to accurate event recording. If, for example, a student left his seat momentarily several times during the day, event recording could be used to count this behavior. But, if he left his seat once to take a two-hour stroll around the school grounds, event recording would grossly underestimate the actual time away.

Event recording can be performed easily by classroom teachers. It has an advantage over interval and duration recording in that the teacher does not have to observe a student's behavior continuously in order to determine its level. Also, since teachers are familiar with the procedures of tallying the number of times a behavior occurs, they are more likely to use event recording rather than other observation measures.

Reliability of Direct Observation Techniques

A *reliability check* is a measure taken by an independent observer, using the same observation procedure as the teacher, for the purpose of reducing or eliminating inaccuracies or bias (Axelrod, 1977). For instance, if a teacher noted nine occurrences of a target behavior and the consultant recorded ten occurrences of the same behavior within the same time frame, the reliability would be 90 percent, and the teacher could be confident that there was high agreement between her and the consultant on the level of the behavior. Conversely, if she recorded four instances of the behavior and the consultant recorded ten, it would indicate that they were not observing the target behavior at the same time, or that they had differing definitions of the target behavior, or both.

To calculate reliability for interval sampling and time sampling, each observed interval must be compared to determine agreement (see Figure 8–5).

Once the number of agreements has been determined, the following formula can be used to calculate the reliability index:

$$\text{Reliability} = \frac{\text{Number of agreements}}{\text{Total intervals observed}} = 100$$

Reliability over 80 percent is usually considered acceptable for most applied settings (Cooper, 1981). Reliability checks are not only performed on observational data, they are needed for permanent product data as well. To obtain a reliability index for product data, it is necessary for one observer to record on a separate sheet, for example, the number of math problems with correct answers, and then the reliability observer conducts her check on the same data without seeing how the other observer scored each response. In this way the reliability check is performed independently, and the reliability observer is not influenced by the primary observer's recording.

If student responses cannot be obtained with paper and pencil procedures, a tape recorder can be substituted. This situation occurs when the teacher wants the student to respond orally to questions or exam items. To conduct the reliability check, each observer would listen to the tape independently to record the student's responses and then determine the number of agreements. To illustrate, suppose a teacher gave a student a ten item, oral spelling test in which the student spelled the words directly on the tape. After the test the teacher would rewind the tape and listen to each word to determine whether it was spelled correctly. The reliability observer would follow the same procedure as the teacher, except that her recordings of the student's responses would be made on a separate sheet. Once both observers had scored the test, a percentage of agreement (the reliability) could be calculated. This is an effective strategy to employ when the second observer (a consultant, for example) cannot be there to listen to the student as he makes his responses.

Figure 8–5 The number of agreements between two observers during daily five-minute observations.

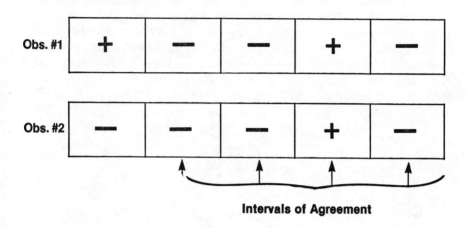

Intervals of Agreement

Applied Examples

In permanent product measures the consultant simply notes the number of errors in the raw data (for example, the completed math paper). However, if data are collected by direct observation, it is usually necessary to sample the behavior over a number of days and under a number of different stimulus conditions. The consultant might note that Peter's on-task performance is high during reading and math, but decreases appreciably during social studies. If this pattern continues, the consultant might suggest to the classroom teacher that the student be allowed to do his reading or math only after he completes his social studies assignments. The consultant could help the teacher plan an appropriate intervention based on the observation of the target behavior.

A general rule of thumb is that at least three to five days worth of data should be gathered before initiating or changing an instructional or behavior approach. Most educators (e.g., Lovitt, 1977; Cooper, 1981) feel that three to five days represents a "fair trial" for the observation.

For example, Figure 8–6 shows that the percentage of Ann's talking-out behavior increased over the first three sessions of baseline. Baseline refers to the magnitude of the behavior before an intervention is introduced, and serves as a standard for comparing the effects of the intervention (Sulzer-Azaroff & Mayer, 1977). These data are sufficient because a trend has been established; talk-outs are increasing. Since the intent of the intervention is to reverse the talking-out, the teacher could initiate an intervention after the third day.

Figure 8–7, on the other hand, shows hypothetical data on the number of times Stephen is out of his seat during a fifty-minute math period. During baseline the data show a decrease, that is, a decelerating trend is evident. It would not be advisable to begin an intervention phase at this point because the trend of the data is already in the desired direction.

In summary, a decision should be made to introduce an instructional or behavioral intervention only when the data show stability or movement in a direction opposite to that of the intervention. For more information on baseline trends and their meanings the reader is referred to Cooper (1981).

Figure 8–6 Percentage of talk-outs during baseline.

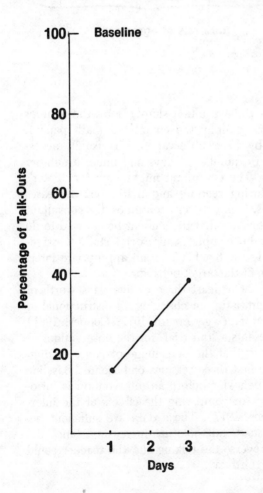

Figure 8–7 Number of out-of-seats during baseline.

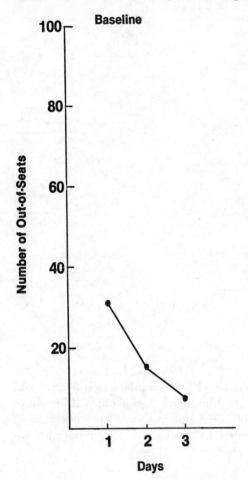

Figure 8–8 shows hypothetical data for rate correct per minute performance in math. These data were collected to determine math proficiency. Since the data reveal a relatively stable pattern, it is acceptable to begin intervention after the fifth day.

INTERACTION ANALYSIS

Interaction analysis refers to the observation of teacher behaviors with individual children or the whole class. There are many interaction analy-

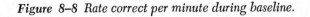

Figure 8–8 Rate correct per minute during baseline.

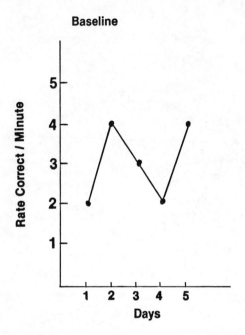

sis techniques that can be used in the classroom. In this chapter, we present an overview of the Brophy-Good Dyadic Interaction System and Flanders Interaction Analysis. Hamilton and Delamont (1974) have noted the successful application of interaction analysis in teacher-training programs. We would like the reader to be aware of classroom applications of interaction analysis systems.

Brophy-Good Dyadic Interaction System

The *Brophy-Good Dyadic Interaction System* was introduced in 1969, and has been used extensively in educational research (Brophy & Good, 1969). One of the reasons for its popularity is that it affords the observer the opportunity to code several types of dyadic interactions, exchanges between a teacher and an individual student. Also, the system treats each individual as a separate unit of analysis.

The dyadic interaction system has a number of distinct advantages compared to applied behavior analysis observation systems and observation approaches that use the whole classroom as the unit of analysis. First, the system measures the verbal interactions that take place between the teacher and student. Second, as we shall discuss later, the system is designed to record many behaviors. Of course, the more behaviors that are measured, the more information that is obtained. Third, it is relatively easy to learn how to code behaviors within this system. Given practice, anyone with experience as a classroom observer should be able to use the system competently. Fourth, adequate reliability scoring between observers is facilitated by the clear description of each behavioral category in the training manual. The 80 percent reliability level can be readily achieved.

Unlike applied behavior analysis which permits the teacher to obtain the observation data herself, the Brophy-Good system requires additional personnel. This may be a disadvantage, especially in districts where consultants are not readily available. A second disadvantage is that only verbal interactions can be measured. Experienced supervisors and teachers realize the powerful effects nonverbal behaviors have on student behavior, but the Brophy-Good system simply does not measure them.

Procedure

The Brophy-Good system measures five types of dyadic interactions in the classroom: (1) response opportunity, (2) recitation, (3) procedural contacts, (4) work-related contacts, and (5) behavioral contacts. These categories will be broadly defined below. The reader is referred to the Brophy-Good manual for a more detailed description of each category.

For an interaction to be coded as a response opportunity, three criteria must be met: (1) the interaction between the teacher and student is public, and heard by the entire class; (2) the teacher initiates the interaction by asking questions, and (3) only one child responds to the teacher. Choral responses, students responding in unison, or student "callouts" to teacher questions are not considered response opportunities.

If a child reads aloud, makes an oral presentation to the class, or recounts an incident to the class in response to a teacher direction, a recitation response is scored.

Procedural contacts are scored when there is an interaction between teacher and child that facilitates the management of personal needs or the distribution of supplies. In a sense, the teacher or child is obtaining the other's compliance in performing a task. Procedural contacts initiated by the teacher may include asking the child to be a messenger, pass out papers, or take roll. Procedural contacts initiated by the child might be asking the teacher's permission to sharpen a pencil, go to the bathroom, or calling the teacher's attention to a specific object or event.

Any interaction between the teacher and child that relates specifically to some aspect of classwork, homework, or other assigned tasks in the classroom is coded as a work-related contact.

Any verbal statement made by the teacher to a student that makes reference to his classroom behavior would be coded as behavioral contact. The three categories under behavioral contacts include praise, behavioral warnings, or behavioral criticism.

Applied example. It would be appropriate to use the Brophy-Good Dyadic Interaction System in situations where the consultant wanted to record the amount of praise given by teachers not only to entire classes but also to individual students, especially mainstreamed handicapped students. Suppose that after conducting observations in two classrooms, it was found that both teachers praised their students during 80 percent of the observed intervals. At first it might appear that the two teachers were comparable in terms of the amount of praise they issued to the students in their rooms. If data were obtained using the dyadic interaction code, it is possible that a different interpretation of the data could be obtained. That is, the first teacher might distribute her praise across all students in the classroom, while the second teacher might praise only a small minority of students. In short, 10 percent of the students might receive 80 percent of the praise. By looking at individual interactions, using the dyadic system, the consultant could determine that the interaction patterns in the two classrooms were different.

Flanders Interaction Analysis

The *Flanders Interaction Analysis System* is one of the early structured observation systems to measure teacher-student interaction (Flanders, 1967). As with the Brophy-Good System the teacher and student behaviors measured are strictly verbal. One category of measurement within the system is reserved for silence or confusion. Again, like Brophy-Good, a basic assumption is that the verbal behavior of the teacher or student is an adequate sample of his total behavior.

Although teacher-student verbal behaviors are observed, the primary focus of this approach is on the teacher. The purpose is to determine the teacher's influence upon pupil participation in class by recording and analyzing his or her spontaneous verbal behavior.

Procedure

The use of this system requires an observer who is not engaged in classroom interaction. According to Flanders (1967), the observer sits in the classroom in the best position to see and hear the classroom participants. At the end of a three-second period, the observer decides which of ten categories best represents the interaction just completed. Seven itemized categories relate to teacher verbalizations, and two categories (eight and nine) are reserved for student talk. The tenth category is for silence or confusion. The observer records the appropriate category number in a column as teacher and student behavior is observed. Whenever there is a major transition in the classroom, like a change in activity, the observer indicates the time on his recording form because changes in interaction patterns may coincide with changes in activity. When the observation is completed, the observer leaves the classroom and writes a general description of each observation period. The description provides the observer with an overall view of the classroom and supplements the data obtained in the observation.

The Flanders Interaction Analysis System has been used successfully to train classroom teachers and researchers. The training involves three basic steps. First, the trainees memorize the teacher and student categories. Second, the trainees attempt to code taped recordings of classroom verbal interactions. Here group discussion can lead to the development of more reliable judgments.

The third step in the training process involves direct classroom observation. The presence of an experienced trainer during the observation facilitates the recording of reliable data. The trainer is able to answer questions regarding the recording of teacher or pupil talk. Hence, higher levels of agreement can be achieved.

Applied example. There are at least three different situations in which the use of the Flanders Interaction Analysis System would yield helpful information. First, suppose success in the mainstream classroom can be fostered by teachers who provide structure and direction for all students, especially the handicapped. The Flanders Interaction Analysis System could be used by the consultant to quantify the amount of direct teacher influence on a handicapped child.

Second, it may be necessary for the success of a mainstreamed placement to identify a teacher who exhibits an indirect influence upon students. Sometimes handicapped students react negatively when faced with a teacher who is directive. In such a case, it may be helpful to place this student with a teacher who uses students' ideas and accepts the feelings of students rather than a teacher who manages the class by primarily lecturing and issuing directions. The Flanders Interaction Analysis System can help identify a teacher with this particular teaching style.

Third, interaction analysis systems are used commonly to provide feedback to teachers on their behavior. Since each system analyzes classroom events from a different perspective and uses different recording procedures, each can be of value to the teacher who is interested in developing specific interaction skills. Morine (1975) suggests that teachers be provided with feedback from a variety of systems, thereby exposing them to different perspectives.

Consultants should also recognize that the teacher behaviors selected for observation will probably reflect the evaluator's viewpoint. For the most accurate evaluative use, the interaction analysis system should also reflect the views of the teacher being evaluated.

Finally, the consultant should also be aware that interaction analysis systems may seem to the teacher to lack relevance. The teacher may simply not be interested in the data generated by the system because he does not view interaction patterns as particularly good indicators of successful teaching. For whatever purpose an interaction analysis system is chosen, it is advisable to survey several techniques before making the most appropriate choice for each teacher.

SOCIOMETRIC ANALYSIS

Sociometric analysis using the peer-nominating technique was originally developed by Moreno (1953). In this procedure each child's social position in the class is determined by analyzing his responses with respect to specific questions. For example, each student might be asked to name someone he would like to play with. It is assumed that the student who is named most frequently enjoys the highest status in the class.

Sociometric analysis is not a direct observation technique. However, it can provide the teacher and consultant with information useful for understanding classroom dynamics or interactions because it focuses on student-student interaction in the classroom.

Procedure

As discussed by Hammill and Bartel (1978) and Wiederholt, Hammill, and Brown (1978) sociometric analysis involves students responding to a questionnaire. For example, each student may be asked to choose two or three children in the class with whom he would most (or least) like to play, or most (or least) like to work with on a project.

The students' responses are confidential. Students are not asked to make their nominations aloud, but usually write the names of their choices on pieces of paper. An alternative is to assign a number to each child. Then each student, in response to a question, writes on paper the number of the selected child. It is also possible to provide a multiple-choice situation. That is, for each question, the student may have the names or numbers of the other students before him, and then indicate his selection by circling or underlining the appropriate name or number. Whatever the method, it should take into account each student's response capability.

Once the peer nominations have been made, they are plotted on a *sociogram*. A sociogram is a schematic representation of all student responses. Figure 8–9 shows a schematic representation of the responses by a third-grade class to the question, "Who would you most like to sit next to?" This sociogram shows us that Yolanda was not picked by any student nor did she select any student to sit next to. Carl chose two students, Bethanne and Stephen, but was not chosen himself. Also, one may suspect that Kathleen and Christine as well as Blaine and Marge are close friends since they chose each other.

After the sociogram is analyzed, the consultant might help the teacher plan a program to change for the better the social relationships of the students in the classroom.

Figure 8–9 Example of a sociogram.

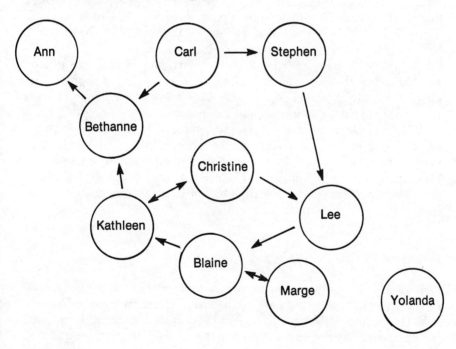

Applied example. It is apparent from Figure 8–9 that Yolanda is an isolate in this class. If Yolanda also exhibited withdrawn behavior (she did not participate in class discussions, raise her hand, or talk with her teacher or classmates outside the classroom) the results of this sociometric analysis might confirm why and help the consultant understand how Yolanda's peers felt about her and she about them. Steps could then be taken to engineer positive social interactions between Yolanda and one or two selected classmates. A subsequent sociometric analysis could measure any change that might result in the social status of Yolanda with respect to her peers and vice versa. In this way, some estimate as to the success of the consultant's intervention plan for Yolanda and her classmates could be made.

ECOLOGICAL ASSESSMENT

Ecological assessment can be defined within two broad perspectives. First, the student's behavior is considered interactive. That is, a change in performance of one behavior may affect other behaviors. Second, behavior is viewed in relation to its environmental context. That is, a change in one setting or context may produce changes in other environments and, in turn, affect student performance (Rogers-Warren & Warren, 1976).

Ecological assessment is usually conducted when a more representative sample of the student's behavior and environment than can usually be obtained in the classroom is desired. As Hardin (1979) suggests, before an effective intervention can be conducted, the student and his relationship to the environment must be assessed.

A basic assumption in an ecological approach is that there is an intrinsic order to human events and behavior, and that behaviors and events occur within and in response to the surrounding environment (Gutmann, 1969). As Brandt (1975) notes, it then becomes the task of the observer to gather enough information to make this order and behavioral consistency apparent.

Procedure

Due to the comprehensive nature of an ecological assessment, the consultant should consider the student's behavior in several settings. Wiederholt, Hammill and Brown (1978) have identified the school, home, and the community as the major environments in an educational, ecological assessment. Depending upon the situation, of course, numerous settings within the school may also be identified as influential variables (for example, the regular classroom, the special education setting, the gym, the lunchroom, or the playground). Heron and Heward (1981) note the possible importance of the physical aspects of a given classroom; that is, the amount of space each student has, how the seating is arranged, the amount of classroom lighting, and the noise level. These variables have been shown to affect student performance.

Heron and Heward (1981) also identify other factors that seem related to student performance. These include: student physiological aspects (for example, medical history, medication, or dietary consideration); the nature of student-student interaction; the nature of teacher-student interaction; and the previous reinforcement history of the student. The last is considered worth study, since current student behavior can be affected by the behaviors which have been reinforced across the various settings of the regular classroom, the special education placement, or the home in the past.

To conduct a comprehensive ecological assessment several sources of data may need analysis. One readily available source of information is the student's permanent record. According to Heron and Heward (1981) student records should indicate the level (and possibly the rate) of student achievement, as well as provide important information on pertinent physical or psychological characteristics. Such records should not be viewed as the sole source of information, nor should they be viewed as verification of a student's problem. Rather, student records should serve as a stimulus to continue the inquiry.

Also, a consultant can probe areas identified through student records by interviewing relevant individuals, such as teachers, students, parents, or physicians. By using interviewing techniques described by Stewart and Cash (1974) and Gorden (1969) the consultant can confirm, clarify, and possibly add to information in the student records.

Another useful way to investigate student behavior and the environment is direct observation. The various observation techniques discussed in this chapter can be used to accomplish this objective. For instance, the use of interaction analysis might help the consultant define the nature of teacher-student interactions. Student-student relationships can be explored through sociometric analysis. Direct, daily observation can be used to assess physical aspects of an environment, such as the amount of space in the room, as well as the behavioral aspects of an environment, such as the frequency and duration of student behavior.

When is it appropriate to conduct a full-scale ecological assessment? Heron and Heward (1981) suggest that this time-consuming activity be undertaken only when a planned intervention has the potential to produce unexpected consequences, or could presumably be jeopardized because salient ecological variables were ignored.

Applied example. A consultant may wish to conduct an ecological assessment if faced with the following type of situation. Suppose a new student moves into the school district and he is suspected of having a handicapping condition. He has not been previously classified as handicapped in his other school placements. However, two of his teachers at the new school have reported serious behavior problems.

There are a number of avenues that the consultant may wish to explore in an effort to define this problem. Interviews with teachers mentioned in the student's school record might determine whether he experienced earlier school problems. Also, it may be helpful to talk to the parents to find out whether the student had undergone any recent changes in diet or medication. The consultant might learn, too, from the parents whether the student had difficulties in other schools. The parent might be able to describe the previous school setting, so that the consultant could compare it with the current placement to determine any differences between the two that could account for the student's behavior. Observations made of teacher-student and student-student interaction, as well as the physical structure of the classroom, might yield significant information regarding the student's behavior. Finally, the consultant may wish to talk directly with the student to gain his perspectives on the situation, and see whether or not he perceives himself as exhibiting inappropriate behaviors.

INFORMATION PROCESSING

An information-processing approach is not strictly an observation technique. Although observations may be conducted, other sources of data are used to gain an understanding of the situation. Typically, other sources of data include teacher reports and interviews.

Information processing has been used in education with observation data to analyze teacher intention (Clark, 1978–1979; Smith & Geoffrey, 1968; Yinger, 1977). It is based on the premise that one must consider both the ecological and the psychological contexts of the educational process (Clark, 1978, 1979). The *ecological context* includes all the resources, external events, and settings which influence a given situation. The *psychological context* for teacher behavior involves the teacher's theories, beliefs, and values about teaching and learning. Analyzing the psychological context is important because it is assumed that teacher beliefs and values affect the way instruction is presented and the classroom is managed (Joyce, 1978–1979).

Procedure

The information-processing approach is based on the ethnographic tradition. Extensive observation is considered an essential component of this approach because it is important to have a context in which to understand the descriptions of the teacher's thought processes and the nature of the teaching acts (McNair and Joyce, 1978–1979). Observation measures commonly used in information processing are discussed under field study later in the chapter.

Another important source of data in the information-processing approach is the self-report of the teacher. These reports can be obtained in two ways. The consultant might use a traditional interview or a questionnaire.

For example, the teacher may be asked to keep a journal in which classroom events and her thoughts about the events are recorded. Clark and Yinger (1979) used this technique to study teacher planning and implementation in the language arts. Specifically, each teacher kept a detailed journal documenting her planning and thought processes related to the planning. Biweekly interviews and classroom observations were used to elaborate on and confirm the journal data. The intent of the approach was to determine why the teacher chose certain activities and teaching strategies.

In another variation, the teacher may be asked to "think aloud" or verbalize her thoughts and decisions on an audiotape as they take place. By analyzing the teacher's comments on the tape, a judgment can be made as to why a specific course of action was taken. Several educators have used this approach in studying teacher planning (Peterson, Marx, & Clark, 1978; Yinger, 1977).

Another possible technique is the use of stimulated recall. In this procedure, the teacher is given a record of her planning or teaching behavior, such as written notes (Smith & Geoffrey, 1968) or a videotape (Mackay & Marland, 1978; McNair, 1978–1979), and she is asked to recall or recreate the thoughts and decisions that were taking place while planning or teaching. In effect the notes or videotape prompt the teacher to remember what she was thinking. Again, the intent is to discover the teacher's thought processes while planning or teaching. By identifying these thought processes and relating them to known outcomes of the instruction, a decision can be made on the effectiveness of the plan or instruction.

As Clark (1978–1979) notes, however, there are few recognized tests of the validity or reliability of these procedures. Nevertheless, consultants might consider the information-processing approach when there is a need to fully understand the effects of a complex program and the teacher's participation in it.

Applied example. This approach might be used by a consultant who is involved in the evaluation of the effects of "open education" on regular and special education elementary students. Analysis of product measures (for example, achievement scores) and daily observations would provide the consultant with data on how the program was implemented and its effectiveness. However, using an information-processing approach, such as teacher reports, the consultant would learn why the program was implemented as observed. The data could provide the consultant with valuable knowledge necessary for possible program modification. For example, as a result of teacher reports, the consultant would know how teachers defined and valued "open education," upon what principles teachers based their instructional decisions, and whether or not these principles were in accordance with open education program goals. Such information would be helpful in determining what teaching skills or principles of open education needed to be addressed or whether program goals, especially for special education students, were being met.

FIELD STUDY

The *field study* procedure described next has also been referred to by educators as educational ethnography, participant observation, qualitative observation and case study (Smith & Geoffrey, 1968; Stake, 1978; Smith, 1979). It is useful when the consultant wants to understand the context in which specific behaviors are being measured, define problems or behaviors to be measured, or needs additional information before proceeding with specific assessment activities. It may involve a considerable investment of time and energy by the consultant. Thus, it is used most efficiently when important judgments or decisions need to be made or nebulous problems defined.

The field study is based on the assumption that human behavior is significantly influenced by the settings in which it occurs (Wilson, 1977). Its purpose is to provide an on-site, holistic study of a group, program, or individual that furnishes a rich description of the situation. This description can be used to generate further observation and measurement of relevant specific behaviors.

Procedure

The essential elements of this method are three. First, the focus of observation, the so-called bounded system (Stake, 1978), must be identified.

The focus could be a person, an institution or a program. The purpose is not to measure prespecified behaviors, but rather to identify behaviors which may need to be assessed. What is happening and deemed important with respect to the person, institution, or program determines what is observed and studied.

Second, it is essential that the evaluation be on-site with the consultant present at all times. With other structured observation systems (for example, ABA techniques) it may be possible to train another observer who could actually collect the data; the consultant need not be on-site. But because the purpose of the field study is to identify behaviors in need of further definition or assessment, the consultant must be there. The observation process evolves as it proceeds, and thus the consultant must be engaged in all its aspects.

Finally, the data are based upon a narrative description of the bounded system but the approach is constructed to allow and actually foster *multi-modal data collection*. That is, the consultant may begin with a narrative description of what is happening in a given situation for a period of time, similar to an anecdotal record. Observations are usually conducted over a long enough period of time (hours and weeks as opposed to minutes and days) to ascertain patterns of behavior. The descriptive narrative then provides the basis for other means of data collection. *Narrative recording* is used to generate questions and to help the consultant learn what additional data will be necessary to answer questions. Since multi-modal data come from many sources, they provide the consultant with a wider data base and lend objectivity to this method.

Wilson (1977) describes the procedure generally used in field study. First, the consultant, acting as observer, must establish his role within a particular situation. For example, if the consultant intends to study an elementary, self-contained, special education classroom for learning disabled students, he would first establish his role in the classroom as an unobtrusive observer. Only after complete acceptance would the consultant consider his field notes a valid reflection of the situation. Otherwise the bounded system of this room might be greatly influenced by the consultant's presence, and thereby not truly reflect the actual class situation to be studied.

Second, since the data collected are multi-modal, the consultant may attempt to do the following: describe the physical setting; describe how that setting changes with modification in activity or personnel; and describe both the form and content of verbal as well as nonverbal interactions between participants. The various modes of data collection evolve from the basic narrative in the field notes. The consultant develops questions based on his notes, and in the process develops additional sources of data to answer these questions. For example, the consultant might record activities that the classroom aide performs. After reflecting on the descriptions of the activities, the consultant may question whether the teacher uses the aide primarily for instructional or clerical assistance. The consultant may then decide to engage the teacher in a simulated activity whereby the teacher is asked to plan for the same class at the same point in time during the year, but without the aide's assistance. Or, the consultant may decide to interview the teacher about the aide's duties in the classroom. Either activity would provide an additional data source to the field notes about the role of the aide in the room.

Third, objectivity is achieved through a representative sampling of information. It is established by using long-term and multi-modal data collection, and interpreting the data in terms of the context in which it was gathered. The observer must be sure to conduct field observations in all relevant situations and over a sufficient period of time to detect behavioral patterns. For example, in a field observation of a class of elementary learning-disabled students the physical setting of the classroom, playground, lunchroom, and gym as well as various aspects of the teacher-student interaction and student-student interaction, the amount of time spent on academic tasks, and the nature of the educational program should be observed.

Fourth, data are analyzed by using a comparative method. Smith (1979) describes himself when analyzing the field study data as being engaged in two processes: comparing and contrasting information, and looking for antecedents and consequences. He actively searches for overall patterns. For Smith, the final analysis of the field study involves understanding the particular situation in comparison to his general knowledge of all situations of this type.

Applied example. A field study might be used by the consultant who wants to ascertain, for example, whether or not a physically handicapped student had been fully integrated and accepted in a mainstream educational program. The consultant would try to determine the student's level of achievement and also whether the student was being treated differently from his peers. (For example, the consultant might try to determine if he was being overprotected or if he was being ignored by his classmates.)

The consultant might observe the physically handicapped student as well as his normal peers, noting the behaviors of the student, important features of the classroom environment, and the actions of others in different environments (other classrooms, the playground, and the lunchroom). Based on the written field notes, the consultant may decide to use other means of data collection, such as interviews and systematic observation, to determine the rationale for why the physically handicapped student was being treated as he was. After a representative amount of information has been obtained, the consultant could analyze it to determine why the physically handicapped student has or has not been fully integrated and accepted into the educational program.

CHECKLIST AND RATING SCALES

According to Brandt (1975) observational data can generally be reduced to three types: narratives, ratings, and checklists. Narrative observation has been described earlier in this section. A *rating scale* represents an estimate of the degree to which a particular characteristic is evident along a basic continuum, and a *checklist* reflects the presence or absence of a particular characteristic according to some predetermined set of categories. Therefore, if the degree or frequency of behavior is important, a checklist would not be appropriate. Checklists are suggested for use as initial sources of assessment data, not as definitive sources (Wallace & Larsen, 1978). There are published rating scales and checklists available, many of which are reviewed in the first volume of Buros' *The Seventh Mental Measurements Yearbook* (1972) and Brandt (1972).

Procedure

Bower and Lambert (1971) in their discussion of teacher-made behavior checklists suggest that three general areas be included on them: (1) behaviors seen in the target child; (2) behaviors seen in the target child's interaction with other students in the class; and (3) behaviors seen in the teacher's interaction with the target child. Based on recommendations from teachers, Wiederholt, Hammill, and Brown (1978) have developed these same three areas into a sample checklist. The authors suggest that the sample checklist serve as a guide for teachers (see Table 8–2).

In addition to checklists designed to indicate the presence or absence of problem behaviors, consultants and teachers can develop checklists which will indicate the presence or absence of specific skills, such as those related to student readiness for school, self-help (dressing, grooming, toileting), arithmetic, and reading.

Some sample items that might be found on a school readiness scale are the following:

1. Does the child appear to be in good general health?

2. Can the child name the days of the week?

Table 8–2 Teacher-made Checklist for Measuring Problems in Social and Emotional Development.

This list was designed to be used by teachers in any classroom to make them more aware of their students' behavior. It can help identify behavior that otherwise might be overlooked or misunderstood. From here the teacher may want to take frequency counts of identified behavior, or in some other way further analyze the situation.

	Frequently	*Not Frequently*

I. Self-image
  A. Makes "I can't" statements
  B. Reacts negatively to correction
  C. Gets frustrated easily
  D. Makes self-critical statements
  E. Integrity: cheats, tattles, steals, destroys property
  F. Makes excessive physical complaints
  G. Takes responsibility for actions
  H. Reacts appropriately to praise

II. Social Interaction
  A. Seeks attention by acting immaturely: thumbsucking, baby talking, etc.
  B. Interacts negatively
  C. Fails to interact
  D. Initiates positive interaction
  E. Initiates negative interaction
  F. Reacts with anger, verbally
  G. Reacts with anger, physically

III. Adult/Teacher Relationships
  A. Seeks attention by acting immaturely
  B. Excessively demands attention
  C. Reacts appropriately to teacher requests
  D. Inappropriately reacts to authority figures

IV. School-Related Activities
  A. Attends to task
  B. Exhibits off-task behavior
  C. Interferes with the other students' learning
  D. Show flexibility to routine changes

    Date the checklist and complete one for each child. Once the checklist has been completed and reviewed, a narrative report can be written with explanations and suggestions for the future. For the list to be effective, the teacher must use the results to actually make changes in the classroom.

Source: Wiederholt, J. L., Hammill, D. D., & Brown, V. *The Resource Teacher,* Boston: Allyn & Bacon, 1978, p. 212–213.

3. Can the child count aloud from one to twenty?

4. Does the child follow classroom rules?

Laurent (1978) proposes the following guidelines for developing informal assessment checklists for handicapped students: (1) skills should be sequenced according to difficulty under their appropriate subject headings; (2) the range of skills should be broad enough so that almost all students in the class will be included; and (3) the skills should be based on the curriculum.

Listed below are some sample items from an informal checklist.

Basic Knowledge	*Achievement Date*
1. Identifies body parts	_____
2. Sorts by color, shape, size, and class	_____
3. Counts ten subjects	_____
4. States name, address, and phone number	_____
5. Selects coins to make sums up to $1.00	_____

The consultant may also tap knowledge of specific arithmetic and reading skills with a teacher-made checklist. The teacher can list, hierarchically, those skills necessary to master a particular reading or arithmetic program and check off mastery of each skill as the child achieves it. Some sample items from an arithmetic skills checklist that may be used at the elementary level follow: (Note: the items are not arranged hierarchically.)

1. Sort according to a particular quality (physical property, form, color, size, shape)

2. Count from one to twenty

3. Add two place numbers by counting objects

4. Rewrite subtraction problem as an addition problem

5. Demonstrate that multiplication is repeated addition

6. Demonstrate successful understanding of division using 2, 3, or 4 place divisors

The consultant may also want to consider the use of rating scales. Though requiring a degree of judgment, rating scales may provide more specific information than checklists. For example, a rating scale can indicate not only the presence or absence of a behavior but also the frequency with which the behavior occurs. The reader is referred to Wallace and Larsen (1978) for a discussion of types of rating scales useful in ecological assessment.

A rating scale developed by Iscoe and Payne (1972) for evaluating exceptional children with respect to environmental influences focuses on three general areas. They are the physical domain, the adjustment domain, and the educational domain, areas of particular relevance to the successful functioning of the handicapped student. Each domain is divided into the categories of visibility, locomotion, and communication. (See Table 8–3.)

In each of the nine resulting subareas, Iscoe and Payne have established a seven-point rating scale, one indicating the absence of a problem

Table 8–3 Hypothetical Rating Profile According to the Iscoe-Payne Classification System.

	Visibility	Locomotion	Communication
Physical Domain	**7**	**5**	**2**
	Peer	Family	Self
Adjustment Domain	**4**	**2**	**2**
	Motivation	Achievement	Potential
Education Domain	**1**	**2**	**1**

and seven indicating extreme problems. Each exceptional child is judged with respect to a normal peer. Inspection of Table 8–3 shows a hypothetical rating profile for Ted. Based upon the summary information in this table, we can conclude that Ted has no apparent difficulties in academic achievement, but he is experiencing some problems relating to his classmates, and his adjustment problem may be related to a highly visible handicap which interferes with his mobility.

SUMMARY

Two broad purposes of observation for the consultant were presented. Also, the purpose and general procedure for eight observational approaches were described, along with applied examples of each. The eight approaches were representative of the two basic observational methodologies used in this country, one based in psychometry and the other based in ethnography.

All observation systems have advantages and disadvantages. Consultants interested in assisting teachers will need to decide upon the use of an observational approach that will be sufficient to answer the proposed questions. If a consultant is able to reconcile concerns of need and efficiency, then he is well on his way to deciding the type of observation technique best suited to a particular situation.

Regardless of the observation approach selected, the observer should adhere to the following guidelines: (1) announce the intention to observe prior to implementing the observation; (2) be as unobtrusive in the observations as possible; (3) conduct reliability checks; and (4) provide appropriate feedback to all interested parties following the observation period.

Questions

1. What are the two broad purposes of observation?

2. What is the difference between formative and summative evaluation?

3. What are some of the advantages of observation techniques based in psychometry?

4. What are some of the disadvantages of psychometrically based obser-

vation techniques for which ethnographic observation techniques attempt to account?

5. Name three permanent product measures.

6. Identify a situation when collection of frequency data would yield helpful information.

7. Rate data is an index of what?

8. What is the name of the observational technique whereby the occurrence of the target behavior at any time during a prescribed interval is scored?

9. What is the name of an observational technique appropriate for the determination of the total amount of a given behavior per unit of time?

10. Why is it important to conduct reliability checks?

11. Name one purpose for which the use of an interaction analysis system would be appropriate.

12. What observation system codes verbal interactions between teacher and individual students and treats each individual as a separate unit of analysis?

13. Describe a situation in which use of the Brophy-Good Dyadic Interaction System would yield useful information.

14. What observation system provides information as to the teacher's influence upon a class of students by coding verbal interaction during schoolwork?

15. What is the name of an approach that can provide useful information concerning the process of student-student interaction in the classroom?

16. What is the purpose of an ecological assessment?

17. What are some of the factors that should be considered in an ecological assessment?

18. Name three sources of information a consultant may draw upon in conducting an ecological assessment.

19. Describe a situation in which the use of the information-processing approach would be necessary.

20. Name three examples of teacher reports.

21. What approach attempts to provide an on-site, holistic study of a group, program, or individual?

22. What is the basic difference between a checklist and a rating scale?

Discussion Points and Exercises

1. Interview and observe the consultants and supervisors in your school district to determine for what purposes student observations are conducted. Identify the types of observational approaches used, and what the observers feel are their strengths and weaknesses.

2. Based on a teacher referral on a student who is exhibiting behavior problems, devise an observational approach that will identify and measure the problem behavior. If possible, construct and implement an intervention. Measure the effectiveness of that intervention.

3. Inspect the annual goals and short-term objectives from the IEP of a handicapped child. Which of the short-term objectives can be assessed through the use of observational approaches? Which observational techniques would be most appropriate? Why?

4. Identify a curriculum or instructional program that teachers have been asked to implement in your school. Describe an observational approach that will be sensitive to the way in which each teacher is implementing this program. Explain why the program is being implemented in this fashion.

REFERENCES

ANGRIST, S. S. Evaluation research: Possibilities and limitations. *The Journal of Applied Behavioral Science,* 1975, *11* (1), 75–91.

AXELROD, S. *Behavior modification for the classroom teacher.* New York: McGraw-Hill, 1977.

BOWER, E. M., & LAMBERT, N. M. In-school screening of children with emotional handicaps. In N. J. Long, W. C. Morse, and R. G. Newman (Eds.), *Conflict in the classroom.* Belmont, California: Wadsworth, 1971.

BRANDT, R. M. *Studying behavior in natural settings.* New York: Holt, Rinehart & Winston, 1972.

BRANDT, R. M. An historical overview of systematic approaches to observation in school settings. In R. A. Weinberg and F. H. Wood (Eds.), *Observation of pupils and teachers in mainstream and special education settings: Alternative strategies.* Reston, Virginia: Council for Exceptional Children, 1975.

BROPHY, J. E., & GOOD, T. L. *Teacher-child dyadic interaction: A manual for coding classroom behavior.* Austin, Texas: The Research and Development Center for Teacher Education, The University of Texas at Austin, 1969.

BROPHY, J. E., & GOOD, T. *Teacher-student interactions: Causes and consequences.* New York: Holt, Rinehart & Winston, 1974.

BUROS, O. K. *The seventh mental measurements yearbook.* Highland Park, New Jersey: Gryphon, 1972.

BUSSIS, A. M., CHITTENDEN, E. A. & AMAREL, M. *Beyond surface curriculum.* Boulder, Colorado: Westview Press, 1976.

CARINI, P. F. *Observation and description: An alternative methodology for the investigation of human phenomena.* Grand Forks, North Dakota: University of North Dakota Study Group on Evaluation, Center for Teaching and Learning, 1975.

CARO, F. G. Issues in the evaluation of social programs. *Review of Educational Research,* 1971, 41, 87–114.

CLARK, C. A new question for research on teaching. *Educational Research Quarterly,* 1978–1979, *3* (4), 53–58.

CLARK, C. M., & YINGER, R. J. Research on teacher planning: A progress report. *Journal of Curriculum Studies,* 1979, *11* (2), 175–177.

COOPER, J. O. *Measuring behavior* (2nd ed.). Columbus, Ohio: Charles E. Merrill, 1981.

FLANDERS, N. A. Interaction analysis in the classroom: A manual for observers. In Anita Simon and E. Gil Boyer (Eds.), *Mirrors for behavior: An anthology of classroom observation instruments,* Vol. 2. Philadelphia: Research for Better Schools, Inc., 1967.

GORDEN, R. L. *Interviewing: Strategy, techniques, and tactics.* Homewood, Illinois: Dorsey, 1969.

GUTMANN, D. Psychological naturalism in cross-cultural studies. In E. P. Willens and H. L. Rausch (Eds.), *Naturalistic viewpoints in psychological research.* New York: Holt, Rinehart & Winston, 1969.

HAMILTON, D., & DELAMONT, S. Classroom research: A cautionary tale. *Research in Education,* 1974, *11,* 1–16.

HAMMILL, D. D., & BARTEL, N. R. *Teaching children with learning and behavior problems* (2nd ed.). Boston: Allyn & Bacon, 1978.

HARDIN, V. Ecological assessment and intervention for learning disabled students. *Learning Disability Quarterly,* 1978, *1* (2), 15–20.

HERON, T. E., & HEWARD, W. L. Ecological assessment: Implications for teachers of learning disabled students. *Learning Disability Quarterly,* 1981, (in press).

ISCOE, I., & PAYNE, S. Development of a revised scale for the functional classification of exceptional children. In E. P. Trapp and P. Himelstein (Eds.), *Readings on the exceptional child.* New York: Appleton-Century-Crofts, 1972, p. 7–29.

JOYCE, B. Toward a theory of information processing in teaching. *Educational Research Quarterly,* 1978–79, 3 (4), 66–77.

LAURENT, P. *Collecting additional information.* Unpublished paper, National Learning Resource Center of Pennsylvania, 1978.

LOVITT, T. *In spite of my resistance . . . I've learned from children.* Columbus, Ohio: Charles E. Merrill, 1977.

LOVITT, T., KUNZELMANN, H. R., NOLAN, P. A., & HUTTEN, W. J. The dimensions of classroom data. *Journal of Learning Disabilities,* 1968, *1* (12), 20–31.

MACKAY, D. A., & MARLAND, P. *Thought processes of teachers.* Canada: University of Alberta, 1978. (ERIC Document Reproduction Service, No. ED 151328).

MARTIN, R., & KELLER, A. Teacher awareness of classroom dyadic interactions. *Journal of School Psychology,* 1976, *14* (1), 47–55.

McNAIR, K. Capturing inflight decisions: Thoughts while teaching. *Educational Research Quarterly,* 1978–79, 3 (4), 26–42.

McNAIR, K., & JOYCE, B. Thought and action, a frozen section: The South Bay Study. *Educational Research Quarterly,* 1978–79, 3 (4), 16–25.

MORENO, J. *Who shall survive? Foundations of sociometry, group psychotherapy, and sociodrama* (2nd ed.). New York: Beacon House, 1953.

MORINE, G. Interaction analysis in the classroom: Alternative applications. In R. A. Weinberg and F. H. Wood (Eds.), *Observation of pupils and teachers in mainstream and special education settings: Alternative strategies.* Reston, Virginia: Council for Exceptional Children, 1975.

North Dakota Study Group on Evaluation. *First California Conference on Educational Evaluation and Public Policy, 1976,* Grand Forks, North Dakota: University of North Dakota, Center for Teaching and Learning, 1977.

PARTLETT, M., & HAMILTON, D. Evaluation as illumination: A new approach to the study of innovative programs. In D. Hamilton et al. (Eds.), *Beyond the numbers game: A reader in educational evaluation.* Berkeley, California: McCretchan, 1977.

PETERSON, P. L., MARX, R. W., & CLARK, C. M. Teacher planning, teacher behavior, and student achievement. *American Educational Research Journal,* 1978, *15* (3), 417–432.

ROGERS-WARREN, A., & WARREN, S. F. *Ecological perspectives in behavior analysis.* Baltimore: University Park Press, 1977.

SIMON, A., & BOYER, E. G. *Mirrors for behavior III: An anthology of observation instruments.* Wyncote, Pennsylvania: Communication Materials Center, 1974.

SMITH, L. M. An evolving logic of participant observation, educational ethnography, and other case studies. In Lee S. Shulman (Ed.), *Review of research in education: 6.* Itasca, Illinois: F. E. Peacock, 1979.

SMITH, L. M., & GEOFFREY, W. *Complexities of an urban classroom.* New York: Holt, Rinehart & Winston, 1968.

STAKE, R. E. The case study method in social inquiry. *Educational Research,* 1978, 2, 5–8.

STEPHENS, T. M. *Teaching skills to children with learning and behavior disorders.* Columbus, Ohio: Charles E. Merrill, 1977.

STEWART, C. J., & CASH, W. B. *Interviewing: Principles and practices.* Dubuque, Iowa: Brown, 1974.

WALLACE, G., & LARSEN, S. C. *Educational assessment of learning problems: Testing for teaching.* Boston: Allyn & Bacon, 1978.

WIEDERHOLT, J. L., HAMMILL, D. D., & BROWN, V. *The resource teacher: A guide to effective practices.* Boston: Allyn & Bacon, 1978.

WILSON, S. The use of ethnographic techniques in educational research. *Review of Educational Research,* 1977, 47 (1), 245–265.

YINGER, R. J. A study of teacher planning: Description and theory development using ethnographic and information processing methods. Unpublished doctoral dissertation, Michigan State University, 1977.

ZELDITCH, M., JR. Some methodological problems of field studies. In G. J. McCall & J. L. Simmons (Eds.), *Issues in participant observation: A text and reader.* Reading, Massachusetts: Addison-Wesley, 1969, p. 5–19.

9

Selecting and Implementing Appropriate Behavior Management Strategies

Each day teachers are faced with innumerable decisions. They must decide what lessons should be reviewed, what teaching material to use, which skills should be taught, and what behavior management strategies to employ.

The emphasis of this chapter is on the management needs of students. Specifically, the purpose is to describe a number of procedures which a consultant can recommend to the regular educator to increase appropriate behavior in the classroom and decrease inappropriate behavior. Training strategies will be discussed along with recommended procedures for implementing a given strategy. Examples from the authors' classroom teaching experience with handicapped and nonhandicapped populations, as well as examples from research studies, will be presented.

Objectives

After reading this chapter, the reader will be able to:

1. define the terms *positive reinforcer* and *positive reinforcement,* and give applied examples of each.

2. define the terms *negative reinforcer* and *negative reinforcement* and give applied examples of each.

3. name two variables which enhance modeling, and provide classroom examples.

4. write a functional contingency contract with task and reward components.

5. distinguish between the terms *time-out, response cost,* and *punishment.*

6. describe the appropriate steps to use to establish, maintain, and fade a token economy system.

7. describe the conditions under which an individual consequence should be applied, and the circumstances under which a group consequence should be applied.

8. describe several positive reductive procedures and give applied examples of each.

9. state under what conditions each of the above management strategies should be employed.

Key Terms

Positive reinforcement	Negative reinforcement
Positive reinforcer	Negative reinforcer
Unconditioned reinforcer	Extinction
Conditioned reinforcer	Punishment

Levels of reinforcers	Response cost
Token reinforcer	Time-out
Contingency contracting	Positive reductive procedures
Premack principle	Group consequences

PROCEDURES TO INCREASE SATISFACTORY ACADEMIC AND SOCIAL BEHAVIOR

The classroom teacher has a number of procedures at her disposal for improving academic and social behavior. These procedures have been thoroughly researched and field tested and have been used by the authors in many classroom circumstances.

It is important for teachers, especially teachers who have handicapped children in their classrooms, to be well-grounded in learning theory and applied behavior analysis. It is important because handicapped children and youth offer such a variety of challenges, which the classroom teacher must be prepared to meet in a constructive way. A classroom teacher who has numerous ways of managing student behavior will be more successful than a teacher who has a limited repertoire of reinforcing alternatives.

Positive Reinforcement

According to Martin and Pear (1978) *positive reinforcement* is defined in two parts. In part one, a behavior is performed which is followed immediately by a consequence. In the second part, the likelihood of that same behavior occurring again is increased. The consequence or stimulus which follows the behavior is called the *positive reinforcer*. For example, if a student raises his hand to answer a question in class (the behavior), and the teacher calls on him (the positive reinforcer), the likelihood of the student raising his hand in the future is increased. It should be noted that a reinforcer can be so labeled only if it increases the likelihood of a behavior's reoccurrence. Table 9-1 contains a list of potential positive reinforcers. Whether any one is a true reinforcer will depend on its effect on the student's behavior. Reinforcers are determined in a functional manner, what might be a reinforcer for one student may not work for another.

Some reinforcers affect an individual's behavior without the individual having prior experience with them. These reinforcers are termed *un-*

Table 9-1 Potential Positive Reinforcers for School-Aged Students

ELEMENTARY LEVEL STUDENTS	INTERMEDIATE LEVEL STUDENTS	SECONDARY LEVEL STUDENTS
Popcorn	Graphs of behavior	Soft drinks
Soft drinks	Points/tokens	Radio listening time
Crayons	Calculators	Popular magazines
Comic books	Science activities	Free time in gym
Play money	Fast food gift certificates	Romantic novels
Stars/stickers	Pictures of TV stars	Graphs of behavior
Graphs	Radio listening time	Praise
Toy	Structured free time	Rock star posters
Notes home	Sports and car magazines	T-shirts
Balls	Soft drinks	Plants
Raisins	Diary	Calculators
Chalkboard work	Games	Tickets to sports events

conditioned reinforcers. Unconditioned reinforcers are biologically determined, and tend to satisfy basic human needs for food, drink, sleep, and sex.

The great majority of reinforcers are acquired. These reinforcers are termed *conditioned reinforcers.* Conditioned reinforcers acquire their reinforcing capability when paired repeatedly with unconditioned reinforcers or previously acquired conditioned reinforcers.

Levels of Reinforcers

Sulzer-Azaroff and Mayer (1977) indicate that five *levels of reinforcers* exist. These levels, arranged hierarchically, are edible, tangible, exchangeable, activity, and social. It is important for the consultant to be aware of these levels so that she can provide recommendations to a regular education teacher that will work with the handicapped students in the class. Further, the consultant must be able to recognize conditions in the classroom that would suggest a shift to more natural reinforcers such as social praise. Each level of reinforcer will be presented with an anecdote that illustrates its use. An analysis will also illustrate the role of consultant in dealing with a particular management problem in a mainstreamed classroom.

Edible reinforcers. The most basic reinforcers are those which are consumable and satisfy basic human needs. Food and drink are edible reinforcers. Another term often used to describe edible reinforcers is *primary reinforcers*. Numerous researchers have demonstrated the effectiveness of edible reinforcers in improving a wide range of school behaviors (Coleman, 1970; Campbell & Sulzer, 1971; Azrin & Lindsley, 1956).

Coleman (1970), for example, implemented a program in a normal classroom whereby target students earned candy for the entire class contingent upon appropriate behavior. As a result, on-task behavior improved and disruptive behavior decreased. Anecdote 9–1 illustrates how a consultant discussed the possibility of using edible reinforcers with a classroom teacher.

Anecdote 9–1

TEACHER: "Yesterday Marc and I had a discussion about the low number of completed assignments he is handing in each day. Both he and I agreed that he is capable of doing much better work. Other students have to wait for Marc to complete his tasks before they go to lunch or go outside, and they are beginning to react negatively."

CONSULTANT: "I see. It sounds like Marc's problem is starting to affect the whole class."

TEACHER: "It is. I've tried to praise him for his work, but it just isn't working out as I thought it would."

CONSULTANT: "Well, I have an idea that might help. Beginning tomorrow, maybe you could tell Marc that for every three assignments he completes he will earn a piece of candy. The candy will be in a container on your desk. At the end of the day the candy will be divided evenly among the class. So, continue to encourage and praise Marc to do his best during the day. When the candy is distributed to the class, mention that Marc's good performance earned the candy."

TEACHER: "That sounds like a great idea. I know the students like candy. My only question is how will I be able to remove the candy later?"

CONSULTANT: "Good question. One way is by continuing to praise Marc as you have been. Eventually, by pairing praise with the candy, the praise will acquire the reinforcing strength of the candy. Also, as Marc's performance improves, increase the number of assignments he has to complete to earn the candy from three to five to seven and so on."

TEACHER: "Okay, I'll give the program a try tomorrow."

Before implementing a program using edible reinforcers the consultant should issue a few words of caution to the teacher. First, from an ethical viewpoint it is critical that the teacher make absolutely sure there is no medical condition which might preclude the use of edible reinforcers. For example, if a handicapped student were allergic to chocolate or sugar and the teacher issued chocolate bits for appropriate behavior, a serious situation could develop. Second, edible reinforcers can lose their effectiveness rather quickly as a student becomes satiated. That is, the student has received an overabundance of a reinforcer. A Coke break immediately after lunch is not likely to be an effective reinforcer either. Finally, even though edibles can be used successfully to establish desired behavior, to maintain the behavior over long periods of time it is usually advisable to switch to other reinforcers in the hierarchy, such as praise, which occur more naturally in the environment. The teacher should use edible reinforcers only in those situations where other reinforcers in the hierarchy are not likely to be effective.

Tangible reinforcers. A tangible reinforcer, the next level on the hierarchy, can be considered any type of concrete object offered as a reinforcer. For example, if a learning disabled student remembered to clean his desk each week, the teacher might reward him with a puzzle or small trinket. Recall Table 9–1 and its list of reinforcers? Many of these reinforcers can be considered tangible rewards because the student receives a physical object contingent upon performance. Anecdote 9–2 describes how a regular classroom teacher structured tangible rewards for two physically handicapped students based on a prior discussion with her supervisor.

Anecdote 9–2

TEACHER: "Nancy and Barbara, I've noticed that you girls have a difficult time getting your work completed each day."

NANCY: "That's for sure. There is so much to do, I barely have time to breathe."

BARBARA: "That's right. It seems like we are always working."

TEACHER: "Well, to help you get more done I want to present a plan to you. I've discussed the plan with Mr. Bobb, the supervisor, and we both feel that it's worth a try. When you complete your assigned tasks for the week, you'll earn a cassette tape on which I've recorded your favorite records. The tape will be yours to keep."

BARBARA: "That sounds great."

NANCY: "And we get to keep the tape?"

TEACHER: "That's right, and to get things off to a good start, here is a cassette tape bin to store your tapes. I think you'll be earning a number of them."

GIRLS: "You bet!"

The supervisor and teacher had jointly agreed to use the cassette tapes because they knew the students enjoyed listening to music. They also chose tapes because they are powerful reinforcers, can be prepared easily, and used in other environments, such as at home.

Also, according to Sulzer-Azaroff and Mayer (1977), a teacher may want to issue a noncontingent reinforcer, one which the students do not have to earn, to prime them to respond. In this case, the tape bin served as the noncontingent reinforcer. The teacher could have just as easily made the first few assignments simple enough so that the students could have earned the tape bin. Either strategy is acceptable.

Exchangeable reinforcers. A token, check mark, or star that is earned by a student for appropriate behavior and later traded for another reinforcing object or event is considered an exchangeable reinforcer. Exchangeable reinforcers serve a dual function. First, they reinforce the target behavior immediately, and second, they remind the student that a stronger reinforcer will be issued in the near future. More description of token reinforcers and an illustration of how tokens serve as exchangeable reinforcers is found later in this chapter. Anecdote 9-5 discusses the use of a token economy in a classroom.

Activity reinforcer. Phillips, Phillips, Fixsen, and Wolf (1971) demonstrated that providing access to activities contingent upon performance can increase appropriate academic and social behavior. It is important to remember that when using activity reinforcers (free time, field trips, etc.) students should not have access to the activity at other times. It would hardly be effective to say to a student who had an articulation problem that contingent upon three correct verbal initiations to other students he would earn fifteen minutes of free time, if access to free time was available at recess or lunch. Students will more likely perform under the stated contingencies, if other sources of activity reinforcers are controlled.

Anecdote 9–3 shows how a supervisor and regular class teacher structured an activity reinforcer for a hard-of-hearing student mainstreamed into a regular junior high school class. The student has concomitant speech difficulties.

Anecdote 9–3

TEACHER: "Mrs. Frank, I'm having a problem with one of my students in the class. I thought you might be able to help me."

SUPERVISOR: "I'll be glad to help if I can. What seems to be the difficulty?"

TEACHER: "Megan, a hearing-impaired student in the class, has extreme difficulty talking to the other students. I think she is afraid they will either ignore her or make fun of her."

SUPERVISOR: "I see."

TEACHER: "There are a few students who talk to her occasionally, but most of the students ignore her."

SUPERVISOR: "I see. Let me think about what we can do."

TEACHER: "Okay."

SUPERVISOR (*meeting with the teacher a few days later*): "I recall you said that there were a few students who talked a little bit to Megan?"

TEACHER: "Yes, that's right."

SUPERVISOR: "How would you feel if I suggested to these students that they could earn extra gym if they interacted with Megan?"

TEACHER: "That would be fine. I'm sure we could arrange the time with Mr. Howard, the physical education teacher."

SUPERVISOR: "Good."

SUPERVISOR (*approaches the two students who occasionally talk to Megan*): "Chris and Bill, I have an idea that might interest the two of you."

BILL: "Really, what is it?"

SUPERVISOR: "As you know, Megan has difficulty talking to other students."

CHRIS: "We know. She is hard to understand sometimes."

SUPERVISOR: "I realize that some of what Megan says is difficult to understand, but I'd like the two of you to make an effort to talk to her, maybe between classes or during project work in class. Let me also say that whenever the teacher notices either of you saying something to Megan, you'll earn one extra minute of gym with Mr. Howard."

BILL: "That's all we have to do?"

SUPERVISOR: "That's right. Any time either of you begins a conversation with Megan, both of you will earn one extra minute of gym time."

MEGAN (*approaches the teacher some time later*): "Mrs. Jones, things have really gotten better. Two students in my classes are talking to me more, and even listening to me when I talk. School isn't such a drag anymore."

The supervisor and the teacher could have arranged the contingency the other way around. That is, they could have made free time for Megan contingent upon her initiating conversations with other students. The rationale for structuring the activity reward for the nonhandicapped students is that the teacher knew that free time was a powerful reinforcer for Chris and Bill and there might be more occasions for Chris and Bill to initiate a conversation with Megan than the reverse.

Social rewards. Social reinforcement is the least intrusive level of reward that a classroom teacher can use to establish and maintain behavior. Praise is the foremost example of a social reward. Other types of social reinforcement include smiles, pats on the back, facial gestures, and teacher attention. The use of contingent praise has been demonstrated frequently in the literature (Hall, Lund, & Jackson, 1968; Broden, Bruce,

Mitchell, Carter, & Hall, 1970; Kazdin & Klock, 1973). Surprisingly, however, social praise is not given in the classroom with the frequency that one might expect despite its demonstrated effectiveness. While "hard data" still remain to be gathered, some researchers (e.g., Stuart, 1971; Madsen & Madsen, 1974) indicate that a functional ratio of about four praise statements to one disciplinary statement should be the goal of teachers in most learning settings. These data are in contrast to Madsen, Madsen, Saudargas, Hammond, and Egar's (1970) study which found that approximately 77 percent of teacher interactions with children were negative whereas 23 percent were positive.

Anecdote 9–4 illustrates how a consultant showed a group of regular classroom teachers how to use social praise effectively and systematically in a classroom where handicapped and nonhandicapped students were enrolled.

Anecdote 9–4

CONSULTANT: "Thank you for inviting me to your team meeting. I hope that the demonstration I have prepared will help you use social praise more effectively in the class."

TEACHER: "I hope so, too. (*Gestures to the other team members.*) We all have handicapped students in the class, together with our normal class size of thirty, and we're looking forward to learning a technique that will make teaching more enjoyable for us and the students."

CONSULTANT (*Suggests to the five teachers that they role play a lesson. Each teacher assumes the role of a student. The consultant takes the role of the teacher. The lesson is in math.*)

CONSULTANT: "Sally, can you tell me the sum of 15 + 5?"

TEACHER (*thinking a minute*): "Twenty."

CONSULTANT: "Very good!"

CONSULTANT (*observing one of the teachers playing with his pencils, but waiting to comment until he begins to write on his worksheet*): "George, I am glad to see you are doing your work. Keep it up."

TEACHER (*has a slight smile on his face*): "Thanks."

CONSULTANT (*mentioning the other three teachers by name*): "I'm glad to see that you three students are working so productively. Super job!"

During the discussion which followed the short role-playing demonstration the consultant indicated that social praise was used in the first instance to reinforce a correct response, in the second case to increase attending behavior, and in the third example to maintain appropriate work behavior.

The consultant also stressed that praise is the most natural reinforcer that teachers use, and it has a number of distinct advantages over the other levels of reinforcement. First, given the variety of praising statements which teachers can use, satiation is not likely to occur. Second, praise and attention are cost-effective. The teacher does not have to spend money to deliver the reinforcement. With other levels of reinforcers (edibles, tangibles, and exchangeables) the cost of purchasing items is a factor. Third, it is convenient and efficient. Teachers do not have the potential messiness associated with edible reinforcers, nor do they have to be concerned with the potential delays in student response while the candy is eaten or the exchangeable reinforcers are handled. Finally, student performance is much more likely to be maintained in different learning settings under social reinforcement than under other levels of reinforcement.

Token Reinforcers

According to Axelrod (1977) token reinforcers can be considered generalized reinforcers because they are associated with a large number of rewards. A *token reinforcer* can be a physical object, such as a chip or a star, or it can be a written symbol, such as a check mark. Tokens can be reinforcing themselves, and they acquire stronger reinforcing capability when they are exchanged for back-up reinforcers, such as free time or activity reinforcers.

Initiating a Token Economy in the Classroom

Token economies have been used in a wide variety of settings including classrooms for the retarded (Bijou, Birnbrauer, Kidder, & Tague, 1967); culturally deprived (Wolf, Giles, & Hall, 1972); and normal student (McLaughlin & Malaby, 1972).

When initiating a token economy the first step is to determine the target behavior to be modified. Once the target behavior has been identified, the teacher describes the rules of the token economy. The teacher tells the students the conditions under which tokens can be earned, the back-up reinforcers which are available, and the exchange procedure. Anecdote 9–5 describes how a teacher established a token economy system in a regular classroom where a handicapped student was emitting a host of disruptive behaviors. The teacher had extensive discussions with her supervisor and the principal and, after eliminating the possibility of a less intrusive program, they agreed to implement a token system. Anecdote 9–5 also provides an example of an exchangeable reinforcer.

Anecdote 9–5

TEACHER: "Barry, I'd like to talk about your behavior."

BARRY: "What about it?"

TEACHER: "Your behavior over the last two weeks has become unacceptable, and I have a plan I think you will like which will help you get back on track."

BARRY: "What is it?"

TEACHER: "Beginning today every time you raise your hand to answer a question rather than call out, I'll place a chalk mark on the side of the blackboard. For every two chalk marks that you have you will earn one extra minute of free time each day. At 2:30 this afternoon we'll tally the number of chalk marks on the board, and you can have that amount of free time."

BARRY: "Suppose I don't use all of my check marks?"

TEACHER: "We'll carry them over to the next day. You'll be able to save your checks if you like to a maximum number of twenty. Do you have any questions?"

BARRY: "You mean the only thing I have to do is raise my hand instead of calling out and you'll give me a check mark?"

TEACHER: "That's right. Except that I'm not giving you anything. You will earn a check mark for raising your hand. Any more questions?"

BARRY (*raising his hand*): "No."

TEACHER (*placing a check mark on the board*): "Very good. I'm glad you understand the program. You've earned your first check mark already."

Maintaining a Token Economy in the Classroom

Once the token system is established, maintaining it is a relatively simple task. The teacher needs only to follow the rules which were initially formed. Reinforcing students with the token as soon as possible after the occurrence of the desired behavior, providing a variety of back-up reinforcers, and maintaining a functional exchange procedure are essential components of maintenance. Also, it is to the teacher's advantage to begin to increase the response requirements while simultaneously decreasing the amount of tokens earned. It is important to incorporate this strategy because the primary goal of the token program should be to move to a higher level of reinforcement (for example, praise) as soon as possible. By repeatedly pairing praise with the delivery of the token, it will acquire the reinforcing capability of the token. For a complete description of the guidelines for establishing and maintaining token economy systems in the classroom, the reader is referred to Kazdin and Bootzin (1972) and Martin and Pear (1978).

Financing a Token Economy

Consultants who recommend the use of token economies, edible reinforcers, or other exchangeable reward systems must be able to suggest ways for teachers to finance these systems. A few alternatives will be presented.

Grant-in-aid. Many state and local departments of education offer grants for teachers to develop, implement, and evaluate instructional approaches. If the use of tokens, exchangeables, or edibles are essential components of the overall instructional methodology, the cost of these items could be incorporated into the budget. The obvious disadvantage of this approach is that competition for funding is often keen and many proposals have to be reviewed, so there may be a considerable delay between application and receipt of the grant. The teacher may have to wait to implement the program until a decision is rendered by the granting source.

District support. Some school districts allocate money each year for expendable items, such as reinforcers. Often the principal has a petty cash account that might be used to reduce the cost of the token economy.

Parent-teacher groups. In many districts parent-teacher associations (PTA's) sponsor fund-raising events each year to reduce or eliminate costs for worthwhile school projects. Petitioning the PTA to sponsor a fund raiser to support a token economy might help.

Personal expenditure. Many teachers purchase the exchangeable reinforcers with their own money. While an undesirable option from a cost standpoint, many teachers feel that the benefit the students derive from having the program outweighs the cost they incur.

Contingency Contracting

Contingency contracting refers to a behavioral approach in which tasks and rewards are specified before the assignment is begun. The use of contracts is frequent in our daily lives. Examples of such contracts are paying a mortgage, purchasing items with credit cards, and signing an employment agreement. Although each of these activities is different, a common feature exists. In any contract there are specifications about the terms of the agreement and responsibilities of each party.

While contracts are a necessary and important part of business, it has only been within the last decade that educators (notably Homme, Csanyi, Gonzales, and Rechs, 1969) have begun to investigate the use of contracts in school environments. Homme et al. outlined ten specifications for contracts, and suggested that contracts can be used with any population of students for any subject matter (see Table 9–2).

Table 9–2 Homme et al's. Ten Rules for Contingency Contracting

---

Rule   1.   The contract payoff (reward) should be immediate.

Rule   2.   Initial contracts should call for and reward small approximations.

Rule   3.   Reward frequently with small amounts.

Rule   4.   The contract should call for and reward accomplishment rather than obedience.

Rule   5.   Reward the performance after it occurs.

Rule   6.   The contract must be fair.

Rule   7.   The terms of the contract must be clear.

Rule   8.   The contract must be honest.

Rule   9.   The contract must be positive.

Rule 10.   Contracting as a method must be used systematically.

SOURCE: Homme, L., Csanyi, A. P., Gonzales, M. A., & Rechs, J. R. *How to use contingency contracting in the classroom.* Champaign, Illinois: Research Press, 1969.

Taken as a whole, Homme et al's. specifications provide the consultant or supervisor with clear guidelines for assisting teachers in developing working contracts. Embedded in the rules are the behavioral principles of immediate reinforcement, rewarding small approximations of behavior, and systematic application.

Teachers who use contingency contracting according to Homme et al's. guidelines become more directive teachers, even for subject areas in which contracts are not employed. Teachers begin to recognize the value of positive directions, immediate feedback, frequent rewards, and consistency. In classrooms where handicapped students are enrolled, teachers frequently report that the shared responsibility of developing the contract, in conjunction with the monitoring process, increases student academic and social performance.

More recently, Dardig and Heward (1976) and Heward, Dardig, and Rossett (1979) have indicated that contracts can be used with children in home or school settings to increase and maintain a wide variety of behaviors. These authors suggest that contracts be written so that the task and reward components are clearly specified.

As Figure 9–1 shows, four items are completed under the task component portion: who, what, when, how well. Under the reward component the items who, what, when, and how much reinforcement are listed. In this contract Ron must attend to his tasks each day with a minimum of two prompts from the teacher. When this behavior occurs he will earn ten minutes of free time from his teacher, Mrs. Pauley.

Ideally, contracts should be written jointly with students. Students specify tasks or rewards. For example, when beginning to contract with students, the teacher or the parent may specify the task components, while the student completes the reward categories. As the student develops more and more competence in task completion, the teacher or parent may let her suggest tasks as well. As a student becomes more self-directed, more responsibility is provided for stating the terms of the contract.

As Dardig and Heward suggest, contracts can also be employed across settings. For example, a handicapped student who completes her work on time and at criterion in the regular classroom might have the reward issued at home. She might be able to stay up later in the evening, earn a trip to the movies, or have a job, such as doing dishes, removed from her chore list.

Contracts have been used at the elementary and secondary level for students for whom previous types of reinforcement strategies failed. Anecdote 9–6 shows how a consultant helped a teacher in a junior high school earth science class initiate a contingency contract with a mildly handicapped student.

Figure 9–1 SOURCE: Dardig, J. B. and Heward, W. L. *Sign Here: A Contracting Book for Children and Their Parents.* Copyright © 1976 by F. Fournes and Associates, Inc., Bridgewater, N.J. (unnumbered page in text) Reprinted with permission.

Contract

Task	Reward
WHO: Ron Johnson	**WHO:** Mrs. Pauley
WHAT: Attending to task,	**WHAT:** Extra free time
WHEN: Each school day	**WHEN:** Each day
HOW WELL: Not more than two reminders may be given each day	**HOW MUCH:** 10 minutes

Sign Here: Ronald Johnson Date 1|5|82

Sign Here: Mrs. J. Pauley Date 1/5/82

Task Record

Anecdote 9–6

MRS. PHILBIN: "Ruth, I've been having a considerable amount of difficulty getting Brian to complete his assignments on time."

CONSULTANT: "Really? What seems to be the problem?"

MRS. PHILBIN: "Brian has a number of earth science projects to complete this semester, and he hasn't made progress on any of them. He seems to do his assignments in the resource room, but he just can't or won't do them in class like the other students."

CONSULTANT: "What strategies have you tried to help his performance?"

MRS. PHILBIN: "I've tried praising him, giving him more time to complete the assignments, and finally I've kept him after school."

CONSULTANT: "You're sure he is able to do the assignments?"

MRS. PHILBIN: "Absolutely. The resource room teacher helped me design his program so that he'd be able to do the work."

CONSULTANT: "That's good. Have you thought about using contingency contracting?"

MRS. PHILBIN: "No. What's involved?"

CONSULTANT: "Actually it's a matter of sitting down with Brian to discuss the tasks he has to complete, how well they have to be completed, and when they are due. Then, you would discuss the rewards he would earn upon completing the tasks."

MRS. PHILBIN: "Sounds interesting. Will it take a lot of time?"

CONSULTANT: "Not necessarily. The first discussion probably will take the most time, perhaps fifteen to twenty minutes. I'd like to recommend that you set up a session with Brian to do this."

MRS. PHILBIN: "I'm willing to try anything at this point."

CONSULTANT: "Fine. When you meet with Brian, come prepared with the list of tasks you'd like him to complete, and give him several reward options you know he would enjoy. Then ask Brian to complete the reward side of the contract using one of the options. Encourage him to be reasonable with the rewards in the same way you were reasonable with the task side."

MRS. PHILBIN: "Anything else?"

CONSULTANT: "Yes. Make sure he understands the contract before he leaves the session, give him a copy of it, and see that your signature and his signature appear at the bottom of the contract."

MRS. PHILBIN: "Thank you. I'll give the contingency contract a try."

CONSULTANT: "I'll call you in a couple of days to see how things are going. In the meantime, here is a list of guidelines that may help you when you write the initial contract with Brian." (*Consultant hands teacher a list of guidelines by Dardig and Heward.*)

Supervisors or consultants who recommend contingency contracting should emphasize that it may take a couple of trials with students before the contracting process is completely successful. They must also stress to teachers that contracting is a mechanism to increase student performance when other procedures have failed, as it provides students with a voice in determining either the tasks they have to perform or the reinforcement they will earn. For many handicapped students having a say about the curriculum can enhance their performance within it.

Premack Principle

The Premack Principle is often dubbed Grandma's Law, which may be best explained in Grandma's own words: "When you finish your meat and beans, you'll be able to have your ice cream." In the present context the *Premack Principle* means that access to a high probability behavior (eating ice cream) is contingent upon the performance of low frequency behavior (eating meat and beans). Teachers can use the Premack Principle in their classrooms if they can determine high and low frequency behaviors.

Determining High Frequency Behaviors

One of the easiest ways to determine high frequency behavior is to observe student activity during free time. For example, during recess or lunchtime, what activities does the student engage in? Does he like to play games, listen to records, talk to a friend, or read a book?

Another way a teacher can determine high frequency behavior is to ask the student, "What do you like to do when you have free time?"

Finally, a third way is to systematically arrange tasks for students to choose. For example, a teacher could give a student the option of doing one of the three possible tasks, writing a report, preparing a collage, or listening to a slide-tape presentation. It can be inferred that the task the student chooses will be the one that he finds the most reinforcing.

Once the high frequency behavior has been determined, the teacher need only make access to it contingent upon performance of a low frequency behavior. For purposes of discussion, academic school work will be considered low frequency behavior, conceding that the example does not hold in all cases.

It should be noted that the Premack Principle can be used with either individuals or groups, and can be applied with equal success across grade levels and academic subject areas.

Modeling

Despite the extensive research that indicates the powerful effects modeling has on increasing student performance (e.g., Broden, Bruce, Mitchel, Carter, & Hall, 1971; Bandura, 1969), consultants may overlook this procedure when recommending strategies to teachers for solving academic and social problems in the classroom. It may be overlooked because consultants do not fully understand how modeling can be used.

Broden et al. (1971), for example, demonstrated the effect of contingent teacher attention on the disruptive behavior of second-grade students. Specifically, when the teacher attended to one student, the behavior of another student also improved, albeit to a lesser degree, even though the teacher's attention was not directed to the second student. Broden et al. suggested modeling may have played a part in the improved performance of the nontarget child. In essence, the nontarget student saw the target student receive the teacher's attention only when he was not disrupting the class. Therefore, to gain the teacher's attention the nontarget student may have begun to imitate the behavior of the target student.

Other researchers (e.g., Bell, 1977; Blankenship, 1978) have shown how modeling can be used to teach mathematic skills to students. Bell, for instance, demonstrated that when a teacher modeled the performance of a given mathematics problem (showed students how to do the problem), and gave them verbal feedback about the accuracy of their responses, student performance improved.

In summary, when students already possess many of the component skills required in a task, whether they be academic or social skills, teachers can use a modeling procedure to refine the performance of the student.

Negative Reinforcement

Probably no term is misused or misunderstood more often than negative reinforcement. Simply stated, *negative reinforcement* occurs when an aversive stimulus is removed contingent upon a particular behavior. Consequently, the likelihood of that particular behavior occurring in the future is increased. Negative reinforcement has the effect of increasing the desired behavior, not decreasing it. Negative reinforcement is not synonymous with punishment. In fact, it has the opposite meaning and effect.

Negative reinforcement and *negative reinforcers* are used repeatedly by skilled classroom teachers to improve student performance. For example, a teacher says, "If each person in the class receives eighty-five percent or better on the first two math pages today, the third page of the assignment will be cancelled." In effect the teacher is removing the aversive stimulus (the third page of math) contingent upon the successful completion of the first two pages. The negative reinforcer is the third page of math.

Consultants or supervisors should not hesitate to recommend a negative reinforcement contingency to a regular classroom teacher. In many instances the use of a negative reinforcement approach can serve the teacher's purpose better than a positive one. For example, suppose that a learning disabled student consistently returned homework that was sloppy and inaccurate. The consultant might suggest that the teacher set up a contingency whereby neater and more accurate papers were negatively reinforced by the removal of the student's homework requirements one day per week.

Extinction

Extinction refers to the discontinuation of reinforcement for a previously reinforced behavior (Sulzer-Azaroff & Mayer, 1977). When a teacher ignores a student behavior which she previously reinforced extinction is in effect. Zimmerman and Zimmerman (1962) and Hall, Lund, and Jackson (1968) have indicated that extinction (ignoring) will produce desirable reductions in inappropriate behavior. If the other sources of reinforcement, such as peer attention to a student's misbehavior, cannot be eliminated, however, the extinction procedure will be compromised.

The teacher's systematic use of an extinction procedure can have a dramatic effect on student performance in the classroom. Suppose that a teacher feels she may be reinforcing poor behavior. For example, calling on students who shout their responses may reinforce shouting. To use extinction on shouting behavior, the teacher would stop attending to students who shouted. The only students who would receive attention would be those who raised their hands.

While extinction can be a powerful technique for reducing inappropriate behavior in a nonaversive manner, it has shortcomings. For example, it may take several sessions to be effective. For problems that require quick solutions, such as fighting, verbal abuse, or self-destructive behavior, the consultant would be advised to recommend other alternatives to the teacher. Further, when extinction is introduced, the teacher may notice a temporary increase in the rate of the inappropriate behavior. Consultants need to advise teachers to prepare for this temporary increase, lest they abandon the procedure prematurely.

PROCEDURES TO DECREASE INAPPROPRIATE BEHAVIOR

The use of aversive techniques in classroom settings has been investigated with the same rigor as other approaches. Just as the teacher has a wide range of strategies at her disposal to increase appropriate behavior, likewise does she have a variety of aversive techniques to reduce or eliminate inappropriate academic or social behavior.

Punishment

The term *punishment* has many connotations and meanings. According to Sulzer-Azaroff and Mayer (1977), punishment frequently implies physical pain. In behavioral terms, punishment refers to the presentation of an aversive stimulus following a behavior (Azrin & Holz, 1966). Like reinforcement, punishment is defined in terms of its effect on behavior. That is, if a behavior is suppressed after the presentation of the stimulus, punishment has occurred. If not, punishment has not occurred.

Given recent court decisions (e.g., *Wyatt* v. *Stickney*, 1972), school boards are more careful how they sanction or condone the use of any punishment contingency, especially those that might involve the use of an aversive stimulus. Sometimes, however, student behavior can be physically harmful and an efficient and reliable means must be employed to suppress it quickly.

Hall, Axelrod, Foundopoulos, Shellman, Campbell, and Cranston (1971) report a study in which punishment was used to stop a seven-year-old retarded girl from biting and pinching herself. The teacher simply pointed to the student and shouted "No!" following each self-inflicted bite or pinch. Figure 9-2 shows that the student's biting and pinching were virtually eliminated when the punishment condition was in effect, and that high levels of biting and pinching were evident when the punishment condition was absent.

Consultants must temper their recommendations to use punishment procedures because of the unpredictable side effects punishment can have, perhaps increasing aggressive or avoidance behavior, and their own sense of the potential effectiveness of the procedure. Heron (1978) proposed several guidelines to aid the consultant in deciding when and how to recommend punishment procedures to teachers with handicapped chil-

Figure 9–2 The number of times Andrea bit or pinched herself or others each day. SOURCE: Hall, R. V., Axelrod, S., Foundopoulos, M., Shellman, J., Campbell, R. A., and Cranston, S. S. The effective use of punishment to modify behavior in the classroom. *Educational Technology,* 1971, *11*(4). P. 25. Reprinted with permission.

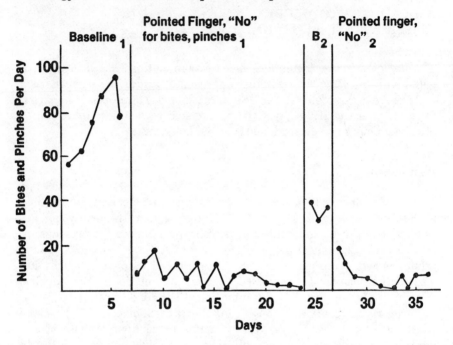

dren in their classrooms (see Table 9–3). These guidelines summarize the major limitations and procedures for using punishment.

Response Cost

Response cost is defined as the loss of a specific amount of positive reinforcement contingent upon a behavior. The response or behavior is going to "cost" the child something he or she finds reinforcing. Like other forms of punishment, a response-cost contingency has the effect of temporarily reducing or suppressing the inappropriate behavior. Fortunately, response cost does not involve the application of any physically aversive stimulus.

There are a number of examples which demonstrate the efficacy of the response-cost procedure. For example, Gallagher, Sulzbacher, and Shores (1976) and Leonardi, Duggan, Hoffheins, and Axelrod (1972) demon-

Table 9–3 Limitations of and Recommended Procedures for Punishment

---

Limitations

1. Disruptive or inappropriate behavior can be reduced using punishment procedures. However, if students are motivated to perform the punished behavior, and have the opportunity to perform the punished behavior, it is likely that the inappropriate behavior will occur again in the future.

2. If a teacher uses a punishment technique to remove an aversive stimulus (for example, yelling at students to be quiet), the teacher may be negatively reinforced. She may tend to use punishment again in the future to reduce inappropriate student behavior.

3. Punishment may produce undesirable side effects. Student aggression, escape, or avoidance behavior may result. If punishment occurs in the same environment repeatedly (for example, in the classroom), the environment may become a conditioned aversive setting that students avoid.

4. Punishment may produce "spillover effects." That is, the behavior of nontarget students may be adversely affected by punishment directed toward target students.

Procedures

1. Vary the types of punishments that are used. If the same type of aversive stimuli are used repeatedly, the students may become satiated.

2. Use a high enough intensity of punishment to suppress the behavior, but refrain from gradually increasing the intensity less the student develop a tolerance for punishment.

3. Punishment delivered at the beginning of a sequence of disruptive or inappropriate behavior will often reduce the level of that behavior faster than punishment delivered at the end of the sequence.

---

strated how a response-cost technique can be used to reduce inappropriate behaviors in the classroom. In both studies the teachers wrote a series of numbers on the blackboard that indicated the amount of available free time. When students disrupted the class, the teacher placed a slash through the highest remaining number on the blackboard depriving them of one minute of free time.

Anecdote 9–7 shows how a building principal recommended a response-cost procedure to a teacher who had two behaviorally disordered students mainstreamed into her junior high school classroom.

Anecdote 9–7

TEACHER: "Mrs. Jackson, the two boys who are mainstreamed into my classroom have completely disrupted my regular program."

PRINCIPAL: "Does the problem lie with only these two students or are there other students involved?"

TEACHER: "Initially it was just the two students, but the problem has spread to many others as well. I've tried talking to the boys, talking to their parents, and reinforcing them for their good behavior, but nothing seems to be working. I'm afraid someone is going to get hurt."

PRINCIPAL: "You feel there is a danger that someone might get injured?"

TEACHER: "I do. Several arguments have already broken out. I'm afraid that a fight might break out at any time."

PRINCIPAL: "Given the circumstances, let's try a response-cost procedure. Here's what I'd like you to do. First, place the numbers twenty to one on the chalkboard so that everyone can see them. Then tell the students that any time anyone in the classroom is out-of-seat or calls out that the top number will be crossed off. Emphasize that the number left after the period is over indicates the amount of free time they'll have in class the next day, or that day, if possible. Teach the class as you normally do, and make certain that every time one of the disruptive behaviors occurs you cross off the highest remaining number. Any questions?"

TEACHER: "What happens if the disruptive behavior continues?"

PRINCIPAL: "Let's wait to see what happens before we plan other alternatives. I'm prepared to recommend some options, but I'll hold off until after you've had a chance to try this procedure."

TEACHER: "I'm willing to try it for a day or so."

PRINCIPAL: "Let's meet again tomorrow."

In this case the principal recommended the response-cost procedure because the threat of student injury in the classroom was so high. He made his decision knowing that the response-cost procedure has several possible advantages, including rapid suppression of the behavior, possible long lasting effects, and convenience for the teacher (Sulzer-Azaroff & Mayer, 1977).

While an informed principal would be aware of the disadvantages of response cost—it may generate escape or aggressive behavior—he might choose not to outline these at the time to the teacher. Perhaps here the principal felt that the teacher could implement the procedure more effectively if the possible disadvantages were outlined at a later time. Planning a meeting for the next day would give the teacher time to field test the principal's recommendation and report the findings.

Time-out

Time-out is said to be in effect when either the student is removed physically from the reinforcing environment or the student loses the opportunity to receive reinforcement while remaining in the environment. Both variations can be extremely powerful reducers of inappropriate classroom behavior.

It should be noted that the physical removal of the student from the environment can be done successfully only under certain conditions. If the time-out environment is appealing, it is unlikely that the procedure would be beneficial. If a teacher sends a student to the principal's office only to have the student enjoy talking with school staff, visitors, or other students, time-out will be ineffective. Also, the time away from the classroom should be relatively short. Sulzer-Azaroff and Mayer (1977) recommend time-out durations which do not exceed fifteen minutes. Longer time-out intervals become self-defeating because students have the opportunity to engage in other behaviors which may not be desirable.

The second time-out method—removing the opportunity to earn reinforcement—can be integrated in a token economy system. Instead of removing a student from the classroom, the teacher merely tells the student, "For the next ten minutes you are ineligible to earn tokens because of your inappropriate behavior." Therefore, regardless of how well the student might behave, tokens would not be delivered until the ten minutes have expired. This type of time-out has the obvious advantage of avoiding physical confrontations with students, and can be conducted within the regular classroom.

Before a time-out procedure is implemented the consultant should make sure that district policy does not preclude its use. Some school systems, reacting to public pressure and court mandates, have ruled that time-out can not be employed. Several court cases (e.g., *Morales* v. *Turnman*, 1973) have set mandatory guidelines and time limitations for physically secluding students from their normal environment. The reader is referred to Budd and Baer (1976) for a review of the legal implications of time-out.

POSITIVE REDUCTIVE PROCEDURES

Students emit a number of behaviors in the classroom that, while not totally disruptive, could be considered annoying or obnoxious. For example, a student who sings or hums to himself may distract other students who are trying to complete their work. Under different circumstances, the humming and singing could be perfectly acceptable, and the teacher might encourage such behavior. With such a student, teachers are not interested in eliminating the singing, rather they want to reduce the level of the behavior or teach the child when to sing and hum and when not to.

Positive reductive procedures can be employed successfully when the teacher wants to reduce the level of behavior. Additionally, positive reductive procedures avoid the potential side effects associated with the punishment techniques presented earlier.

Differential Reinforcement of Other Behavior (DRO)

Differential Reinforcement of Other Behavior (DRO) or omission training is a relatively simple procedure to reduce unwanted behavior. To use a DRO procedure: (1) choose a target behavior; (2) establish a time interval for nonoccurrence of the behavior; and (3) deliver reinforcement if the time interval passes without the target behavior occurring.

For example, a fifth-grade teacher had a learning disabled student in her classroom who did a competent job on her assignments, but often daydreamed. Ms. Abbott decided to reduce the amount of daydreaming. To accomplish her objective Ms. Abbott discussed the situation with her supervisor who suggested that she collect baseline data on the student's daydreaming during the last twenty minutes of each period. Then the supervisor, along with Ms. Abbott, established a series of four five-minute intervals for each period. At the end of each five-minute interval, a kitchen timer sounded. If daydreaming was not occurring, the student was rewarded. However, if daydreaming behavior occurred at the end of the interval, reinforcement was postponed. Any behavior which occurred at the end of the five-minute period except daydreaming produced reinforcement.

It should be obvious that one of the major shortcomings of the DRO procedure is that a wide range of behaviors could occur at the close of the interval and the teacher would still have to give reinforcement. This student, for example, could be hitting another student at the end of the five-minute interval, but as long as she was not daydreaming reinforcement would follow. Inappropriate behavior, therefore, could be reinforced.

Given the possibility of adventitious reinforcement of inappropriate behavior, and the fact that differential reinforcement of other behavior requires consistent observation, consultants should recommend a DRO procedure for those behaviors that can be clearly observed (for example, talking-out, swearing, fighting).

Differential Reinforcement of Low Rates (DRL)

Students who occasionally call out jokes or other humorous anecdotes in class can help to maintain an informal atmosphere that makes learning more enjoyable. Students who tell jokes constantly, however (for example, the class clown), can be annoying.

To use a differential reinforcement of low rates (DRL) procedure, the teacher structures the management plan so that the emission of lesser amounts of the behavior lead to reinforcement. Anecdote 9–8 describes how a consultant helped a teacher plan a DRL procedure to systematically reduce the verbal joking of behaviorally disordered students in a high school English class.

Anecdote 9–8

TEACHER: "Harry has become the class clown lately. He tells jokes constantly, and while I don't mind a joke now and then to lighten the atmosphere, he has gone too far."

CONSULTANT: "Then you don't want to eliminate Harry's joking altogether?"

TEACHER: "No. He is really quite funny, and it seems to help the other students do their work—if it is not too excessive."

CONSULTANT: "May I propose a DRL procedure? Typically the way it works is that you tell Harry he has a limit on the number of jokes he can tell each day, say maybe ten jokes. If he does not exceed that limit, he would earn reinforcement—maybe running the movie projector or collecting the attendance sheets from teachers."

TEACHER: "I see. But how do I reduce the level of joking?"

CONSULTANT: "After a couple of days reduce the limit of allowable jokes to eight and then six, and so forth to earn reinforcement."

TEACHER: "What if he exceeds the limit?"

CONSULTANT: "Reinforcement would not be delivered."

TEACHER: "I'll give the DRL procedure a try for a week, and I'll let you know how it goes."

CONSULTANT: "Fine. I'll look forward to our next meeting."

According to Sulzer-Azaroff and Mayer (1977), the DRL procedure has several advantages and disadvantages. First, it is positive. Students can earn reinforcers. Second, it is tolerant. It does not require the total elimination of a behavior. Rather DRL is designed to progressively reduce the inappropriate behavior. Third, DRL is convenient and effective. Teachers can incorporate DRL in the classroom without rearranging their entire management program.

On the other hand, DRL is slow. It takes time to reduce the inappropriate behavior to tolerable levels. Consultants would not recommend a DRL procedure to a teacher to reduce aggressive or violent behavior. Also, this procedure does focus on the inappropriate behavior. Teachers who are not careful might fall into the trap of attending to undesirable behavior more than to desirable behavior, and, in effect, inadvertently reinforce it.

Differential Reinforcement of High Rates (DRH)

Differential reinforcement of high response rates (DRH) is the opposite of the DRL procedure. With DRH students are reinforced for responding that exceeds previously established rates. Suppose that a hard-of-hearing student, integrated in a junior high school class, was only completing 20 percent of her daily assignments. Using a DRH schedule, contingent reinforcement would be given when the student increased her assignment completion performance over 20 percent. The DRH schedule could be increased systematically so that future performance would have to meet or exceed 30 percent, 50 percent and so on.

According to Sulzer-Azaroff and Mayer (1977), when using DRH it is important to gradually increase the response requirements. If the criterion for higher response rates is increased abruptly, performance will falter. If the performance does disintegrate, the temporary lowering of the DRH criterion is usually recommended.

Reinforcing Alternative Behavior (Alt-R)

When a teacher reinforces a behavior that is incompatible with another behavior, Alt-R is said to be in effect. Skilled consultants recommend Alt-R because they have learned that it accomplishes a twofold purpose with one strategy. An inappropriate behavior is reduced or eliminated, and an appropriate behavior is strengthened. Reinforcing alternative behaviors seems to blend the best of reductive and reinforcement techniques (Sulzer-Azaroff & Mayer, 1977).

How does one choose an incompatible behavior? Usually all that is required is to select a behavior which physically can not occur at the same time as the target behavior. For instance, if an educable mentally retarded student emits "nomad" behavior—continues to walk around the room—the teacher would be wise to choose in-seat behavior as the incompatible behavior to reinforce. Likewise, if a student repeatedly blurts out answers, the teacher might choose quiet hand-raising as the incompatible behavior. Ayllon and Roberts (1974), for example, found that disruptive behavior decreased when students were consistently reinforced for appropriate academic performance.

GROUP CONTINGENCIES IN THE CLASSROOM

Rationale

Thus far a number of procedures for increasing appropriate and decreasing inappropriate behavior in the classroom have been discussed. It should be noted that many of these procedures can be employed within a group context. Teachers who have serious problems with many students in the room usually do not have the luxury of time to apply a series of individual contingencies. Teachers need an effective and convenient approach to deal with multiple misbehaviors. *Group consequences* serve this purpose because the contingencies are applied to the whole class regardless of individual behavior.

Barrish, Saunders, and Wolf (1969) devised a group strategy that regular education teachers could use in their classrooms to reduce inappropriate social behavior. They called their strategy "The Good Behavior Game." The procedure involved dividing the students in the room into two teams. Each time there was an occurrence of a target behavior (for example, talking-out or out-of-seat) the teacher placed a mark on the chalkboard. The team with the fewest marks at the end of the day was the winner. If both teams had fewer than a set criterion of marks, both teams won victory tags, access to free time, and stars next to their names on a chart.

The results of the Barrish et al. study were dramatic. Prior to the initiation of "The Good Behavior Game," out-of-seat behavior and talking-out were occurring over 80 percent of the time. After the game was played seventeen times both teams won 82 percent of the time, indicating a substantial reduction in the undesirable behavior.

Litow and Pumroy (1975) suggest that group management strategies can be arranged in three ways:

1. Dependent group-oriented systems—the whole class is rewarded if one student performs the stated behavior.

2. Independent group-oriented systems—individuals are rewarded if they *each* perform the desired behavior.

3. Interdependent group-oriented systems—the whole class is rewarded when all students perform the acceptable behavior.

Advantages of Group Contingencies

Group contingencies have a number of advantages which teachers might find appealing. First, most students enjoy playing games, and group games usually generate enthusiasm. As Axelrod (1977) indicates, teachers can capitalize on student willingness to participate in these games. Second, many student behaviors, appropriate and inappropriate, are the result of conformity to peer pressure. For older students, especially junior and senior high school students, performance of appropriate and inappropriate social behavior may be reinforced by the peer group (Minuchin, Chamberlin, & Graubard, 1967). Academic behavior, as well, may be controlled by peer pressure (Hamblin, Hathaway, & Wodarski, 1971). In the latter study, when group reinforcement was based on the improved performance of the bottom three students on a test, the more able students helped to tutor the low-scoring students. This contrasts with data acquired during the study's individual contingency phase where the more able students did not tutor the other students. Third, group contingencies are often easy to carry out in the classroom. Axelrod (1973), for example, compared individual and group contingencies in two classrooms to determine which would be more efficient in reducing disruptive behavior. He found that both techniques were equally effective, but that the group consequence was far easier to implement in the room, since the consequence for any inappropriate behavior only had to be administered to the group rather than to each individual. Finally, simpler record keeping can be facilitated using group consequences. Individual data would not have to be gathered on thirty to forty students. Rather the occurrence of each target behavior would be recorded for the class as a whole.

Disadvantages of Group Contingencies

The most obvious disadvantage for the use of group consequences in the classroom is that all students, regardless of behavior, share the same outcome. For example, when a teacher uses a response cost group contingency in a class to reduce call-outs, all students lose a minute of recess for each call-out. Students who do not call out share the same punishment as those who do. However, if only a few students in the class are responsible for the call-outs, the teacher could set up a specific response-cost contingency just for them. In this case, the rest of the class would not be penalized for the inappropriate behavior of a few students.

Second, group procedures may not be sensitive to individual student performance. If a teacher only uses group data, individual student performance will be masked.

Finally, aversive peer group pressure may be generated. Students who lose reinforcement because of a peer's behavior may threaten or intimidate that peer to force him to conform to group standards. Consultants who recommend group contingencies to teachers need to emphasize that the peer pressure can work both for and against them.

SUMMARY

Positive reinforcement is defined as the presentation of a stimulus or event subsequent to the performance of a behavior which increases the probability of the behavior occurring again. Reinforcers can be edible, tangible, exchangeable, activity, or social. Reinforcers are determined solely by their effect on behavior.

Tokens, or exchangeable reinforcers, can be employed in classroom situations where conventional reinforcers have been ineffective. Token programs permit the teacher to use a wide variety of back-up reinforcers to establish and maintain behavior. Tokens should be paired with social praise so that when the tokens are reduced or removed, student performance will be maintained by the social praise. Teachers need to be knowledgeable about procedures to initiate, maintain, and finance a token reinforcement program.

Contingency contracts state the task and reward components for the teacher and student. Contracts should be written, and, if possible, students should help to write them. Contracts can be employed with individuals or groups of students, and should be drawn using appropriate guidelines.

Negative reinforcement is defined as the removal of an aversive stimulus contingent upon a response and has the effect of increasing the probability of the behavior in the future. Teachers use negative reinforcement procedures in the classroom when they remove student assignments contingent upon the successful completion of prior tasks.

When a teacher wants to increase the performance of students who already possess many components of target behaviors, a modeling procedure may be employed. Modeling, or imitation, can be effective for a wide range of academic or social behavior.

If a teacher discontinues the reinforcing of a previously reinforced behavior, extinction is said to be in effect. Extinction must be used cautiously in the classroom, because other sources of reinforcement for inappropriate student behavior might interfere. Further, extinction usually has a delayed effect on behavior rather than an immediate one.

Inappropriate behavior can also be reduced with punishment techniques and positive reductive approaches. Whereas punishment techniques usually suppress the behavior immediately, positive reductive approaches reinforce reduced amounts of the inappropriate behavior over time. Positive reductive approaches also do not have the aversive side effects that are often characteristic of punishment procedures.

Group consequences are contingencies designed to reduce the inappropriate and increase the desirable behavior of a class as a whole. Group consequences can be applied to a variety of academic or social problems. "The Good Behavior Game" is an excellent example of a group consequence which can be applied in regular classroom settings where handicapped and nonhandicapped students are enrolled.

Questions

1. Define and give one example of positive reinforcement, negative reinforcement, punishment, and extinction.

2. Identify the components of a contingency contract. Why are contracts effective when other management procedures are not?

3. List three ways to decrease inappropriate social behavior and provide an example of each.

4. List three advantages of group contingencies.

5. Describe two ways to phase out an established token economy system.

Discussion Points and Exercises

1. Discuss the notion that there is no substitute for objective data in teaching in terms of (1) deciding whether or not a problem exists; (2) determining appropriate intervention strategies; and (3) the effect of an applied intervention.

2. Identify your school system's procedures for dealing with truant students, students who abuse drugs and alcohol, and destructive students. Do the data indicate existing procedures are effective?

3. How would you apply the procedures outlined in the chapter to the following situations?
   a. A student who is consistently late for class.
   b. A student who will not attempt assigned work.

4. List five potential reinforcers for students at each of the following grade levels: primary, intermediate, junior high, and high school.

5. Present regular teachers who have a handicapped student in their classrooms with a blank contract (see Figure 9–1). Ask the teachers to complete the full contract for one handicapped student and one nonhandicapped student in the classroom. Check each contract for consistency with Homme's recommendations and Dardig and Heward's guidelines. Praise teachers for correct performance.

6. During an in-service presentation demonstrate how to pair social praise with the delivery of tokens. Stress how to remove tokens once performance begins to improve. Have teachers practice token delivery during in-service sessions, and monitor their performances in the classroom.

7. Show a videotape of a skilled teacher using response cost and time-out procedures with handicapped and nonhandicapped students. Have regular education teachers in attendance identify the specific teaching behaviors that make these approaches work. Solicit their options as to how these techniques could be used in their classrooms.

REFERENCES

AXELROD, S. Comparison of individual and group contingencies in two special classes. *Behavior Therapy.* 1973, 4, 83–90.

AXELROD, S. *Behavior modification for the classroom teacher.* New York: McGraw-Hill, 1977.

AYLLON, T., & ROBERTS, M. D. Eliminating discipline problems by strengthening academic performance. *Journal of Applied Behavior Analysis,* 1974, 7, 71–76.

AZRIN, N. H., & HOLZ, W. E. Punishment. In W. K. Honig (Ed.), *Operant behavior: Areas of research and application.* New York: Appleton-Century-Crofts, 1966.

AZRIN, N. H., & LINDSLEY, O. R. The reinforcement of cooperation between children. *Journal of Abnormal and Social Psychology,* 1956, 52, 100–102.

BANDURA, A. *Principles of behavior modification.* New York: Holt, Rinehart and Winston, 1969.

BARRISH, H. H., SAUNDERS, M., & WOLF, M. M. Good behavior games: Effects of individual contingencies for group consequences on disruptive behavior in a classroom. *Journal of Applied Behavior Analysis,* 1969, 2, 199–224.

BELL, L. Effects of modeling and verbal feedback on math performance of educable mentally retarded children. Unpublished thesis, The Ohio State University, 1977.

BIJOU, W. W., BIRNBRAUER, J. S., KIDDER, J. D., & TAGUE, C. Programmed instruction as an approach to teaching reading, writing, and arithmetic to retarded children. In S. W. Bijou and D. M. Baer (Eds.), *Child development: Readings in experimental analysis.* New York: Appleton-Century-Crofts, 1967.

BLANKENSHIP, C. S. Remediating systematic inversion errors in subtraction through the use of demonstration and feedback. *Learning Disability Quarterly,* 1978, 1, 12–22.

BRODEN, M., BRUCE, C., MITCHELL, M. A., CARTER, V. C., & HALL, R. V. Effects of teacher attention on attending behavior of two boys in adjacent desks. *Journal of Applied Behavior Analysis,* 1970, 3, 199–203.

BUDD, K., & BAER, D. M. Behavior modification and the law: Implications of recent judicial decisions. *The Journal of Psychiatry and Law,* Summer, 1976, 171–244.

CAMPBELL, A., & SULZER, B. Naturally available reinforcers as motivators toward reading and spelling achievement by educable mentally handicapped students. Paper presented at the meeting of the American Educational Research Association meeting, New York, February, 1971.

COLEMAN, R. A. A conditioning technique applicable to elementary school classrooms. *Journal of Applied Behavior Analysis,* 1970, 3, 293–297.

DARDIG, J., & HEWARD, W. L. *Sign here: A contracting book for children and their parents.* Bridgewater, New Jersey: F. Fournies and Associates, 1976.

GALLAGHER, P. A., SULZBACHER, S. I., & SHORES, R. E. A group contingency for classroom management of emotionally disturbed children. Paper presented at the meeting of the Kansas Council for Exceptional Children, Wichita, March, 1976.

HALL, R. V., AXELROD, S., FOUNDOPOULOS, M., SHELLMAN, J., CAMPBELL, R. A., & CRANSTON, S. The effective use of punishment to modify behavior in the classroom. *Educational Technology*, 1971, 11, 24–26.

HALL, R. V., LUND, D., & JACKSON, D. Effects of teacher attention on study behavior. *Journal of Applied Behavior Analysis*, 1968, 1, 1–12.

HAMBLIN, R. L., HATHAWAY, C., & WODARSKI, J. S. Group contingencies, peer tutoring, and accelerating academic achievement. In E. A. Ramp and B. I. Hopkins (Eds.), *A new direction for education: Behavior Analysis*, 1971, Vol. 1. University of Kansas, Lawrence, Kansas, 1971.

HERON, T. E. Punishment: A review of the literature with implications for the teacher of mainstreamed children. *Journal of Special Education*, 1978, 12, 243–252.

HEWARD, W., DARDIG, J., & ROSSETT, A. *Working with parents of handicapped children*. Columbus, Ohio: Charles E. Merrill, 1979.

HOMME, L., CSANYI, A. P., GONZALES, M. A., & RECHS, J. R. *How to use contingency contracting in the classroom*. Champaign, Illinois: Research Press, 1969.

KAZDIN, A. E., & BOOTZIN, R. R. The token economy: An evaluative review. *Journal of Applied Behavior Analysis*, 1972, 5, 343–372.

KAZDIN, A. E., & KLOCK, J. The effect of nonverbal teacher approval on student attentive behavior. *Journal of Applied Behavior Analysis*, 1973, 6, 643–654.

LEONARDI, A., DUGGAN, T., HOFFHEINS, J., & AXELROD, S. Use of group contingencies to reduce three types of inappropriate classroom behaviors. Paper presented at the meeting of the Council for Exceptional Children, Washington, D.C., March, 1972.

LITOW, L., & PUMROY, D. K. A brief review of classroom group-oriented contingencies. *Journal of Applied Behavior Analysis*, 1975, 8, 341–347.

MADSEN, C. H., & MADSEN, C. R. *Teaching discipline: Behavior principles towards a positive approach*. Boston: Allyn & Bacon, 1974.

MADSEN, C. H., MADSEN, C. R., SAUDARGAS, R. A., HAMMOND, W. R., & EGAR, D. E. Classroom RAID (Rules, Approval, Ignore, Disapproval): A cooperative approach for professionals and volunteers. Unpublished manuscript, University of Florida, 1970.

MARTIN, G., & PEAR, J. *Behavior modification: What it is and how to do it*. Englewood Cliffs, New Jersey: Prentice-Hall, 1978.

MCLAUGHLIN, T. F., & MALABY, J. E. Intrinsic reinforcers in a classroom token economy. *Journal of Applied Behavior Analysis*, 1972, 5, 263–270.

MINUCHIN, S., CHAMBERLAIN, P., & GRAUBARD, P. A project to teach learning skills to disturbed delinquent children. *American Journal of Orthopsychiatry*, 1967, 37, 558–567.

MORALES v. TURMAN, 364, F. Supp. 166, (Ed.D., Texas, 1973).

PHILLIPS, E. L., PHILLIPS, E. A., FIXSEN, D., & WOLF, M. Achievement place: Modification of behavior of predelinquent boys within a token economy. *Journal of Applied Behavior Analysis*, 1971, 4, 45–61.

STUART, R. B. Assessment and change of communication patterns of juvenile delinquents and their parents. In R. D. Rubin, H. Fensterheim, A. A. Lazarus, and C. M. Franks (Eds.), *Advances in behavior therapy.* New York: Academic Press, 1971, 183–196.

SULZER-AZAROFF, B., & MAYER, G. R. *Applying behavior-analysis procedures with children and youth.* New York: Holt, Rinehart and Winston, 1977.

WOLF, M. M., GILES, D. K., & HALL, V. R. Experiments with token reinforcement in a remedial classroom. *Behavior Research and Therapy,* 1968, 6, 305–312.

Wyatt v. *Stickney,* 344 F. Supp. 387 (M.D. Ala. 1972).

ZIMMERMAN, E. H., & ZIMMERMAN, J. The alteration of behavior in a special classroom situation. *Journal of Experimental Analysis of Behavior,* 1962, 5, 59–60.

10

The Consultant's Role in Career Education Programs for Handicapped Students

This chapter was written by David S. Hill, The Ohio State University.

The ability of elementary and secondary education programs to prepare handicapped students for meaningful participation in the American society is being scrutinized. The reason for the close examination is that special programs for the mentally retarded which initially were intended to prepare these students for gainful employment after leaving high school have been disappointing (Kolstoe, 1976a). High unemployment within this population, as well as within other handicapped groups, indicates that existing programs are not providing basic skills for obtaining and maintaining jobs. In addition, since recent federal legislation requires training of handicapped students in skill areas related to successful participation not only in the labor force but also in the community, changes in elementary and secondary programs in the next several years will undoubtedly reflect a concern for "life after high school."

Special education's interest in the orientation and curricula embodied in the field of life skills or career education reflects a concern for the future of identified handicapped children. Special education professionals are beginning to provide a range of alternative programs which focus on the living skills these students must possess. An increased emphasis is being placed on assisting handicapped students with identifying employment and life goals, given the student's motivation, ability skill, and interest levels. In addition, professionals from vocational education counseling, elementary and secondary education, are working with special educators to identify programs currently available for nonhandicapped students which may, with possible modification, meet the educational needs of handicapped students.

251

The purpose of this chapter is to define career education as an emerging and important element of elementary and secondary programming for handicapped students, to identify a strategy for providing career education programs for handicapped students, and to discuss how consultants and supervisors of regular and special education teachers can facilitate a career education orientation in mainstreamed classrooms.

Objectives

After reading this chapter, the reader will be able to:

1. identify the three dimensions of a career education curriculum.

2. identify a research-based and a legislation-related rationale for career education programming for handicapped students.

3. write long- and short-term objectives for an individualized educational program (IEP) designed for an elementary and secondary student. The objectives will reflect a career education orientation.

4. list regular class placement alternatives that address the career education needs of handicapped students.

5. describe the tasks that must be accomplished in providing career education programs for the handicapped.

Key Terms

Career education	Work coordinator
Career awareness	Daily living skills
Career exploration	Personal-social skills
Career preparation	Occupational guidance and
Vocational counselor	preparation skills

THE CAREER EDUCATION CONCEPT

Definition of Career Education

The recent interest in *career education* as a curriculum approach and instructional orientation was initiated at the national level in 1971 by former U.S. Commissioner of Education, Sidney Marland (Brolin & D'Alonzo, 1979). To date several education professionals at federal, state, and local levels have endorsed career education and have worked to include the concept in school programs. The products of these efforts differ greatly due to the number of different definitions of career education. Present differences make definition one of the more critical issues in career education for handicapped and nonhandicapped students (Brolin & D'Alonzo, 1979). Present definitions of career education differ according to how the term *career* is defined.

A narrow definition. In its narrowest sense, a career is defined as the source of an individual's employment. Educators who define career in these terms consider career education as ". . . preparation for entry into the world of work" (Dellefield, 1974, p. 11). Thus, career education programs consist of experiences typically provided in vocational education programs.

A broad definition. A more comprehensive definition of career is provided by Super (1976).

> [A career is] the sequence of major positions occupied by a person throughout his preoccupational, occupational, and postoccupational life: including work-related roles such as those of student, employee, and pensioner, together with complementary avocational, familial and civic roles. (p. 18).

Educators, such as Super (1976), who define career in these terms consider career education as a means to prepare students for full participation in all aspects of life: economic, social, and personal. It is more than the occupational skill training provided by vocational programs.

This chapter will consider the comprehensive definition provided by Super to meet the total needs of handicapped students for economic and social survival. Several other reasons exist for using Super's definition. First, it is compatible with the focus of educational programs provided for mentally retarded populations. Kolstoe (1976a) pointed out that curricula designed to train retarded individuals in life skills, including occupational skills, are common and have been in existence and use for some time. A career education orientation to programs for handicapped students is not completely new to the field of special education.

A second reason for favoring a broad conceptualization of career education is that it does not suggest instructional programming in a single discipline (i.e., vocational education). Rather, it encompasses all program areas in schools, from academic instruction in content areas, such as math, English, or science, to nonacademic areas, such as homemaking, physical education, and vocational education. Career education, broadly defined, is compatible with the current trend toward providing a range of program alternatives to the handicapped population.

Third, a broad conceptualization of career education implies a purpose and relevance for schooling which goes beyond the mastery of academic or vocational skills. Also, it suggests the need to teach students to apply basic skills in real life situations. The real life situations that both handicapped and nonhandicapped individuals might face in the future will be related not only to securing employment, but also to all aspects of living in our complex society.

Finally, a broad conceptualization of career education is consistent with a recent Council for Exceptional Children (CEC) position paper. The position was adopted as CEC policy by the governing body of the organization and includes the following career education objectives for exceptional children:

1. To help exceptional students develop realistic self-concepts, with esteem for themselves and others, as a basis for career decisions.

2. To provide exceptional students with appropriate career guidance, counseling and placement services utilizing counselors, teachers, parents, and community resource personnel.

3. To help students know and appreciate the many changing avocational, domestic, and civic outlets for developed interests and abilities, outlets which in an automated society often supplement, complement, or even supplant paid work in making a satisfying career.

4. To provide the physical, psychological, and financial accommodations necessary to serve the career education needs of exceptional children.

5. To infuse career education concepts throughout all subject matter in the curricula of exceptional children in all educational settings from early childhood through post-secondary.

6. To provide the student with the opportunity to leave the school program with an entry level saleable skill.

7. To provide career awareness experiences which aim to acquaint the individual with a broad view of the nature of the world of work, including both unpaid and paid work.

8. To provide career exploration experiences which help individuals to consider occupations which coincide with their interests and aptitudes.

9. To provide exceptional individual programs with occupational preparation opportunities for a continuum of occupational choices covering the widest possible range of opportunities.

10. To help insure successful career adjustment of exceptional students through collaborative efforts of school and community.

(Brolin, Cegelka, Jackson & Wrobel, 1977)

Rationale for Career Education for the Handicapped

While there are many forces that might be credited with directing special educators to infuse career education into programs designed for handicapped students (such as parent pressure, changes within secondary education programs) two other compelling reasons for career education are related to projections of employment of handicapped youth, and recent legislation related to school programming for the handicapped. A brief consideration of these statistical forecasts and legal realities might serve to identify a broad range of educational programs which may meet the needs of individual handicapped students.

Employment. While empirical evidence is somewhat sparse, a few reports suggest that handicapped individuals may have difficulty obtaining employment commensurate with their skills and interests. Martin (1972) and Barone (1977) predicted that of the 2.5 million handicapped students who left high school between 1972 and 1975, 21 percent were fully employed or went to college, 40 percent were underemployed, 8 percent to 10 percent were idle much of the time, and 3 percent were totally dependent and institutionalized.

Brolin and D'Alonzo (1979) and Kolstoe (1976b) reviewed research that investigated the employment and community adjustment of educable mentally retarded (EMR) students. They concluded that EMR students who are not enrolled in work-study or other vocational programs during high school may tend to have employment and community adjustment problems. However, their reviews suggested that when appropriate occupational and life skills programs were provided, employment and community adjustment improved.

The research which investigated the efficacy of career education for EMR students raises an important question: "Will increases in employment and community adjustment be realized when career education is provided for other handicapped populations?" The possibility of an affirmative response to this question together with the need to increase employment of handicapped individuals provides a compelling reason for adoption of a career education orientation.

Legislation. Public Law 94–142 is compatible with a career education in two ways. First, the law requires the participation of parents and professionals in the identification of handicapped children and in the development of educational programs for them. Through participation, parents and educators have the opportunity to translate their concern for the future of the handicapped into procedures for assessing occupational and living skill levels. Further, parents and professionals can insure that the programs designed for handicapped students attend to career needs.

Public Law 94–142 also requires that vocational education programs be provided for the handicapped (Razeghi & Davis, 1979). These may be either specially designed programs or programs currently accessible to nonhandicapped students, depending on the abilities of the handicapped students to benefit from such programs. In addition, nonacademic and extracurricular activities and programs are to be made available (Razeghi & Davis, 1979).

Under Public Law 94–482, The Education Amendments of 1976, states must spend 10 percent of their funds for vocational programs to meet the training needs of the handicapped (Brolin & Kokaska, 1979). Public Law 94–482 is an extension of the Vocational Education Act of 1963 and the Vocational Education Amendments of 1968 in that it requires monies to be spent to the maximum extent possible on assisting handicapped students to participate in regular vocational programs. State spending must be compatible with the state plan for providing Individualized Educational Programs under Public Law 94–142.

Two parts of the Rehabilitation Act Amendments of 1973 (P.L. 93–112) pertain to career education for the handicapped. Section 503 requires that private business under contract with the federal government make every effort to recruit, hire, train, and promote handicapped individuals. Businesses can request assistance from vocational programs in the public schools to meet these requirements (Razeghi & Davis, 1979). Section 504 of the act requires the accessibility of vocational education programs to the handicapped. Vocational and other educational services cannot be denied because an individual is handicapped.

In addition to mandating appropriate educational opportunities for handicapped students, federal legislation provides for the development of career education programs for all students. Public Law 93–380, the Education Amendments Act of 1974, authorized the establishment of a United States Office of Career Education and provided funds for the development of career education. The Education Amendments Act of 1976 (P.L. 94–482) provided federal assistance for state planning and development of career education programs (Part C, Title III, "Career Education and Career Development"). Finally, the Career Education Implementation Incentive Act of 1977 (P.L. 95–207) provided $400 million over a five-year period to merge existing school curricula and career education (Brolin & Kokaska, 1979).

These major pieces of legislation have provided for the development of career education programs for both nonhandicapped and handicapped individuals. They have provided financial support, and have mandated career-oriented programs to meet the individual needs of all students.

THE CAREER EDUCATION CURRICULUM

The various conceptualizations of career education have led to the development of curriculum models to structure instructional practices and activities. As stated previously, while the authors of the models may differ in their definitions of the term *career*, the levels required of a career education program usually include career awareness, exploration, and preparation.

Career Awareness

Career awareness begins with an examination of the different roles and responsibilities of living. These initial investigations begin during the elementary grades. Kolstoe (1976c) identified three aspects of career awareness: attitude formation, career information, and self-understanding.

Attitude formation. Attitude formation involves learning that work ". . . is a conscious effort aimed at producing some benefit and it is something one chooses to do" (p. 40). In addition, children must learn that the reason for work is not only to provide money for purchasing goods, but also to develop a sense of identity and self-worth and to insure the survival of the society.

Career information. The second aspect of career awareness involves informing students of the many ways people earn a living (Kolstoe, 1976c). Teachers may begin by having students identify and describe the occupations of family members. Next, activities such as field trips are designed to acquaint students with occupations of people in the school and community. At later ages, information on occupations within different job clusters is presented.

Self-understanding. The self-understanding aspect of career awareness involves arranging experiences which allow students to relate their skills, abilities, and interests to different adult roles. Students might make more satisfactory career choices and adjustments to living when they have developed a realistic understanding of themselves and the world in which they must survive.

Career Exploration

The *career exploration* level of career education begins during the later elementary school years and continues into junior high and high school (Brolin & Kokaska, 1979). At this level, students are directed to examine more closely the alternatives that they may eventually select within occupational, recreational, or familial areas related to career development. Students are encouraged to refine their skills, abilities, and interests through hands-on activities. For example, practical experiences may be provided so that students learn specific strategies for managing personal finances. These activities may include generating a personal budget, beginning and managing a checking account, and using newspaper want ads to compare prices of necessary items. It is at this level that students begin to identify, learn, and master a variety of living skills.

Career Preparation

The *career preparation* level of career education occurs during high school. At this level students learn specific occupational and living skills through work experiences, vocational courses, or academic coursework. Goldhamer and Taylor (1972) discuss the following six features of a career preparation program for high school students:

1. Continuous refinement and application of basic skills.

2. Development of specific knowledge and skills needed for family life, avocational citizenship, and cultural careers.

3. Exploration of the vocational opportunities within a specific cluster or area.

4. Provision of the opportunity for students to select a specific career.

5. Provision of opportunities for students to engage in initial preparatory knowledge and skill-building experiences while they explore post-secondary preparatory potentials.

6. Acquisition by every student of some saleable skills before graduation.

Career preparation is the final level of career education in the public schools. Cegelka (1979) pointed out, however, that the tasks encompassed by these career education levels do not end for the individual upon leaving high school. The process of becoming aware of, exploring, and preparing for the multitude of tasks associated with managing living in the society never ends.

Theaters of Career Education

One of the more dynamic and far-reaching implications of a broad-based definition of career education is that instruction could take place in a variety of settings and could involve a variety of personnel. Since school personnel cannot be experts in all career areas, parents and individuals from surrounding communities or local businesses might be included in the school career education program.

School personnel. The school is the primary setting for career education because it is the school's responsibility to provide instruction appropriate to the needs of individual students. Career needs vary according to the abilities of the individual student and may range from academic instruction that prepares students for continuing studies in post-secondary settings to vocational instruction that prepares students to enter the work world upon graduation from high school. The career education orientation emphasizes that skills taught in academic (i.e., social studies, science, math) and nonacademic (i.e., homemaking, industrial arts, physical education) courses should be directly related to the career needs of students. Teachers are responsible for this instruction.

The involvement of other school personnel is necessary in a comprehensive career education program. Of particular importance are professionals who administer, score, and interpret group and individual assessments to identify the abilities and interests of individual learners. These include the school psychologist, who assesses aptitudes and abilities, and the guidance counselor, who assists in determining career goals and planning coursework to meet those goals. In addition, the school nurse or occupational therapist can provide information on any physical limitations which might limit occupational choices. The speech therapist may assess the listening and speaking abilities of a student and indicate how deficiencies in these areas may affect career decisions.

At the secondary level, the *vocational counselor* is a key person (Smith & Payne, 1980). Brolin and Kokaska (1979) list the following activities of vocational counselors:

1. Assist the individual to learn about the world of work.

2. Determine appropriate experiences, courses, and persons who can assist in occupational awareness and exploration activities.

3. Ascertain more specific vocational aptitudes, interests, and needs.

4. Determine occupational training areas.

5. Instruct in job seeking and securing skills.

(p. 214)

The *work coordinator* is another key individual in vocational programs in secondary schools. Through identifying the requirements of jobs available in the community, coordinating school programs that involve both working and attending classes, and monitoring student performance and progress in job placements, the work coordinator provides valuable information for planning each student's occupational training program. In addition he matches each student's occupational interests and abilities with job requirements and arranges a number of work experiences (Smith & Payne, 1980). Thus the work coordinator is responsible for a vocational training program's success in selecting appropriate occupations, and increasing the employment possibilities of program graduates.

Involvement in the home. The home environment provides students in a career education program with opportunities to observe and practice living skills. Maximum involvement with parents, however, depends on the teacher's abilities to coordinate instructional efforts. For example, a teacher who is instructing on financial management may enlist parental assistance in providing examples of family budgets. Young children receiving instruction in planning and preparing meals may be asked to assist family members in that task in order to practice skills learned in school. In the area of occupational awareness, parents can provide first-hand knowledge of their occupations as well as providing experiences that acquaint students with other occupations (for example, visiting parent's place of employment, speaking to neighbors). Finally, as indicated in Chapter 5, parents are participants in the educational planning for their children. As members in parent organizations and, in the case of handicapped students, participants in the specification of the educational program, parents can be advocates for the infusion of career education into school curricula (Brolin & Kokaska, 1979; Smith & Payne, 1980).

Involvement of the business community. The business community can provide three important sources of information to teachers with career education programs. First, business professionals can assist teachers in the identification of occupational alternatives within the community, including the educational, skill level, and job requirements. This information is important for teachers and vocational counselors to have so that more appropriate career awareness and preparation activities can be developed. Second, businesses provide jobs for work-study students. A variety of work-study placements is essential to facilitate realistic occupational decision making. Finally, business leaders in the community can help educators to determine the need for vocational programs as well as the scope and sequence of the training. When vocational programs train students in skills and occupations that are needed in business, then handicapped students might be more likely to secure and maintain employment. The involvement of business professionals is necessary to secure information relative to these tasks.

Career Education Program Competencies

The number of competencies specified in a career education program varies according to the definition of career education adapted by the designer. Professionals who favor a narrow definition will include competencies that are related to occupational guidance and preparation. However, a broad conceptualization of career education includes competencies that are not directly related to earning a living. The following section outlines a curriculum model proposed by Brolin and Kokaska (1979).

CURRICULUM AREA	COMPETENCY		
	1. Managing family finances	1. Identify money and make correct change	2. Make wise expenditures
	2. Selecting, Managing, and Maintaining a Home	6. Select adequate housing	7. Maintain a home
	3. Caring for Personal Needs	10. Dress properly	11. Exhibit proper grooming and hygiene
	4. Raising Children, Family Living	14. Prepare for adjustment to marriage	15. Prepare for raising children (physical care)
DAILY LIVING SKILLS	5. Buying and Preparing Food	18. Demonstrate appropriate eating skills	19. Plan balanced meals
	6. Buying and Caring for Clothing	24. Wash clothing	25. Iron and store clothing
	7. Engaging in Civic Activities	28. Generally understand local laws & government	29. Generally understand Federal Government
	8. Utilizing Recreation and Leisure	34. Participate actively in group activities	35. Know activities and available community resources
	9. Getting Around the Community (Mobility)	40. Demonstrate knowledge of traffic rules & safety practices	41. Demonstrate knowledge & use of various means of transportation
	10. Achieving Self-Awareness	43. Attain a sense of body	44. Identify interests and abilities
	11. Acquiring Self-Confidence	48. Express feelings of worth	49. Tell how others see him / her
	12. Achieving Socially Responsible Behavior	53. Know character traits needed for acceptance	54. Know proper behavior in public places
PERSONAL SOCIAL SKILLS	13. Maintaining Good Interpersonal Skills	58. Know how to listen and respond	59. Know how to make & maintain friendships
	14. Achieving Independence	62. Understand impact of behaviors upon others	63. Understand self-organization
	15. Achieving Problem-Solving Skills	66. Differentiate bipolar concepts	67. Understand the need for goals
	16. Communicating Adequately with Others	71. Recognize emergency situations	72. Read at level needed for future goals
	17. Knowing & Exploring Occupational Possibilities	76. Identify the personal values met through work	77. Identify the societal values met through work
	18. Selecting and Planning Occupational Choices	82. Identify major occupational needs	83. Identify major occupational interests
	19. Exhibiting Appropriate Work Habits & Behaviors	87. Follow directions	88. Work with others
OCCUPATIONAL GUIDANCE & PREPARATION	20. Exhibiting Sufficient Physical-Manual Skills	94. Demonstrate satisfactory balance and coordination	95. Demonstrate satisfactory manual dexterity
	21. Obtaining a Specific Occupational Skill		
	22. Seeking, Securing, & Maintaining Employment	98. Search for a job	99. Apply for a job

Figure 10–1 Competencies and subcompetencies related to daily living skills, personal-social skills, and occupational guidance and preparation. SOURCE: Brolin, D. E., & Kokaska, C. J. *Career Education*

3. Obtain and use bank and credit facilities	4. Keep basic financial records	5. Calculate and pay taxes		
8. Use basic appliances and tools	9. Maintain home exterior			
12. Demonstrate knowledge of physical fitness, nutrition and weight control	13. Demonstrate knowledge of common illness prevention and treatment			
16. Prepare for raising children (psychological care)	17. Practice family safety in the home			
20. Purchase food	21. Prepare meals	22. Clean food preparation areas	23. Store food	
26. Perform simple mending	27. Purchase clothing			
30. Understand citizenship rights and responsibilities	31. Understand registration and voting procedures	32. Understand Selective Service procedures	33. Understand civil rights & responsibilities when questioned by the law	
36. Understand recreational values	37. Use recreational facilities in the community	38. Plan and choose activities wisely	39. Plan vacations	
42. Drive a car				
45. Identify emotions	46. Identify needs	47. Understand the physical self		
50. Accept praise	51. Accept criticism	52. Develop confidence in self		
55. Develop respect for the rights and properties of others	56. Recognize authority and follow instructions	57. Recognize personal roles		
60. Establish appropriate heterosexual relationships	61. Know how to establish close relationships			
64. Develop goal-seeking behavior	65. Strive toward self-actualization			
68. Look at alternatives	69. Anticipate consequences	70. Know where to find good advice		
73. Write at the level needed for future goals	74. Speak adequately for understanding	75. Understand the subtleties of communication		
78. Identify the remunerative aspects of work	79. Understand classification jobs into different occupational systems	80. Identify occupational opportunities available locally	81. Identify sources of occupational information	
84. Identify occupational aptitudes	85. Identify requirements of appropriate and available jobs	86. Make realistic occupational choices		
89. Work at a satisfactory rate	90. Accept supervision	91. Recognize the importance of attendance and punctuality	92. Meet demands for quality work	93. Demonstrate occupational safety
96. Demonstrate satisfactory stamina and endurance	97. Demonstrate satisfactory sensory discrimination			
100. Interview for a job	101. Adjust to competitive standards	102. Maintain post-school occupational adjustment		

for Handicapped Children and Youth. Columbus, Ohio: Charles E. Merrill Publishing Co., 1979, p. 108–109.

While there are other models (e.g., Phelps & Lutz, 1977) the Brolin and Kokaska model is discussed here because it is consistent with the broad definition presented in this chapter. Also, it has one of the more comprehensive sets of competencies available, and it includes a vocational orientation. The entire set of competencies and subcompetencies is presented in Figure 10–1.

The competencies are categorized under the headings *Daily Living Skills, Personal Social Skills,* and *Occupational Guidance and Preparation Skills.* Collectively these competencies include a wide range of skills related to living, social interaction, and obtaining employment. It is not feasible to present in this chapter extensive lists of activities for teaching each of the subcompetencies. Other sources, such as Brolin and Kokaska (1979), Kolstoe (1976a), and Smith and Payne (1980), provide excellent comprehensive discussions of ways to teach the subcompetencies. In addition, the Council for Exceptional Children has recently published two compendia of teaching activities as part of the *Education and Work* series (Johnson, 1980; Lamkin, 1980). The curriculum model is presented here only to illustrate the scope of a career education program and as a reference for examples to follow in the chapter.

In sum, given that career education should be provided for all handicapped students, the problem of infusing career education into programs for the handicapped remains. The career education concept suggests that special education professionals should consider both the ability of the handicapped student to master the more traditional academic material and the competencies needed for that individual to lead a successful and productive life. In addition, the career education concept requires that special educators work with experts in other education areas (such as vocational education), professionals in the business community, and parents of handicapped students to design and implement appropriate educational programs. Finally, the career education concept embraces the mandates of recent legislation which require the education of handicapped students in the least restrictive environment. That is, many goals and objectives of a career-oriented program may be most easily met by program alternatives available to the nonhandicapped. Handicapped students must be given access to these programs to the extent that they can benefit from the training provided.

CAREER EDUCATION PROGRAMMING FOR THE HANDICAPPED

Current law requires the participation of special educators, parents, and other education professionals in the identification, programming, and placement of handicapped students. The requirement for generating an Individualized Educational Program (IEP) for each handicapped student together with the required provision of vocational guidance and education services suggests that the inclusion of career education concepts and competencies in education for the handicapped might logically begin with the IEP development process. Some ways in which consultants can participate in the assessment, program writing, program management, and evaluation of the IEP are discussed in the remainder of the chapter.

Involvement of Consultants in Assessment

Assessment consists of determining a child's performance levels before the IEP program is written and as part of the annual IEP review. The career education concept implies that assessments should include identification of the child's interests and abilities relative to occupational, daily living, and personal-social skills (Cegelka & Phillips, 1978). Brolin (1976), Brolin and Kokaska (1979), Kolstoe (1976a), Phelps and Lutz (1977), and Smith and Payne (1980) provide excellent reviews of both formal, norm-referenced evaluation instruments and teacher constructed, criterion-referenced evaluation procedures for these areas.

Special education professionals can contribute to the assessment process in two important ways. First, as potential IEP team members they can be advocates for assessments in the daily living, personal-social, and occupational preparation and guidance areas. For example, a special education teacher serving on an IEP team which is reviewing the referral of a ten-year-old with a tested IQ of sixty-five, may request assessment information in the areas of manual dexterity, balance and coordination, and ability to work with others. These areas are subcompetencies under the Occupational Preparation and Guidance category in Figure 10–1. Information on levels of performance in these areas would assist the team in developing a program to prepare the child for entrance into a vocational program.

The second contribution special educators can make in the area of assessment is to provide the IEP team with evaluative data on performance levels of handicapped students in career education subcompetency areas. For example, suppose a special education teacher for the partially sighted is planning a unit on buying and preparing food at an awareness level of instruction. She might collect data that indicate that a fifteen-year-old student in her class is ready to proceed to the orientation level of instruction. The teacher might consider changing the IEP program to reflect the new instructional need and recommend placement in a regular education homemaking class. With the assessment data from the teacher in hand, the placement team can make program placement decisions relative to the handicapped student's career needs.

Involvement of Consultants in Writing IEP Goals

Consultants, as members of the IEP team, could help to formulate long-term goals and short-term objectives related to career education. Brolin and Kokaska (1979) state that the twenty-two competencies listed in Figure 10–1 are appropriate long-term (annual) goals for IEPs while the subcompetencies could be considered short-term objectives.

Consultants may also suggest the time required to meet the short-term objectives, given the current performance levels of the individual and the scope and sequence of instruction. Figure 10–2 presents an example of the specification of long-term goals and short-term objectives using the Brolin and Kokaska curriculum. The curriculum areas in the example are from the Brolin-Kokaska model. The annual goals are selected from the model's twenty-two competencies. The short-term objectives in the example are some of the subcompetencies given in Figure 10–1. The cur-

Figure 10–2 Example of long-term goals, short-term objectives, and time estimates (expressed in months) in an IEP.

Curriculum Areas Requiring Special Education and Related Services	Annual Goals	Short-term Objectives	Time Required
Daily Living	Buying and Preparing Food	1. Demonstrate appropriate eating skill	9-15 to 10-31
		2. Plan balanced meals	11-3 to 12-15
		3. Purchase food	1-3 to 3-1
Occupational	Selecting and Planning Occupational Choices	1. Identify major occupational interests	9-15 to 10-15
		2. Identify occupational aptitudes	10-16 to 12-1

riculum areas, annual goals, and short-term objectives are selected on the basis of a student's performance levels and skill needs relative to the curriculum model.

Involvement of Consultants in Placement Decisions

As previously indicated, placement of handicapped students depends on the program specified for them in the IEP process. It is not the availability of placements which dictates the nature of the program. Rather, placements must be determined and then designed to meet the needs of individual handicapped students. The consultant, with her knowledge of the learning, skill, and interest characteristics of the handicapped student, can be a valuable resource for the IEP team in making a placement decision. The sharing of the characteristics with educators from regular academic and vocational classes will help the team determine whether a regular class would meet the program needs of a handicapped student. The following anecdote provides an example of the participation of the consultant in IEP placement decisions for a fourteen-year-old physically handicapped student.

Anecdote 10–1

TEAM CHAIRPERSON: "We have considered Allen's current performance levels and have written annual goals and short-term objectives related to family finances. What placement alternatives can we recommend to meet these goals and objectives?"

CONSULTANT: "The assessment data indicate that Allen is capable of performing the math skills necessary to calculate taxes and manage a bank account. In addition, his social skill levels are appropriate for regular class placement."

BUSINESS TEACHER: "I teach units in those areas in our ninth-grade business math sections. I think that Allen could do the math. However, I wonder about his ability to take notes in class and complete homework assignments given his physical limitations. The assessment report indicates difficulty in writing. Since my course requires homework and note taking he may not be able to do all the assignments."

CONSULTANT: "I've noted that Allen has had great success when he either uses a tape recorder for note taking and homework assignments or when a nonhandicapped peer assists him with note taking. Would either of these arrangements be acceptable to you?"

BUSINESS TEACHER: "Certainly."

PARENT: "I'm in favor of Allen receiving instruction in banking and tax computation. I can take him to the bank to open an account and provide the tape recorder he'll need for class."

TEAM CHAIRPERSON: "We are in agreement then that Allen could be placed in the ninth-grade business math class for instruction related to calculating taxes and managing a bank account. He may use a tape recorder or peer to assist in note taking and homework assignments."

In Anecdote 10–1 the consultant suggested a placement alternative (a regular class in business math) based on the assessment data, his knowledge of the class curriculum, and the compensatory strategies he had known to be successful with Allen. The business teacher was concerned about the student's physical abilities, but found the compensatory measures acceptable. The parent agreed to provide the needed recording equipment and a practical experience related to banking. This example points out another function the consultant can serve in IEP team meetings. She can suggest ways in which regular educators can modify existing classes or assignments to accommodate a handicapped student.

MANAGING CAREER EDUCATION PROGRAMS FOR HANDICAPPED STUDENTS

For many handicapped students, placement may be in self-contained special education classes. Others might be mainstreamed into regular classes appropriate to their needs and abilities. Career education programs may be conducted in a variety of settings by a number of educational professionals. The consultant may be involved in providing direct instruction in career competencies to a regular or special educator, or she may provide supplemental career instructional material for mainstreamed students. As stated previously, she may assist the regular class teacher by suggesting ways to accommodate the handicapped student. Specific tasks associated with these responsibilities will be discussed in the following section.

Managing Programs in Self-Contained Classes

There are three major responsibilities of special education teachers in self-contained classrooms related to career education programming. These include providing instruction, including parents in the program, and arranging for people from the business community to participate. Consultants can provide valuable assistance to self-contained teachers doing these tasks.

Providing instruction. The first task of the special educator is to provide instruction to handicapped students. Career education instruction should include teaching basic skills in the areas of reading and mathematics, together with the applications of these skills to applied situations. In other words, instruction should be directed toward career education competencies and subcompetencies. Kolstoe (1976b) indicates that instruction should also be designed to teach students about the nature and necessity of work and should include opportunities for students to discover relationships between their abilities and work requirements. Finally, instruction should move students toward career goals in a sequential manner.

At first glance, the requirements of career education may appear to be overwhelming. However, since special education teachers usually provide sequential instruction in basic skills, all that usually is needed is an increased emphasis on the application of skills.

Word problems in mathematics, writing or presenting book reports, learning to tell time, or using money are examples of exercises that illustrate applications of skills. In a career education curriculum these exercises are extended into simulations which reflect, in part, real life situations. The practice exercises become the strategies for teaching basic skills as important as more traditional methods. For example, a special education teacher may provide math instruction on addition of three-digit decimals with carrying. Practice exercises may be provided which focus the computation on amounts of money. A teacher with a career education orientation would also teach addition of money but might provide the instruction in place value and decimals concurrently. Also, she may use a classwide token system in the simulation exercise. Tokens may be earned by students for accuracy, completion of assignments, appropriate work behavior, or completion of extra assignments. The tokens could resemble real coins, and could be used to purchase materials or activities of the students' choice. Responsibility for keeping an account of the number of tokens earned can be given to students based on their skill levels in addition and subtraction. At later levels of career instruction, the system can include instruction in banking, obtaining credit, managing family finances, and completing tax forms.

Kolstoe (1976b) indicated that special educators need to provide information on occupations in addition to providing instruction on skill development. The specificity of the information depends on the interests of the students and the level of career preparation (that is, awareness, orientation, preparation). For example, teachers at the elementary level may have students explain the job responsibilities of their parents. To extend awareness of occupations, a teacher may discuss with his class different jobs within the community, (police officer, mail carrier, etc.). Students may also be encouraged to select jobs in the classroom. At the orientation level, teachers may require students to study the skill requirements, educational preparation levels, employment opportunities, and earnings potential of a number of jobs in which they are interested. Students may also be given the opportunity to try out different jobs through simulations provided by vocational programs. At the preparation level, students receive training in a job of their choice.

There are a number of activities a teacher might design. Many of these, whether in the areas of basic skill applications or occupations, will require materials specifically designed for the purpose. While there are many such materials available from publishers, it is difficult for the special education teacher to decide which to buy. The selecting and obtaining of career education materials can be greatly facilitated by administrators, special education consultants, and other teachers. Provision of career education activities and materials appropriate for a teacher's special education class is an important function of these professionals.

Including parents in the program. Chapter 5 outlined ways in which consultants can help parents in the education process. It needs only to be pointed out here that parent involvement is an important aspect of career education.

A creative example of parent involvement in a special education class is described by Kolstoe (1976c). Students in a self-contained special education class learned about different daily living, personal-social, and occupation skills by conducting interviews with their parents. The interview questions related to work were "Do you talk on the job?", "Whom do you talk to?", or "What must you do at work?" Interviews also included a series of questions on managing family finances, disciplining children, and a number of other areas. The students returned the completed questionnaires to class and discussed their findings.

Unfortunately, space limitations do not allow presentation of further examples of parent involvement. Teachers and consultants will find a number of materials and activity suggestions in Brolin and Kokaska (1979) and Smith and Payne (1980).

Business community participation. The success of a career education program depends to a great extent on the involvement of business leaders and professionals in the community. Businessmen and women are a logical source for teachers and consultants who are seeking descriptions of jobs appropriate for handicapped students in the future.

A means of accessing this information was offered by Pollard (1977). Her strategy involved the use of job analysis forms, an example of which is presented in Figure 10–3.

Pollard suggested that teachers and consultants talk to business leaders. During the interview use of the job analysis form may help to determine employment areas appropriate for handicapped individuals. The next step is to have students categorize and compare the jobs described on the forms. Business leaders may be invited to the classroom to assist the students in categorizing the jobs and answering questions. As a final step in involving business leaders, Pollard suggests asking them to serve on an advisory board to help in the development of career education and vocational training programs. The benefit to these potential employers of handicapped persons is readily apparent. Their participation in a special education career education program may lead to more qualified employees.

It is likely that many business professionals will be unable to participate in classroom activities because of busy schedules. An alternative resource is recently retired businessmen and women. For example, the job classification project outlined by Pollard could easily include persons who have been involved in the business community. Retired individuals who participate in classroom instruction might also find the activities a source of personal satisfaction.

THE ROLE OF THE CONSULTANT IN IMPLEMENTING CAREER EDUCATION PROGRAMS IN THE MAINSTREAM

The preceding discussion of career education instruction in special education classes indicated that consultants can work together with special education teachers to provide instructional activities and materials and involve business leaders. This cooperative relationship is extended when IEPs specify involvement in regular classes. Consultants continue to provide activity and material ideas for special education teachers who instruct students in career competencies and subcompetencies. In addition, consultants work together to provide support to regular class teachers, to monitor the progress of students toward annual goals and short-term objectives, and to provide assessment information for subsequent program planning.

Job Analysis Form

Job Title _____ DOT Title _____

Name of Firm _____ Code Number _____

Date of Analysis _____ Name of Analyst _____

A. Description of Work Performed _____
_____

**B. Job Requirements. Circle number of those required
and comment if needed.**

1. Adding _____   11. Use telephone _____
2. Subtracting _____   12. Lift, carry, push, pull _____
3. Multiplying _____   13. Walk, run, climb, balance _____
4. Dividing _____   14. Stoop, kneel, crouch, crawl ____
5. Make change _____   15. Stand or sit _____
6. Use measuring devices _____   16. Use hand tools _____
7. Read _____   17. Operate machines _____
8. Write _____   18. Other _____
9. Talk _____   19. Other _____
10. Follow instructions _____   20. Other _____

**C. Working Conditions. Circle number that describes the job
and comment if needed.**

1. Extremely hot _____   8. Good lighting _____
2. Extremely cold _____   9. Good ventilation _____
3. Humid _____   10. Tension and pressure _____
4. Wet _____   11. Distracting conditions _____
5. Dry _____   12. Hazardous _____
6. Dusty and dirty _____   13. Work with others _____
7. Noisy _____   14. Other _____

D. Training Required _____

E. Salary _____

F. Hours Worked _____

G. Good features of the Job _____
_____

H. Poor features of the Job _____
_____
_____

Figure 10–3 Job analysis form. SOURCE: Brolin, D. E., & Kokaska,
C. J. *Career Education for Handicapped Children and Youth.*
Columbus, Ohio: Charles E. Merrill Publishing Co., 1979. P. 224.
Reprinted wtih permission.

Assisting Regular Class Teachers

Ideally, the consultant has offered assistance regularly to the class teacher at the time placement decisions are made. After placement, there are several areas in which special education consultants can render additional service to regular class teachers.

Providing additional instruction. Perhaps the most apparent task of consultants involved with mainstreamed handicapped students is to provide instruction and practice to supplement regular class activities. The following anecdote illustrates how a special education teacher served as a consultant to a fourth-grade teacher, and provided direct service to a behaviorally disordered boy mainstreamed into the regular fourth-grade class.

Anecdote 10–2

SPECIAL EDUCATOR: "How is John behaving in your class?"

FOURTH-GRADE TEACHER: "He's doing quite well, although there are some social behaviors he needs to work on. I have talked to John about following class rules, respecting the privacy of others, making and maintaining friendships, and considering the impact of behavior on others. While John's behavior in these areas is not a significant problem, he could improve some of these skills."

SPECIAL EDUCATOR: "I might be able to help with John in a couple of ways. First, I can provide some instruction in these areas in the resource room. Also, I have some activity suggestions in my room which you might use with your whole class. The activities include role playing, modeling, and peer tutoring. Your whole class might enjoy some of them."

FOURTH-GRADE TEACHER: "I'd like to look at those materials. In the meantime, I'll try to follow up on the instruction you provide."

The provision of additional instruction need not be limited to the area of student behavior. The special educator may also provide time for students to practice academic tasks using career oriented materials.

Instructional guidelines. The special educator's knowledge of individualized instruction, task analysis, and the learning characteristics of handicapped students can assist regular educators in teaching handicapped students within their classes. For example, a teacher in a main-

streamed classroom may indicate that her students, including the mainstreamed student, are on several different levels in their performance of
math facts. The special educator may suggest a peer-tutoring program
to allow more practice of math facts or offer game activities such as
math bingo. A teaching strategy which presents the tasks in smaller,
sequential steps may be suggested to the auto mechanics teacher who
is having difficulty teaching carburetor repair. The special educator may
also offer additional practice exercise materials for the regular class
teacher to use with the mainstreamed student who is having difficulty
mastering a particular skill.

Compensatory strategies. Handicapped students may have difficulties
in regular classes due to physical limitations. For example, a learning disabled or motorically impaired student may not be able to perform tasks
on electrical machinery in industrial arts classes. A visually impaired student may have difficulty reading assignments from the chalkboard. In
these instances it is important for the consultant to be aware of techniques and services available to help the learner circumvent his handicap.
Examples of strategies and devices include tape recorders, the use of
nonimpaired modalities, and the construction of guards and gigs for
workshop machinery.

Monitoring Programs

Another key role consultants play in the mainstreaming process is to
help monitor handicapped students' progress in their individual programs. The consultant with the assistance of the special education teacher
must evaluate student progress in those instructional areas that are her
responsibility. Brolin and Kokaska (1979) review several norm-referenced
tests that are related to career competencies and can be used for this purpose. Criterion-referenced tests devised by the special education teacher
and consultant should also be used. It is recommended that special class
teachers also employ the daily measurement and recording techniques
described by Cooper (1981).

Special education consultants may also suggest assessment procedures
for regular class teachers. As in the special education class, regular class
teachers should adapt daily measurement and recording techniques to
monitor the progress of mainstreamed handicapped children. For example, a consultant may suggest that regular class teachers record the
number of homework assignments completed, grades on daily quizzes,
and the note-taking behavior of the mainstreamed student. The vocational education teacher might be encouraged to record the rate and accuracy of the completion of vocational tasks. The behaviors that are

monitored should be directly related to the short-term objectives specified in the individual's IEP.

The special education consultant also serves as a facilitator of communication among teachers. The recorded data and the implications for changes in the daily instruction of the mainstreamed student should be relayed to the appropriate teachers. For example, the vocational teacher may observe that a handicapped student is having difficulty mastering a skill component of her most favored occupation. The data may be sent by the consultant to the vocational counselor, who may recommend additional vocational interest and skill evaluators. The consultant may, as an alternative, suggest additional time be spent with the student in the vocational program area to practice the skill. Another alternative is additional instruction provided by a special needs vocational teacher or special education teacher. The daily collection of observational data is important to determine the effectiveness of instruction as well as the effectiveness of the alternatives selected by the professionals involved with the handicapped student. Marsh and Price (1980) suggest that written communication be used to inform teachers of student performance and teaching strategy changes.

Attending IEP meetings. Though suggestions for ways in which special educators can participate in IEP meetings were outlined earlier in this chapter and in Chapter 4, one additional suggestion should be cited. The IEP meeting should be concerned with providing continuity in the handicapped student's career education. The career education competencies and subcompetencies are referents for insuring IEPs which direct the educational program toward career goals. The following anecdote illustrates this point. The program being reviewed is for a sixteen-year-old girl who was identified as learning disabled at age eight. She has been enrolled in special education and regular classes since that time

Anecdote 10–3

TEAM CHAIRPERSON: "Our next task is to review the assessment and program evaluation data for Becky. I note that her teachers have recorded the dates of mastery of the short-term objectives. Are the annual goals specified in her current program appropriate for next year?"

CONSULTANT: "Our evaluation data indicate that the goals of managing family finances, buying and caring for clothes, acquiring self-confidence, and selecting and planning occupational choices are appropriate to continue next year. While Becky mastered many of the short-term objectives listed under these annual goals, others remain unmet. I suggest we include as short-term objectives opening and using bank accounts and performing simple mending. In addition, I suggest we add driving a car as a short-term objective for next year, since Becky is sixteen years old and qualifies for a driver's license."

VOCATIONAL COUNSELOR: "I agree with the recommendations made concerning selecting and planning occupational choices. In the past year we've administered occupational inventories, given occupational information, and provided simulations of jobs of interest to Becky. In the coming year we should design a work-study situation to allow Becky to refine her vocational skills and her interest in the occupations she's chosen."

WORK-STUDY COORDINATOR: "I can arrange placements in the community for Becky in the areas you've identified."

BUSINESS TEACHER: "I agree with the inclusion of the banking objective. Becky did very well in my course in keeping basic financial records. I can provide several units on banking for her this coming year."

HOME ECONOMICS TEACHER: "Becky also performed well in my class. My sewing class would be appropriate for her next year."

TEAM CHAIRPERSON: "Are there any other areas we need to include in Becky's program?"

PARENT: "Becky has expressed an interest in learning about raising children and family living. We've discussed these topics many times at home and I'd like to have her receive instruction in them at school."

TEAM CHAIRPERSON: "Physical care of children and practicing family safety are two short-term goals we can include in the program. We might also include psychological care of children as a short-term goal."

The meeting continued with the writing of the IEP and determination of appropriate placements. The anecdote provides examples of a consultant's contribution to providing continuity in the career education program as well as examples of consultant interactions with other persons involved with Becky's education.

SUMMARY

Broadly defined, career education consists of school experiences and instruction directly related to all facets of life: daily living, personal-social, and occupational. It is a curriculum concept that integrates academic and vocational instruction with relevance to life after high school. When used as a curriculum model, career education suggests the identification of program options according to the needs, abilities, and interests of individual handicapped students.

The roles adapted by consultants and special educators acting in consultant roles under a career education plan are the same as those described in other chapters in this book (working cooperatively with regular class teachers, assessing students, acquiring appropriate materials, participating in IEP meetings, etc.). However, their interactions and activities have as a central focus the competencies students must obtain to lead productive lives.

The major impetus for the integration of a career education orientation in programs for handicapped students has come from federal legislation regarding vocational and career education and from Public Law 94–142. The present chapter indicated that the IEP process identified by these laws is the means by which career education for the handicapped may be insured. Special educators, as participants in the IEP process, must be advocates of career education programming. They must also be knowledgeable in the areas of assessment, instruction, and evaluation approaches to be of assistance to regular educators who are directed to accommodate handicapped students. If these roles are effectively served, we will provide the community with handicapped citizens who are better able to arrange productive and successful lives.

Questions

1. Provide a narrow and a broad definition of career education. Give a rationale for the definition you favor.

2. Develop and describe nine activities designed to integrate basic skills and career education subcompetencies to be used in regular elementary classes. Include three in each of the curriculum areas (daily living, personal-social, and occupational preparation and guidance).

3. Identify one course typically offered at the secondary level appropriate for IEPs that specify instruction in each of the following: maintaining a home, utilizing recreation and leisure time, communicating adequately with others, and exhibiting sufficient physical-manual skills.

4. Describe three ways to accommodate handicapped students (i.e., hearing impaired, visually impaired, learning disabled) in regular

classes. Indicate potential concerns regular educators may have in using the compensatory strategies.

5. To what career education subcompetencies can contingency contracting and group contingencies be related? Provide examples of contingency contracting and a group contingency applied to a career education subcompetency.

6. Describe the roles consultants and supervisors play in providing career education programs for handicapped students in self-contained classes and in mainstreamed classes.

Discussion Points and Exercises

---

1. Conduct a meeting with elementary and secondary teachers to discuss the obstacles they perceive in implementing a career education orientation at their levels. Focus on the problems they feel handicapped students might have with this orientation, and solicit their views of how a consultant might facilitate the implementation of a career education format.

2. Arrange a meeting with a vocational or guidance counselor and a vocational education teacher to discuss assessment instruments and strategies currently used with nonhandicapped students. Identify specific instruments and strategies that might be appropriate for handicapped students. Discuss ways in which the instruments and strategies may need to be modified to accommodate handicapped students.

3. Organize a career education materials day by contacting representatives of publishers of career education materials. Include an in-service program that provides guidelines for selecting appropriate materials. Provide examples of IEP short-term objectives and have special and regular teachers identify materials appropriate for instruction to meet the objectives.

4. Design and present to your local superintendent a plan for involving business leaders in the community in the career education program. Be sure to include provisions for involvement in occupational awareness, vocational preparation, and work-study components of the career education program.

REFERENCES

BARONE, S. *General issues in elementary and secondary education* (Committee on Education and Labor, 95th Congress). Washington, D.C.: U.S. Government Printing Office, 1977.

BROLIN, D. E. *Vocational preparation of retarded citizens.* Columbus, Ohio: Charles E. Merrill, 1976.

BROLIN, D. E., CEGELKA, P. T., JACKSON, S., & WROBEL, C. *Official policy of The Council for Exceptional Children as legislated by the 1978 CEC Delegate Assembly.* Reston, Virginia: Council for Exceptional Children, 1977.

BROLIN, D. E., & D'ALONZO, B. J. Critical issues in career education for handicapped students. *Exceptional Children,* 1979, 45, 246–253.

BROLIN, D. E., & KOKASKA, C. J. *Career education for handicapped children and youth.* Columbus, Ohio: Charles E. Merrill, 1979.

CEGELKA, P. T. Career education. In D. Cullinan and M. H. Epstein (Eds.), *Special education for adolescents: Issues and perspectives.* Columbus, Ohio: Charles E. Merrill, 1979.

CEGELKA, P. T., & PHILLIPS, M. W. Individualized education programming at the secondary level. *Teaching Exceptional Children,* 1978, 10, 84–87.

COOPER, J. O. *Measuring behavior* (2nd ed.). Columbus, Ohio: Charles E. Merrill, 1981.

DELLEFIELD, C. Wanted: A *working* definition of career education. *Educational Leadership,* 1974, 31, 11.

GOLDHAMER, K., & TAYLOR, R. *Career education: Perspective and promise.* Columbus, Ohio: Charles E. Merrill, 1972.

JOHNSON, C. M. *Preparing handicapped students for work: Alternatives for secondary programming.* Reston, Virginia: Council for Exceptional Children, 1980.

KOLSTOE, O. P. *Teaching educable mentally retarded children.* (2nd ed.). New York: Holt, Rinehart and Winston, 1976. (a)

KOLSTOE, O. P. Career education: Where we came from, where we are, and where we should be going. In G. M. Blackburn (Ed.), *Colloquium series on career education for handicapped adolescents.* West Lafayette, Indiana: Purdue University, 1976. (b)

KOLSTOE, O. P. Developing career awareness: The foundation of a career education program. In G. M. Blackburn (Ed.), *Colloquium series on career education for handicapped adolescents.* West Lafayette, Indiana: Purdue University, 1976. (c)

LAMKIN, J. S. *Getting started: Career education activities for exceptional students (K-9).* Reston, Virginia: Council for Exceptional Children, 1980.

MARSH, G. E., II, & PRICE, B. J. *Methods for teaching the handicapped adolescent.* St. Louis, Missouri: C. V. Mosby, 1980.

MARTIN, E. W. Individualism and behaviorism as future trends in educating handicapped children. *Exceptional Children,* 1972, 38, 517–525.

METZ, A. S. *Number of pupils with handicaps in local public schools,* Spring,

1970. (HEW Publication No. OE 11107). Washington, D.C.: U.S. Government Printing Office, 1973.

PHELPS, L. A., & LUTZ, R. J. *Career exploration and preparation for the special needs learner.* Boston: Allyn and Bacon, 1977.

POLLARD, H. E. Career education in the classroom. In R. L. Carpenter (Ed.), *Colloquium series on career education for handicapped adolescents.* West Lafayette, Indiana: Purdue University, 1977.

RAZEGHI, J. A., & DAVIS, S. Federal mandates for the handicapped, vocational education opportunity and employment. *Exceptional Children,* 1979, 45, 353–359.

SMITH, J. E., JR., & PAYNE, J. S. *Teaching exceptional adolescents.* Columbus, Ohio: Charles E. Merrill, 1980.

SUPER, D. E. *Career education and the meaning of work.* Monographs on Career Education, U.S. Department of Health, Education and Welfare. Washington, D.C.: U.S. Government Printing Office, 1976.

11

Litigation and Legislation:
Why and How It Affects
Consultation

Educational services that handicapped children and youth presently receive are, in part, a direct result of litigative and legislative action. Decisions rendered by courts and federal laws enacted by Congress have greatly influenced the structure and operation of our nation's schools. For example, in the past, laws concerning the treatment of the handicapped were permissive. That is, educational service for a school-aged child may or may not have been offered. The state department of education or the local school district had complete discretionary power. With the enactment of recent legislation, however, educational services for the school-aged child are mandated.

Seeking recourse through the courts or through the Congress represents an important change in the way in which educational services are typically secured. No longer can local school districts or state departments of education exclude handicapped children from an education. To the contrary, the specific procedures which local districts must employ to identify and serve the handicapped in the least restrictive setting are delineated in the rules and regulations which accompany federal statutes.

The purpose of this chapter will be to define the terms litigation and legislation, and to establish their importance in the educational process. The implications that these court rulings and federal and state laws have for consultants will also be addressed. In addition, a discussion of funding will be presented. After reading the chapter, consultants working with regular and special education teachers should be aware of key issues regarding the right to education, and how these rights affect their relationships with teachers, administrators, and parents.

Objectives

After reading this chapter, the reader will be able to:

1. define the term *litigation.*

2. define the term *legislation.*

3. cite two important lawsuits concerning the right to education.

4. discuss the meaning and trend of educational opportunity in the United States.

5. discuss the relevance of Section 504 of the Rehabilitation Act of 1973 to the right to education of the handicapped.

6. define the provisions of Public Law 94–142.

7. distinguish between the terms *substantive* and *procedural due process.*

8. discuss three components of a handicapped child's free and appropriate educational program.

9. cite at least one lawsuit pertinent to the assurance of a free and appropriate education for handicapped students.

10. identify the components of a due process hearing.

11. identify several methods of funding educational programs for handicapped students.

Key Terms

Litigation

Class action suit

Consent decree

Pennsylvania Association for Retarded Children v. the Commonwealth of Pennsylvania (1972)

Section 504 of the Rehabilitation Act of 1973

Public Law 93–380

Public Law 94–142

Substantive due process

Procedural due process

Mills v. *Board of Education*
(1972)

Legislation

Rules and regulations

Right to education

Brown v. *Board of Education*
(1954)

Diana v. *State Board of Education*
(1970)

Larry P. v. *Riles* (1972)

LeBanks v. *Spears* (1973)

Nondiscriminatory evaluation

Impartial hearing process

DEFINITION OF LITIGATION

Litigation refers to the act or process of bringing a court suit against another party for the purpose of redressing an alleged injustice. Suits bring a plaintiff and a defendant before a judge or panel of judges. The judge, or panel, is empowered to decide upon an appropriate course of action based on present facts and past precedents. Suits can be filed by individual citizens on their own behalf, or by individuals on the behalf of others in similar circumstances. The latter is referred to as a *class action suit.*

Class Action Litigation

There have been many class action suits involving handicapped individuals. For example, *Pennsylvania Association for Retarded Children* v. *Commonwealth of Pennsylvania,* 1972; *Mills* v. *Board of Education,* 1972; and *Maryland Association for Retarded Children* v. *State of Maryland,* 1974 were class action suits brought before the court by one individual on behalf of other individuals with a similar situation. There are no specified number of plaintiffs required to initiate a class action suit (*Stoner* v. *Miller,* 1974). Rule 23 (a) of the Federal Rules of Civil Procedure (28 USC.A.) lists the following requirements for filing class action suits: (1) there are too many members to have codefendants or coplaintiffs in an individual suit; (2) there are questions of law or fact common to the class; (3) the claims of the defense of the representative parties are typical of the claims of the defenses of the class; and (4) the representative parties will fairly and adequately protect the interest of the class (p. 289).

Advantages of class action suits. Compared to individual lawsuits, class action suits are economical. That is, if an individual or small group

succeeds in persuading the court, a much larger number of people benefit from the action. Likewise, the court's calendar is not consumed with
cases having essentially the same grievance. For example, suppose a class
action suit is filed for a mentally retarded individual on behalf of all
mentally retarded persons alleging that a free and appropriate public
education has been denied. If the court agrees with the plaintiff (that is,
the mentally retarded individual), a decision would be rendered which
would affect not only the plaintiff, but also the population of retarded
individuals specified in the suit.

Disadvantages of class action suits. A distinct disadvantage of the
class action suit occurs when the individual or group fails to achieve a
favorable court decision. In effect, the ability of other individuals or
groups similarly situated to file their suits, individually or collectively,
might be compromised. As Abeson (1976) indicated, litigated cases are
lost despite the presence of competent attorneys, and "what seems the
most noble of causes" (p. 241). Even if a class action suit is lost, however, future cases might not need to be filed if public policy makers and
legislators take steps to correct the injustice through legislation. Such
action extends the process, and the plaintiff is usually not provided with
relief during the interim.

Main Effects of Litigation

As Turnbull and Turnbull (1978) indicate, litigation has been the primary method used to establish and maintain the educational rights of
exceptional children and youth. The litigative decisions or *consent decrees*—agreements between or among parties based on negotiations—
have set the precedent for appropriate legislation. Consent decrees do
not represent judicial decisions resulting from a fully litigated case.
Rather, a consent decree represents a compromise achieved outside of
the court. It has the same effect as a fully litigated case, and can serve
as a legal precedent for future cases. The PARC decision (*Pennsylvania
Association for Retarded Children* v. *Commonwealth of Pennsylvania*,
1972), a class action suit representing the school-age mentally retarded
children in the state of Pennsylvania, was resolved with a consent decree.
    Whether the case be fully litigated through the court, or resolved by
means of a consent decree, the net effect for the plaintiffs is identical.
If a favorable decision is rendered, the case is won. If an unfavorable
decision is obtained, the plaintiff's grievance will probably continue.

Other Effects of Litigation

Although a court may render a decision in favor of handicapped students, increased services are not automatically provided. The defendants

have the right to appeal, and even if their appeal is lost, they are not immediately compelled to comply with the court order. The implementation of several decisions has been delayed because defendants failed to comply with the court mandates (Turnbull & Turnbull, 1978). An important case in the field of special education that illustrates this point is *Mills* v. *Board of Education* (1972).

Mills v. Board of Education (1972). This class action suit was filed by the parents of seven handicapped students against the District of Columbia Board of Education, Department of Human Resources, and the mayor for failure to provide all children with a public education. The court ruled in favor of the parents, and issued a court order on December 20, 1971, stating that by January 3, 1972, all plaintiffs must be provided with a publicly supported education. The defendants (that is, the Board of Education and the Mayor) failed to comply, and further action by the plaintiffs was required. The defendants claimed, in response to this latter action, that they were unable to comply with the court order due to insufficient funds. The court did not find that to be an adequate defense. The following court response resulted:

> The District of Columbia's interest in educating the excluded children clearly must outweigh its interest in preserving its financial resources. If sufficient funds are not available to finance all of the services and programs that are needed and desirable in the system, then the available funds must be expended equitably in such a manner that no child is entirely excluded from a publicly supported education consistent with his needs and ability to benefit therefrom. The inadequacies of the District of Columbia public school system, whether occasioned by insufficient funding or administrative inefficiency, certainly cannot be permitted to bear more heavily on the "exceptional" or handicapped child than on the normal child. (p. 876)

Although the court ruled in favor of the parents in the first action, provision of services did not result until further litigative action had been sought by the plaintiffs. The reader is referred to Turnbull and Turnbull (1978) for a full discussion of options available to plaintiffs in cases where court mandates have been ignored or noncompliance with the court order has occurred.

DEFINITION OF LEGISLATION

Legislation refers to the act or process whereby elected representatives embody within a single document the law that becomes applicable to the general public. The intent of a federal or state statute is to serve the common good, the greatest majority of the citizens. To accomplish this objective, a legislative process has been devised which encourages public participation. One process that a bill—a draft of proposed legislation—might follow before it is enacted into law is shown in Figure 11-1.

Figure 11-1 illustrates that before a bill is enacted into law, the specific provisions within the bill are examined by subcommittees, committees, and finally the full house. At any of these stages the bill is subject to amendments. Conference committees are established to resolve discrepancies between House and Senate versions of a bill. At the federal level, the President has the option to veto a bill, and the Congress has an option to override the veto.

After any federal law is passed, proposed *rules and regulations* are published. These are proposed statements indicating how that law will be implemented and interpreted. Definitions for key terms in the law are provided as well as regulations for implementing the law. The general public is informed of proposed rule changes through the *Federal Register*, a daily publication of the United States Government, and public response to the proposed changes are solicited for a period of months. After reviewing and commenting upon oral and written testimony, the governmental office responsible for the legislation publishes the final rules and regulations relative to the statute.

Often, when federal legislation is enacted, state law is changed so that it conforms to the new federal law. However, the enactment of legislation does not always guarantee that compliance will occur. Implementation is greatly dependent on the publication of clear regulations that specify the consequences for noncompliance.

From an educational perspective it is clear that litigative decisions and federal and state statutes have the potential to affect the population and nature of consultation services. For example, mentally retarded children, who prior to the PARC decision were excluded from school, are currently receiving a free public education. Teachers instructing these children are benefiting and presumably will continue to benefit from direct or indirect consultation services. Further, if educational institutions or systems do not comply with court decisions or federal and state statutes, educational services that may have been offered could be postponed, and consultants would find little demand for the educational service they were trained to supply.

Legislation pertinent to the right to education and, more broadly, to the equal protection of the handicapped can be found in a number of federal statutes (see Table 11-1).

Of the 195 federal laws specific to the handicapped enacted between 1927 and 1975, 61 of these laws were passed in the period from March,

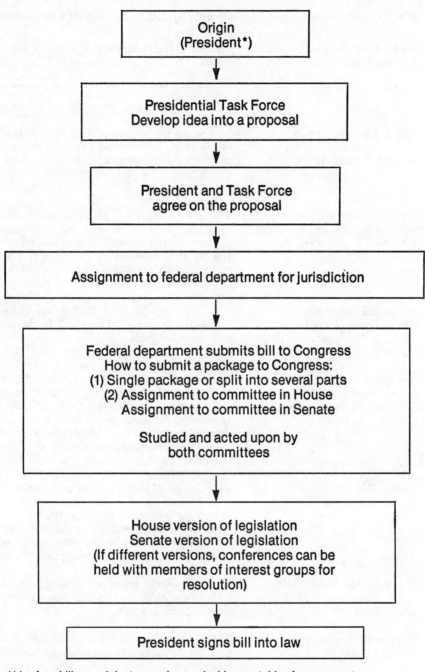

*Idea for a bill can originate anywhere —inside or outside of government

Figure 11–1 Decision points in the development and passage of a bill.

Table 11–1 Federal Legislation Pertinent to the Education of the Handicapped.[1]

TITLE	COMMENTS
Title I, Elementary and Secondary Education Act of 1965, P.L. 89–10	In light of the special educational needs of children of low income families, this act provides federal assistance to local education agencies for the improvement of educational programs in low income areas.
National Technical Institute for the Deaf Act of 1965 P.L. 89–36	This act provides for the construction and operation of a residential institution for postsecondary technical training and education for deaf individuals. The goals of education are to prepare deaf individuals for successful employment.
Vocational Education Amendments of 1968 (Title I—Vocational Education) P.L. 90–576	This act provides that 10% of vocational education funds are to be spent for handicapped individuals.
Developmental Disabilities Services and Facilities Construction Amendments of 1970 P.L. 91–517	This act amends the Mental Retardation Facilities and Community Health Centers Construction Act of 1963 (P.L. 88–164). It provides for assistance to states to furnish comprehensive services to persons affected by mental retardation and other developmental disabilities originating in childhood.
Higher Education Amendments of 1972 P.L. 92–328	This act provides for grants and contracts with institutions of higher education to assist youths with academic potential who are from low-income families but who may lack adequate secondary school preparation or who may be physically handicapped.
The Economic Opportunity Act Amendments of 1972 P.L. 92–424	This act affects preschool services, i.e., it makes enrollment in Headstart available to handicapped children.
The Rehabilitation Act of 1973 P.L. 93–112	This act replaces all Vocational Rehabilitation Act Amendments since P.L. 66–236. It establishes the basis for the Rehabilitation Services Administration. It provides for an individualized written rehabilitation program for each handicapped individual (similar to the IEP required in P.L. 94–142).

Table 11–1 Continued

TITLE	COMMENTS
Title III, Elementary and Secondary Education Act of 1965 (P.L. 89–10) as amended by P.L. 93–380 (1974), Education amendments of 1974.	This act provides funding for supplementary educational programs, including programs for handicapped children.
Education of the Gifted and Talented P.L. 93–380, Title IV, Section 404.	P.L. 93–380 provides for the establishment of an administrative unit within the Office of Education to coordinate programs and activities related to the gifted and talented as well as a national clearinghouse to collect and disseminate relevant information.
The Developmentally Disabled Assistance and Bill of Rights Act of 1974 P.L. 94–103	This act amended P.L. 91–517. Changes made include the following: the definition of the term developmental disability was broadened to include autism and dyslexia, however the latter individuals must also suffer from mental retardation, cerebral palsy, or autism; all developmental disabilities grantees must take affirmative action to employ and advance qualified handicapped individuals; a comprehensive performance-based system for the evaluation of services must be provided.
The Education for All Handicapped Children Act (1975) P.L. 94–142	This act contains the major financial support mechanism and represents the essential educational rights guarantees for handicapped individuals.

[1] The reader is referred to Ballard (1976) and LaVor (1976) for a discussion of these federal education laws.

1970, through November, 1975. In 1974 alone, 36 federal bills which directly or indirectly affected the handicapped were signed into law (LaVor, 1976). It is interesting to note that previous legislation regarding education was primarily permissive, that is, states could provide educational services if they so desired. Legislation in the 1970s, especially P.L. 94–142, has mandated the education of school-aged handicapped children. The enactment of mandatory legislation could be viewed as a reflection of the changing societal approach to providing services for handicapped individuals.

THE RIGHT TO EDUCATION

Many view the movement in the courts by advocates for the handicapped as part of the trend to increase the civil rights of all minority groups. A number of major court decisions have been rendered over the last twenty years, which have greatly influenced the type, variety, and duration of services to handicapped individuals.

The following section will briefly cite litigative and legislative actions pertinent to the *right to education*, the principle that states that all children are entitled to receive free and appropriate instruction, and discuss some of the benefits that have followed. This discussion of specific laws or court decisions is not intended to be exhaustive. Only landmark court cases and legislation relevant to the right to education for handicapped individuals will be presented. It is felt that these litigative and legislative actions have had a significant impact upon the quantity and quality of educational services provided to exceptional individuals. Consultants who are well-grounded in these cases and laws might have a better understanding of their role and function within the school, and how that role and function were determined.

Brown v. Board of Education (1954)

The classic case of separate but equal educational opportunity was tested in *Brown* v. *Board of Education* (1954). This litigation was a class action suit, representing all black children of school age in Topeka, Kansas. Thus, not just one black girl, but all school-age black children in the city of Topeka were represented.

Essentially the case focused on the legality of separate but equal educational opportunity. The plaintiffs contested that their rights under the equal protection clause of the Fourteenth Amendment, Section 1, (i.e., ". . . nor deny to any person within its jurisdiction the equal protection of the laws.") were violated. Equal protection, according to Weintraub and Abeson (1974), means that whatever action is taken with some individuals must be taken with all individuals on equal terms. Judge Warren, ruling on the Brown case, stated that separate educational facilities are inherently unequal. In addition, Judge Warren stated: ". . . it is doubtful that any child may reasonably be expected to succeed in life if he is denied the opportunity of an education" (*Brown* v. *Board of Education*, 1954, p. 493).

Judge Warren's statement had a great impact upon the education of handicapped populations, because in the past there had been legal precedent for excluding the handicapped from educational instruction.

For example, the Wisconsin Supreme Court in the case of *State ex rel Beattie* v. *Board of Education of City of Antigo* (*Wis.*) (1919) upheld the decision that a child's cerebral palsied condition ". . . was harmful to the best interests of the school." (p. 154). The major argument presented by the Board of Education was that such a condition produced "a depressing and nauseating effect on the teachers and school children and that he [the student] required an undue portion of the teacher's time." (p. 154)

The *Brown* v. *Board of Education* case served as the catalyst for providing equal educational opportunity for handicapped students. Also, *Brown* v. *Board of Education* laid the foundation for the eventual reduction of self-contained classrooms for placement of handicapped students.

Pennsylvania Association for Retarded Children v. Commonwealth of Pennsylvania (PARC) (1972)

The exclusion of handicapped individuals from educational opportunity was challenged directly in the PARC case (1972), a class action suit representing school-age mentally retarded children in the Commonwealth of Pennsylvania.

The right of this population to a free public education was argued on several grounds, including the equal protection clause of the Fourteenth Amendment. Essentially, Pennsylvania law stated that a proper education should be provided for all handicapped children. However, the law also stated that children who were uneducable and untrainable, and who had not yet attained a mental age of five years, may be excluded from the public schools (Gilhool, 1973). The plaintiffs used two primary arguments in their case. One argument was based upon the legal decision rendered in *Brown* v. *Board of Education* (1954). The second was based upon the expert testimony of witnesses who stated that handicapped individuals could benefit from an education.

It is important to mention that in the PARC case, expert witnesses challenged the historical arguments for exclusion or segregation of the handicapped from public education. Kubetz (1972) summarizes these historical arguments as follows: (1) retarded individuals could not profit from instruction; (2) retarded students would cause harm to the welfare of other students; and (3) instruction of such individuals, if attempted, would be impractical.

Expert witnesses countered these arguments by testifying that systematic education programs for retarded children would produce learning, and also that education could not be defined solely in terms of academic gains. Rather, "education must be seen as a continuous process by which individuals learn to cope and function within their environment. Thus, for children to learn to clothe and feed themselves is a legitimate outcome achievable through an educational program." (Weintraub & Abeson, 1974, p. 527). This statement of educational goals, developed by experts in the PARC case, should be considered in light of the meaning of equal educational opportunity.

Educational opportunity. Weintraub and Abeson (1974) trace the evolution of the meaning of equal educational opportunity in this country. Initially, as a populist concept, equal education opportunity meant equal access to resources with equal opportunity to meet common objectives. In other words, the resources were the same, the goals were the same, and everyone had equal access to goals. Each student went through the same educational program to achieve his educational goal; for example, the ability to master the skills to achieve a high school diploma. In the 1960s the concept was changed to mean equal access to differing resources to meet common objectives. For everyone to master the skills necessary to achieve a high school diploma, students would not necessarily go through the same educational program. Rather, those who needed it would receive additional remedial assistance. Finally, in the 1970s and 1980s the meaning has changed once again. Now, educational opportunity means equal access to differing resources for the attainment of different objectives. In other words, not only will there be different educational services provided depending on needs, but also the goals of education may not be the same for all students. One need not receive educational services only to achieve a high school diploma; it is also legitimate to receive educational services to learn to clothe and feed oneself.

Thus, the major impact of the PARC case on the education of handicapped children is illustrated by noting the revised definitions of educational opportunity. In short, not only could different educational services be provided, depending on the student's need, but the basic goals of education for each student might not be the same. As Reynolds and Rosen (1976) point out, in the PARC case the court clearly indicated that the enhancement of individual development, rather than potential returns to society, is the critical object of education.

The Rehabilitation Act of 1973, Section 504

Section 504 of the Rehabilitation Act of 1973 is the first federal civil rights law that specifically protects the rights of the handicapped against discrimination on the basis of physical or mental handicap. The nondiscriminatory provisions of the law are almost identical to the nondiscriminatory provisions related to race, which are included in Title VI of the Civil Rights Act of 1964, and to Title IX of the Education Amendments of 1972, Public Law 92–318.[2] Originally, Section 504 was restricted primarily to employment. In 1974, Public Law 93–516 was passed amending Section 504 to include educational services.

In April, 1977, the final regulations for Section 504 were issued for all recipients of funds from the Department of Health, Education and Welfare (HEW), including elementary and secondary schools, colleges, hospitals, social service agencies, and, in some instances, doctors. In a Section 504 Fact Sheet published in July, 1977, the term handicapped was defined as well as the rights of the handicapped highlighted.

The term *handicapped* includes such diseases or conditions as: speech, hearing, visual, and orthopedic impairments, cerebral palsy, epilepsy, muscular dystrophy, multiple sclerosis, cancer, diabetes, heart disease, mental retardation, emotional illness, and specific learning disabilities such as perceptual handicaps, dyslexia, minimal brain dysfunction and developmental aphasia, as well as alcohol and drug addiction. It was noted that physical or mental impairments do not constitute a handicap unless they are severe enough to limit one or more of the major life functions.

Rights of the Handicapped

Several rights for the handicapped are included in Section 504. These rights will be examined briefly.

Program accessibility. Programs as a whole must be accessible to handicapped persons. Structural changes are required to make the program accessible only if an alternative, such as reassignment of classes or home visits, is not possible. The deadline for making structural changes in existing facilities to achieve program accessibility was June 23, 1980.

Free and appropriate education. Every handicapped child at the preschool, elementary, secondary, and adult educational levels is entitled to a free and appropriate public education, regardless of the nature or severity of handicap. School systems have the responsibility of providing transportation for handicapped students to and from educational programs. The compliance date for providing a free and appropriate educa-

[2] P.L. is the abbreviation for Public Law; the number following P.L. indicates the session of Congress; and the number following the dash indicates the number of laws passed to date by that session of Congress. In this case, the law was the 318th passed during the 92nd session of Congress.

tion for children ages three to twenty-one was September 1, 1978 for public elementary and secondary schools.

Colleges and other postsecondary institutions. Recruitment, admission, and the treatment of students must be free of discrimination. Quotas for admission of handicapped persons are not permissible.

Health, welfare, and social services. The provisions for accessibility and reasonable accommodation also apply to health, welfare, and social services. Benefits and services may not be denied on the basis of handicap.

General employment provisions. Employers may not refuse to hire or promote handicapped persons solely because of their disability. Also, accessibility to the employment location is required, and, therefore, reasonable accommodation may have to be made to the person's handicap. The compliance date for those employers who receive federal funds and who employ fifteen or more persons was September 2, 1977.

Failure to comply with Section 504. Another major component of the Section 504 rules and regulations is the provision for failure to comply. The primary consequence for violating Section 504 is that federal funds can be withheld from the state agency, institution, or district until such time as full compliance with Section 504 is achieved.

Impact of Litigation and Legislation for Consultants

The impact of right to education litigation and legislation for consultants is evident in several areas. First, these court rulings and federal and state laws have provided the opportunity to serve, directly and indirectly, populations of handicapped children who were not receiving services previously (for example, trainable mentally retarded children). Second, the structure and administrative procedures of many schools changed as a function of these rulings and laws. Physical barriers for the handicapped have been greatly reduced or eliminated, and administrative procedures for identification, placement, and delivery of service are now required. Finally, consultants should be aware of compliance requirements for Section 504, federal regulations, and state standards. By noting inconsistencies or inadequacies in their districts' programs, and making recommendations to change these deficiencies, the consultants might be able to avoid a federal or state citation for noncompliance, and, therefore, prevent the jeopardizing of existing programs for the handicapped.

ASSURING THE RIGHT TO EDUCATION
FOR ALL HANDICAPPED STUDENTS

Two federal statutes have been instrumental in assuring the right to an appropriate education for all handicapped individuals. *Public Law 93–380* established a national policy of equal educational opportunity by declaring that every citizen is entitled to an education at public expense that is designed to achieve the individual's full potential. *Public Law 94–142* is an amendment to P.L. 93–380 and extends equal educational opportunity specifically to handicapped populations. It has been described as the "Bill of Rights for the Handicapped," because it is designed to correct inequities on behalf of handicapped students.

Brimer and Barudin (1977) outline four basic principles common to both P.L. 93–380 and P.L. 94–142 that are designed to assure that the rights of all handicapped students are observed. They are the following: (1) due process; (2) a free and appropriate public education for all handicapped children; (3) financial assistance to states, and (4) federal training and technical assistance. A close examination of the first three principles will follow. The fourth principle, training and technical assistance, will not be examined because this area has been the responsibility of the former Bureau of Education for the Handicapped, now called the Office of Special Education. Since passage of P.L. 94–142, the Office of Special Education has been responsible for the explanation and implementation of this provision. Suffice it to say that training and technical assistance have been provided to state directors, parents, and teachers.

Due Process

Due process can be defined as a vehicle for judicial protection of liberty and property against unreasonable governmental action. This protection is embodied within the Fifth Amendment of the Constitution: "nor shall any State deprive any person of life, liberty, or property, without due process of law." Essentially due process consists of two components, substantive and procedural. Each will be addressed below.

Substantive due process. Substantive due process refers to the threatened denial or actual denial of life, liberty, or property. It weighs fundamental fairness against arbitrariness or unreasonableness. That is, a court decision cannot be based on whim, but must follow a logical process. Also, a decision that is made must be enforced equally and fairly. Substantive due process can be viewed as the degree of protection under a given set of circumstances before a decision is rendered. The court determines the cut-off point for deciding to hear a case based on alleged violations of substantive due process by weighing the seriousness of the offense and the harm to the individual (Goldstein, 1975). So, as Brimer and Barudin (1977) point out, due process is not a dichotomous situation that is appropriate in some cases and inappropriate in others, but rather a continuum of procedures that offer the appropriate protection of the rights of the individual. As Fischer (1970) emphasized, due process helps to protect a person from an arbitrary or capricious judgment.

Procedural due process. Procedural due process refers to the standards specifying how due process is to be applied. For example, the procedural safeguards delineated in P.L. 94–142 provide an example of procedural due process. This act provides handicapped children and their parents or guardians with procedural safeguards with respect to the provision of free appropriate public education. A summarization of these procedural safeguards can be found in Table 11–2.

Table 11–2 Summarization of the Procedural Safeguards Specified in P.L. 94–142.

---

1. The parents or guardian of a handicapped child are to be provided with the opportunity to examine all records relevant to the educational programming of their child,[3] as well as the opportunity to obtain an independent educational evaluation of the child, if they so desire.[4]

2. If there is no parent or guardian of the handicapped child, an individual who is not involved in the education of the child will be appointed to act as the surrogate for the parent or guardian.

3. Written notice is to be provided to the parent or guardian of a handicapped child when an educational agency proposes or refuses to initiate or change the child's educational program.

4. The parents or guardian of a handicapped child must have the opportunity to present complaints with respect to any matter related to the educational programming of their child.

5. If the parents or guardian of a handicapped child make a complaint regarding the educational programming of their child, they shall have the opportunity for an impartial due process hearing.

---

[3] The Buckley Amendment of 1975 (Title V, Sec. 513, 514, P.L. 93–380) gave to parents of public school students under eighteen the right to see, correct, and control access to school records.
[4] A list of independent evaluators can be obtained from the superintendent of the school district or county program.

As Brimer and Barudin (1977) point out, many of the plaintiff arguments in the PARC case were based upon procedural due process infringements. The parents in the PARC case were not notified as to why their children were excluded from school; neither were they afforded a hearing to counter the school's action. In support of these two arguments, the plaintiffs in the PARC case quoted judicial decisions from prior litigation (i.e., Supreme Court Justice Frankfurter, who stated: "the right to be heard before being condemned to suffer grievous loss of any kind . . . is a principle basic to our society" (Joint Anti-Facist Committee v. McGrath, 1975, p. 168).

Another procedural due process argument used in the PARC case was concerned with the issue of the labelling. The point was that the label *mentally retarded* stigmatized the child, and should not have been attached without prior notice to the parents and an opportunity to challenge the labelling. Justice Douglas of the United States Supreme Court in a previous case related to labelling (*Wisconsin* v. *Constantineau*, 1971) rendered the following decision: "Where a person's good name, reputation, honor or integrity are at stake because of what the government is doing to him, notice and opportunity to be heard are essential." (p. 437). Thus, the Supreme Court made it clear that a label is a stigma and as such cannot be imposed without due process of law.

A fourth argument presented in PARC was that the educational process is a fundamental interest and should not be deprived without notice of the impending deprivation and a chance to be heard. This argument relates to both substantive due process (i.e., the notion of fair play) as well as procedural due process (i.e., the right to be heard before a fundamental interest, such as education, can be denied).

A Free and Appropriate Public Education for All Handicapped Children

According to P.L. 93–380, the education for all children is to be commensurate with each child's needs and in a least restrictive setting. Additionally, parents and guardians are to be involved to the maximum extent possible. P.L. 94–142 expanded procedures of P.L. 93–380 in that an Individualized Educational Program would be used to determine an education commensurate with a handicapped child's needs. This educational program must also meet state educational agency standards. The educational program is to be provided at public expense.

There are three aspects of this educational program which shall be considered: (1) nondiscriminatory evaluation and the placement decision, (2) the Individualized Education Program, and (3) educational placement in the least restrictive environment.

Nondiscriminatory Evaluation and the Placement Decision

There has been a long-standing concern with the nature of programs for children who are provided with special education services. According to Hoffman (1975), special classes during the early part of the twentieth century were often considered a hodgepodge. Non-English speaking students, for example, as well as mentally and behaviorally disordered children, were all grouped together. Classes were disproportionately filled with minority children because of faulty diagnosis and poor administration.

In the 1980s there is still the concern that special education programs are used indiscriminately. It is felt that many minority group children may be inappropriately placed. Advocates for these children are attempting to deal with the problem through the judicial process. Parents are demanding the right to question the appropriateness of a school's classification of their children, and they are demanding the right of due process. A brief discussion of three key lawsuits conducted in the 1970s, pertinent to this aspect of educational programming, will be presented.

In *Diana* v. *State Board of Education of California* (1970), it was argued that nine Mexican-American public school students had been improperly placed in classes for the mentally retarded on the basis of inaccurate and discriminatory tests. That is, individualized intelligence tests were adminstered to these Spanish speaking children by an English speaking examiner. It was argued that the tests relied primarily on verbal aptitude in English, thereby ignoring learning abilities in Spanish. In addition, it was alleged that the intelligence tests were standardized on Americans, and therefore inappropriate for Spanish-speaking, Mexican-American students. The court sustained these arguments.

Further, subsequent legislation passed in California prohibited IQ scores from being used to place students in special education classrooms. The decision rendered in *Diana* set the occasion for subsequent federal legislation P.L. 94–142, which included provisions that intelligence test scores can only be used as *one* measure of a multi-factored evaluation, and tests must be given in the student's native language.

In *Larry P.* v. *Riles* (1972) the plaintiffs sought an injunction restraining the San Francisco school district from administering intelligence tests for purposes of determining the placement of black students in classes for the educable mentally retarded. It was alleged that misplacement in classes for the mentally retarded carried a stigma and a life sentence of illiteracy. The injunction was upheld if the use of the intelligence tests resulted in racial imbalance in the composition of such classes.

In the litigated cases of *Diana* and *Larry P.* the use of standardized tests, especially intelligence tests, for making placement decisions was a main issue. According to Singletary, Collins, and Dennis (1978), two factors that expand on this issue are: no child can be placed in a special education program on the basis of an intelligence test if that placement results in racial imbalance, and those students already enrolled in special programs must be reevaluated periodically.

The *LeBanks* v. *Spears* (1973) case was a class action suit representing students ages five through twenty-one in the public school district of Orleans Parish, Louisiana, who were described, identified, or suspected of being retarded. The plaintiffs asserted that they were denied publicly supported educational programs. A preliminary consent agreement was ordered on May 3, 1973, which expanded the dimension of nondiscriminatory evaluation. The consent decree delineated the steps necessary to ensure that appropriate services were afforded to mentally retarded children.

Subsequent legislation, Section 504 of P.L. 93–112, was based on the rulings issued in *Lebanks* v. *Spears.* In Section 503, procedures for nondiscriminatory materials and evaluation were provided. A summarization of these procedures is found in Table 11–3.

Nondiscriminatory evaluation, specified in Section 503 and P.L. 94–142, means that the standardized tests used to evaluate children and youth should be normed or standardized for that child's particular age, ethnic, or cultural group. Also, testing must be conducted using the child's primary language, and written permission must be obtained from the parents prior to testing.

There are several important implications for educational personnel with respect to nondiscriminatory evaluation. First, the consultant, super-

Table 11–3 Nondiscriminatory Materials and Evaluation Procedures as Specified in Section 504 of P.L. 93–112

1. Tests and evaluation materials are to be validated and administered by qualified evaluators.

2. Tests and other evaluation materials are to assess specific areas of educational need.

3. The tests are to be selected and administered so as not to reflect impairment but accurately reflect aptitude and/or achievement.

4. For educational placement, one must draw upon a variety of sources, carefully document and consider all information, and make group placement decisions.

5. Educational programming must undergo periodic reevaluation.

visor, or school psychologist might be responsible for administering standardized tests to students. Based on the outcome of previous litigation and recent legislation, it is imperative that measures be taken to insure that the test is age and culture appropriate. In addition, the evaluation of the child must assure the careful assessment of all areas of weakness, not just overall general aptitude. If the child's primary language is not English, or the child does not use expressive language, then provisions must be made to test the child through his primary language or mode of communication. Second, the consultant, supervisor, or school psychologist might be responsible for observing that the due process procedures established by the district are carried out. It is important that procedures be followed exactly, especially those procedures which specify the parents' rights. Third, educational placement must be based on a careful consideration of all data obtained through a multi-factored evaluation. The placement decision should reflect the consensus of the placement team, and if there are dissenting opinions regarding the placement, these opinions must be documented. Finally, the consultant, supervisor, or school psychologist might be responsible for scheduling periodic review. The purpose of the review is to reexamine the student's need based on progress observed since the last review. The review is an integral part of the child's Individualized Education Program.

The Individualized Education Program. As stated previously, an Individualized Education Program must be developed for all children who receive special education and related services. The IEP is a written document which specifies the child's educational program, based on assessed need, for a specified period of time, usually an academic year. As defined in Federal Regulations, an IEP must contain the following:

1. a statement of the child's present level of educational performance

2. annual goals and short-term objectives

3. the special education and related services needed by the child

4. the extent to which the child will participate in a regular education program

5. dates for initiation and duration of services

6. evaluation criteria, schedules, and procedures

> (*Federal Register*, Vol. 42, No. 163, August 23, 1977, 121a 346.)

There is a considerable amount of literature describing suggested steps to generate an IEP as well as the guidelines which may be used to assure due process procedures (Meyen, 1976; Meyen, 1978; National Association of State Directors of Special Education, 1976). Basically, all parties involved in the process must come to agreement on the content of the written document, that is, its development and implementation. If there is disagreement, a hearing may be conducted according to due process safeguards. A hearing may be requested by any party in disagreement.

In the *impartial hearing process*, there are three hierarchical steps available to the dissenting party. First, a hearing may be called at the local level to review all pertinent information (e.g., assessment results, placement, related service needs). If the dissenting party is not satisfied, a state level review may be called. Again, if the dissenting party is still aggrieved, civil action through a state or federal district court may be taken. As noted by Abeson, Bolick, and Hass (1975), an impartial hearing includes the right of the dissenting party to receive timely and specific notice of the hearing, all pertinent records, an independent evaluation, if desired, and representation by counsel. Also, the plaintiff is entitled to cross-examine witnesses, and bring witnesses of his own.

Hearing officers are involved in the first two levels. The role of a hearing officer is not to place blame or determine right or wrong, but to achieve resolution of the conflict with a final determination of an appropriate program for the child. As Abeson, Bolick, and Hass (1975) note, the specification of criteria to be used in selecting effective hearing officers in all settings is difficult because of changing circumstances. Nevertheless, the authors provide general guidelines which are presented in Table 11–4.

Dissatisfaction with a decision at the local or state level can result in litigation. It is probable that the courts will become involved in litigation, contesting aspects of the IEP process.

There are several implications that the IEP and impartial hearing processes have for supervisors and consultants. For example, if a supervisor served as the representative from the local education agency during the IEP conference, she would share responsibility for seeing that the services prescribed were actually delivered. Also, the supervisor might bear some responsibility for monitoring the instructional program of the child. The monitoring process might consist of brief contacts or more extensive discussions with the teacher (Bergan, 1977). Further, the consultant might be responsible for scheduling the periodic or annual review. If she is, arrangements for testing may have to be made so that current information would be available for the team.

Finally, in the event that a due process proceeding (i.e., impartial hearing) is initiated, the consultant might be required to document all

Table 11–4 Guidelines for Selecting Hearing Officers

1. The hearing officer should not have been involved in decisions already made about a child regarding identification, evaluation, placement, or review.

2. The hearing officer should possess special knowledge, acquired through training and/or experience, about the nature and needs of exceptional children. An awareness and understanding of the types and quality of programs that are available for exceptional children are essential.

3. The hearing officer should be sufficiently open-minded so that he will not be predisposed toward any decisions that he must make or review. However, he must also be capable of making decisions.

4. The hearing officer should possess the ability to objectively, sensitively, and directly solicit and evaluate both oral and written information that needs to be considered in relation to decision making.

5. The hearing officer should have sufficient experience to effectively structure and operate hearings in conformity with standard requirements and limits, and to encourage the participation of the principal parties and their representatives.

6. The hearing officer should be free enough of other obligations to give sufficient priority to hearing officer responsibilities. He or she must be able to meet the required deadlines for conducting hearings and reporting written decisions.

7. The hearing officer should be aware that this role is unique and relatively new. It will require constant evaluation of the hearing processes and the behavior of all the principals involved, including the hearing officer's. (Abeson, Bolick, & Hass, 1975, p. 72–73)

the steps taken with the student and his parents. It would be important for the consultant to be able to communicate these data effectively to the hearing officer so that an impartial decision could be rendered.

Educational placement in the least restrictive environment. Ennis (1976) stated that the notion of the least restrictive environment is the legal corollary of the social science principle of normalization, that is, existence as close as possible to normal. Wolfensberger (1972) reformulated the normalization principle for application to human management, specifically the management of mentally retarded individuals. He defined normalization as the utilization of means which are as culturally normative as possible, in order to establish or maintain personal behaviors and characteristics which conform to the cultural norm.

There has been considerable litigation concerning the issue of the least restrictive environment. For example, in *Lake* v. *Cameron* (1966), it was made clear that the government may not elect a convenient alternative of service if another would be a more appropriate choice.

In this case, the plaintiff was confined to a hospital for the insane. She was described as senile, with a poor memory, and unable to care for herself, but not insane. The plaintiff was in a hospital because her family was unable to provide care. The ruling in this case was that it was the obligation of the state to explore other possible alternatives to meet the individual's needs. This case demonstrated that the government cannot overextend protection of the individual to the point of deprivation of personal liberty. In other terms, the state was obliged to find the least restrictive placement for the plaintiff, that is, a setting less restrictive than a hospital, but which would meet the plaintiff's needs.

Financial Assistance to States

The distribution of handicapped children and youth affects the cost of special education programs and related services. States or local school districts with small populations of handicapped students receive less money proportionally from the federal government than states or districts with larger handicapped populations.

Also, the degree of a child's handicap affects the cost of special education services. Generally speaking, the more severe the handicap, the more likely the child is to need related services (for example, speech, occupational, or physical therapy, and transportation), and the more costly the program becomes.

Rossmiller, Hale, and Frohreich (1970) produced a cost index for various handicapping conditions. The cost index is the ratio of the average pupil expenditure for a category of exceptionality (for example, blind, deaf, or learning disabled) to the average pupil cost for children in the regular elementary program. Rossmiller et al.'s data indicate that programs for the gifted involved the least cost, while programs for the physically handicapped were the most expensive. Given the broad range of program options for handicapped students, it is unclear whether the relative expenditures for special services for each exceptionality will remain the same. Nevertheless, there are basic costs, common across exceptionalities, which can be identified. Marinelli (1976) cites the following:

Building block resources. These resources involve time, space, equipment, and supplies. Time may be converted into fixed dollar cost, especially if personnel salaries are used.

Organizational units. Instruction, pupil personnel services, transportation, and food services are included in this category. Rossmiller et al. (1970) found that salaries of teachers and teacher aides were the largest single expenditure. Instructional support is an expensive component since guidance, counseling, and rehabilitation personnel, psychologists, therapists, doctors, and nurses are widely used. Also, transportation costs for the physically handicapped are high because orthopedically impaired children require specially equipped buses.

Cost of delivery systems. The educational placement of a handicapped child is often a function of the type and severity of the handicap. Usually, the more severe the handicap the higher the cost. Marinelli indicates that determining the actual costs is difficult due in part to the trend away from the conventional classroom and toward individualized student programs with many student grouping patterns and differentiated staffs.

Federal Government Funding Procedures

As Abeson and Ballard (1976) point out, in 1977 it was estimated that an additional four to five billion dollars was needed to achieve full service for all exceptional children, so the federal appropriation of about $400 million annually was inadequate. However, P.L. 94–142 authorizes a gradual increase in the federal contribution, which would probably reach at least 25 percent of the total contribution from state and local levels. A funding formula established by P.L. 94–142 is based on an escalating percentage of the national average expenditure per public school student multiplied by the number of handicapped children being served in the school districts of each state.

Basically, the formula taxes the National Average Per Pupil Expenditure (NAPPE) for students in public schools and multiplies that figure by the number of handicapped children served in school districts. The formula became effective in fiscal year 1978 and the following percentages were established for the next five years based on national figures available at the time:

1978 @ (5% of NAPPE) × no. of handicapped students = $387 million

1979 @ (10% of NAPPE) × no. of handicapped students = $775 million

1980 @ (20% of NAPPE) × no. of handicapped students = $1.5 billion

1981 @ (20% of NAPPE) × no. of handicapped students = $2.32 billion

1982 @ (40% of NAPPE) × no. of handicapped students = $3.1 billion

The actual allocation to a state is based on the appropriation made by Congress and the total number of handicapped children identified each year. The state's share of pass-through funds after 1979 is 25 percent, and is earmarked for technical assistance and support service programs. The remaining 75 percent is paid directly to eligible local education agencies (Section 611, P.L. 94–142).

To be eligible for federal funds a state must develop a policy which assures that all handicapped children and youth receive a free and appropriate public education. Also, they must submit a state plan to the United States Commissioner of Education. The plan must contain the state's timetable for identifying, locating, evaluating, and serving all handicapped students (Section 612, P.L. 94–142).

State Funding for Special Education

Marinelli (1976) noted that despite the increase of federal funds for special education, the monies would probably not be enough to meet the mandates for educating all handicapped children. State or local funds have been used to cover the deficit.

Historically, programs for special education were financed by categorical state aid that paid for the extra costs. The sources of funding were the regular state funds—a flat amount to pay for a portion of the salary of the special education teacher—and funds generated from local taxes. States also subsidized partial costs of instructional materials, transportation, and personnel. The level of funding and the distribution process were not subjected to special education cost analysis to determine the adequacy or equity of funding (McClure, 1975).

There are several methods of state funding that have been used to assist local education agencies in their provision of services for exceptional children. Several of these methods will be briefly defined.

Unit basis. A unit is defined as a predetermined number of children assigned to a special education class. By this method of funding a state reimburses a local school district based on a fixed sum for the unit. The unit system has prompted the growth of special classes.

Weighted formula. According to this method, special education programs are funded according to a system of weights. The per pupil cost of the least expensive school program (that is, regular elementary program) serves as a base of 1. Each category of exceptionality is weighted. This weight is multiplied by the regular per pupil cost to determine the amount of funding for that special education program. For example, a physically handicapped student receiving therapy may have a weight of

1.8 which means that his program would cost .8 more than the student in the regular program.

Percentage reimbursement. In this approach, the state reimburses a district for a set percentage of all costs incurred in providing special education programs.

Reimbursement for personnel. In this method of funding, a set amount of money is allocated for personnel (for example, special education teachers, administrators and supervisors, and other professional and para-professional staff)

Straight sum reimbursement. This procedure is simply a set amount of money, which may vary according to exceptionality, allocated by the state for each child in a district. A disadvantage of this approach is that school districts are reinforced monetarily for identifying handicapped children.

Extra cost pattern. Excess cost is the amount by which the per pupil expenditure for an exceptional child exceeds the per pupil expenditure for all other children. Calculating excess cost for handicapped children who receive a number of services may be difficult. Data on the true cost of the resources used by the student is often unavailable.

Despite various methods of funding, most states seem to use some form of the categorical label for each handicapping condition to allocate funds. Even in noncategorical funding arrangements, when funds for exceptional children are included in the general fund for use by special education, the local educational agency is in a position to direct some of those funds to other educational programs, unless a strict accounting of the use of those funds for special education is required.

SUMMARY

The terms *litigation* and *legislation* have been defined to assist the reader in understanding litigative and legislative influences upon education for exceptional children and youth. Major litigative and legislative milestones relevant to handicapped populations have been discussed in light of the right to education, and the assurance of an appropriate education for all exceptional students.

Landmark litigative and legislative actions pertinent to the right to education were examined with respect to the developing notion of equal educational opportunity in this country. The assurance of that educational opportunity for handicapped individuals was examined in the context of P.L. 94–142, the key law affecting the education of handicapped children and youth. Aspects of due process, free and appropriate education, and funding were discussed in an effort to provide the consultant with an understanding of how that right to education for handicapped individuals can be sustained.

Questions

1. What are some advantages and disadvantages of class action suits?

2. Define the term *litigation.*

3. Distinguish between a fully litigated case and a case that has been resolved by a consent decree.

4. Define the term *legislation.*

5. Explain the meaning of the term *educational opportunity* over the last thirty years. Provide reasons for any change in meaning.

6. What litigative action had an impact upon the current meaning of educational opportunity in this country?

7. What are two major components of the Section 504 Rules and Regulations?

8. What law is crucial to the assurance of an appropriate education for all handicapped children?

9. What are the basic principles, as outlined by Brimer and Barudin, of P.L. 93–380 and P.L. 94–142?

10. What is a basic distinction between substantive and procedural due process?

11. What are two aspects of nondiscriminatory evaluation resulting from litigated cases?

12. What three hierarchical steps are available to the dissenting party in the impartial due process hearing procedures?

13. According to Ennis (1976), the notion of the least restrictive environment is the legal corollary of which social science principle?

14. List three factors which affect the cost of educating an exceptional child.

15. Describe four methods of state funding that have been used to provide services for handicapped students in local educational systems.

Discussion Points and Exercises

1. Compare the special education programming that existed in your school district in 1970 with the program that exists today.
   a. What are some of the similarities?
   b. What are some of the differences?
   c. Identify federal and state legislation and/or district policy that has affected educational programming in your district.
   d. What have been the consequences of this legislation and/or policy?
   e. Have any problems ensued which could result in litigative action?
   f. What would be the nature of that litigation?
   g. Could you foresee the need to amend recent legislation?
   h. What would be the nature of such amendments?

2. As a consultant in your school district you are involved in the implementation of special education programming. You are requested to make a presentation at the next parent-teacher meeting outlining the service delivery system to your school district. State how all children, handicapped and nonhandicapped, will receive a quality education. Points to consider:
   a. Factors essential for quality education.
   b. Factors unique to handicapped students.
   c. The service delivery procedure best suited to meet the needs of all children in the school district.

3. There has been a complaint regarding the educational program of a mainstreamed special education student in your school system. You are requested to attend the local hearing. What would be the nature of the information you, as a consultant, supervisor, or local education agency representative, should be prepared to supply?

REFERENCES

ABESON, A. Litigation. In F. J. Weintraub, A. Abeson, J. Ballard, & M. L. LaVor (Eds.), *Public policy and the education of exceptional children*. Reston, Virginia: The Council for Exceptional Children, 1976.

ABESON, A., & BALLARD, J. State and federal policy for exceptional children. In F. J. Weintraub, A. Abeson, J. Ballard, and M. L. LaVor (Eds.), *Public policy and the education of exceptional children*. Reston, Virginia: The Council for Exceptional Children, 1976.

ABESON, A., BOLICK, N., & HASS, J. A primer on due process: Education decisions for handicapped children. *Exceptional Children*, 1975, 42, 68–74.

BALLARD, J. Active federal education laws for exceptional persons. In F. J. Weintraub, A. Abeson, J. Ballard, & M. L. LaVor (Eds.), *Public policy and the education of exceptional children*. Reston, Virginia: The Council for Exceptional Children, 1976.

BERGAN, J. *Behavioral consultation*. Columbus, Ohio: Charles E. Merrill, 1977.

BRIMER, R. W., & BARUDIN, S. I. "Due process, right to education and the exceptional child: The road to equality in education." Unpublished manuscript, University of Missouri-Columbia, 1977.

Brown v. Board of Education of Topeka, 347 U.S. 483 (1954).

Diana v. State Board of Education of California, Civil No. C-70, 37 RFP (N.D. Cal., January 7, 1970, and June 18, 1973).

ENNIS, B. J. Reaction comment to Strauss. Due process in civil commitment and elsewhere. In M. Kindred, J. Cohen, D. Penrod, & T. Shaffer (Eds.), *The mentally retarded citizen and the law*. New York: The Free Press, 1976.

Federal Rules Civil Procedure, Rule 23 (a), 28 United States Code Annotated.

FISCHER, T. C. *Due process in the student-institution relationship*. Washington, D.C.: American Association of State Colleges and Universities, 1970. (ERIC Document Reproduction Service No. ED 041 189).

Functions of the placement committee in special education: A resource manual. Washington, D.C.: National Association of State Directors of Special Education, 1976.

GILHOOL, T. K. Education: An inalienable right. *Exceptional Children*, 1973, 39, 597–609.

GOLDSTEIN, S. R. Due process in school disciplinary proceedings: The meaning and implications of *Goss v. Lopez*. *Educational Horizons*, 1975, 54, 4–9.

HOFFMAN, E. The American public school and the deviant child: The origins of their involvement. *Journal of Special Education*, 1975, 9, 415–423.

Joint Anti-Fascist Committee v. McGrath, 341 US 123 (1951).

KUBETZ, B. J. Education equality for the mentally retarded. *Syracuse Law Review*, 1972, 23, 1141–1165.

Lake v. Cameron, 364 F. 2d. 657 (1966).

Larry P. v. Riles, 343 F. Supp. 1306 (1972).

LAVOR, M. L. Federal legislation for exceptional persons: A history. In F. J. Weintraub, A. Abeson, J. Ballard & M. L. LaVor (Eds.), *Public policy*

and the education of exceptional children. Reston, Virginia: The Council
  for Exceptional Children, 1976.

LeBanks v. *Spears,* 60 F.R.D. 135 (1973).

MARINELLI, J. J. Financing the education of exceptional children. In F. J. Weintraub, A. Abeson, J. Ballard & M. L. LaVor (Eds.), *Public policy and the
  education of exceptional children.* Reston, Virginia: Council for Exceptional Children, 1976.

Maryland Association for Retarded Children v. *State of Maryland.* Equity No.
  100-182-77676 (Circuit Court, Baltimore, Maryland, 1974).

McCLURE, W. P. Alternative methods of financing special education. *Journal of
  Education Finance,* 1975, *1,* 36–51.

MEYEN, E. L. *Instructional based approach system (IBAS).* Bellevue, Washington: Edmark Associates, 1976.

MEYEN, E. L. *Exceptional children and youth: An introduction.* Denver: Love,
  1978.

Mills v. *Board of Education of the District of Columbia,* 348 F. Supp. 866
  (1972).

Pennsylvania Association for Retarded Children v. *Commonwealth of Pennsylvania,* 343 F. Supp. 279 (1972).

P.L. 92–318, Education Amendments of 1972, June 23, 1972.

P.L. 93–112, Rehabilitation Act of 1973, July 26, 1973.

P.L. 93–380, Education Amendments of 1974, August 21, 1974.

P.L. 93–516, Rehabilitation Act Amendments of 1974, December 7, 1974.

P.L. 94–142, The Education of All Handicapped Children Act of 1975, November, 1975.

REYNOLDS, M. C., & ROSEN, S. W. Special education: Past, present and future.
  The Educational Forum, 1976, *40,* 551–562.

ROSSMILLER, R. A., HALE, J. A., & FROHREICH, L. E. *Educational programs for
  exceptional children: Resource configurations and costs* (National Educational Finance Project Study No. 2). Madison, Wisconsin: Department
  of Educational Administration, University of Wisconsin, 1970.

*Section 504 of the Rehabilitation Act of 1973. Fact Sheet: Handicapped per-
  sons: Rights under federal law.* (Reprint No. 1977-730. 851/1687 3.1)
  Washington, D.C.: U.S. Government Printing Office, 1977.

SINGLETARY, E. E., COLLINGS, G. D., & DENNIS, H. F. *Law briefs on litigation
  and the rights of exceptional children, youth, and adults.* Washington,
  D.C.: University Press of America, 1978.

State ex. rel. Beattie v. *Board of Education of City of Antigo* (Wis.), 172 NW
  153 (1919).

Stoner v. *Miller,* 377 F. Supp. 177 (1974).

TURNBULL, H. R., & TURNBULL, A. P. *Free appropriate public education: Law
  and implementation.* Denver: Love, 1978.

WEINTRAUB, F. J., & ABESON, A. New education policies for the handicapped:
  The quiet revolution. *Phi Delta Kappan,* 1974, *55* (8), 526–529.

Wisconsin v. *Constantineau,* 400 U.S. 433 (1971).

WOLFENSBERGER, W. *The principle of normalization in human services.* Toronto: National Institute on Mental Retardation, 1972.

Glossary

Annual Goal. Broad statement specifying potential student accomplishment after one calendar year.

Applied Behavior Analysis. Emphasizes direct observation and systematic intervention to solve problems of social significance.

Art, Dance, Music, and Recreational Staff. Each of these professionals provides service to students in his respective "specials" area. These staff can provide invaluable support to the handicapped student experiencing difficulty in the regular curriculum.

Brophy-Good Dyadic Interaction System. A specific coding system to measure the teacher's interaction patterns with one student at a time.

Brown v. Board of Education (1954). Class action suit representing black children of Topeka, Kansas. Court ruled that separate educational facilities are inherently unequal.

Career Awareness. Beginning level of career education that examines the roles and responsibilities of living.

Career Education. Program designed to prepare students for entry into the world of work.

Career Orientation. Program level of career education that integrates career goals with instruction in basic skill or content areas.

Career Preparation. Program level of career education designed to teach secondary-level students specific occupational and living skills.

Checklist. Form which indicates the presence or absence of a particular characteristic.

Class Action Suit. A suit filed by an individual on his own behalf, or by individuals on behalf of others similarly situated.

Conditioned Reinforcer. Refers to a reinforcer which is acquired by repeated pairing with an unconditioned reinforcer or a previously acquired conditioned reinforcer.

Consent Decree. An agreement between or among parties based on negotiations. Consent decrees are not fully litigated cases, but serve as a precedent for future cases.

Consultation Process. A process that includes two or more individuals collaborating to identify and solve a mutually agreed upon problem.

Consulting Teacher. A special education professional who provides regular education teachers with instructional techniques, behavior management strategies, and evaluation guidelines.

Contingency Contracting. A behavioral approach in which tasks and rewards are specified prior to the beginning of an assignment. The contracts are usually written and then signed by all parties.

Countercontrol. Refers to a specific procedure whereby students are trained to employ behavioral principles systematically to change teacher behavior.

Covert Modeling. A procedure in which appropriate teaching (or parenting) behaviors are demonstrated in the presence of the modelee but without his specific knowledge of the behaviors to watch.

Cross-Age Tutoring. Instructional approach in which older students teach younger students. See also Peer Tutoring.

Cue. Prompt, instruction, or signal that sets the occasion for behavior to occur.

Curriculum Adaptations. Changes in instructional methodology or materials to meet the unique learning needs of students.

Daily Living Skills. A wide range of skills related to personal and social behavior and interaction.

Developmental Consultation. A form of consultation that specifically focuses on achieving a long-range goal through the accomplishment of several sequenced subordinate objectives (see Consultation).

Diana v. State Board of Education (1970). Landmark case that revolved around the discriminatory and inaccurate use of standardized tests for the purpose of identifying and placing alleged handicapped students.

Direct Service. Any service that is provided by an agent (consultant) to a target (student) without the use of a mediator. Contrast with Indirect Service.

Duration Recording. The total elapsed time of a behavior usually expressed as a percentage of the total observation time.

Ecological Assessment. Comprehensive assessment approach designed to ascertain a student's behavior across a variety of settings and under a variety of conditions. •

Ecological Context. Includes all the resources, external events, and settings which influence a given situation.

Educational Diagnostician. This professional conducts evaluations using standardized and criterion-referenced tests, and helps to determine the presence of a handicap.

Eligibility. Refers to the criteria used for placement. Criteria are established by state or local education agencies and interpreted by the multidisciplinary team.

Ethnographic Approach. A research methodology, based in sociology and anthropology, which is designed to provide the observer with a means to understand and describe a given situation.

Evaluation. Last step in a systems approach. Helps to determine relative effectiveness of an intervention or course of action (see Formative and Summative Evaluation).

Event Recording. A tally of the number of times a given behavior occurs.

Extinction. Refers to the discontinuation of reinforcement for any behavior that was reinforced in the past.

Feedback. In consultation terms refers to information received by a teacher from a consultant for the purpose of improving instructional or management skills.

Field Study. A long-term observation technique used when an understanding of the context of a behavior is needed, or when the observer needs to acquire more information in order to develop hypotheses concerning a given situation.

Flanders Interaction Analysis. Highly structured observation system designed to measure teacher-student verbal interactions.

Formative Evaluation. Addresses whether an instructional plan was implemented according to the original plan and assesses the interim effects of the plan. Contrast with Summative Evaluation.

Frequency. The total number of occurrences of a behavior.

Functional Curriculum Model. Primarily aimed at teaching independent living skills such as consumerism, banking, finance, or job-related competencies.

Group Consequences. Contingencies applied to a class as a whole irrespective of individual performance.

Guidance Counselor. Provides individual or group sessions to help students solve problems. Offers advice and counseling on career opportunities, curriculum options, and extracurricular activities.

Home-Based Educators. A term reserved for parents who work with their children at home on academic skills.

Home-School Communication. Refers to a broad range of oral or written messages between parents and teachers for the purpose of exchanging information.

Identification. First step in a systems approach. The strengths and weaknesses of the student are assessed.

IEP Conference. Meeting which is conducted to generate, discuss, or revise a student's IEP. Must be held at least annually.

Impartial Hearing Process. The sequence of steps by which complaints or grievances are resolved.

Indirect Service. Any service which is provided by an agent (e.g., a consultant) through a mediator (e.g., a teacher) which is ultimately directed toward the target (e.g., a student). Contrast with Direct Service.

Individualized Education Program (IEP). A document prescribing a handicapped student's specific instructional program.

Individualized Instruction. Instruction based on identified student needs as documented in the IEP.

Information Processing. An approach used in education to study teacher behavior. It involves the examination of on-site observation data in conjunction with teacher self-reports.

In-service Training. A process whereby professionals or parents receive additional training to maintain or improve instructional or management skills.

Instructional and Social Integration. The opportunity for handicapped students to participate in educational and social activities similar to those of their nonhandicapped classmates.

Interaction Analysis. Verbal and nonverbal behaviors of teachers and students are recorded and analyzed.

Intermittent Schedule of Reinforcement. Some, but not all, responses are reinforced.

Interval Sampling. Observation technique in which an observer records the occurrence of a behavior at any time during an interval.

Itinerant Teacher. Usually a special education teacher or related-service professional who travels between schools or districts to work with teachers or students.

Large Group Instruction. Instruction delivered to the whole class.

Larry P. v. Riles (1972). Court case which ruled that intelligence tests resulted in racially imbalanced classrooms.

Learning Strategies Model. Focuses primarily on teaching students how to learn rather than what to learn.

Learning Style. Refers to modality by which instruction is most efficiently processed (e.g., visual, auditory, kinesthetic, or mixed).

Least Restrictive Environment. Any learning environment which meets two criteria: (1) the student is educated with normal peers to the maximum extent possible; and (2) the student is only removed from the setting when the nature of the disability precludes an adequate educational experience even when supplementary learning aids are used. See also Mainstreaming.

LeBanks v. Spears (1973). Class action suit on behalf of mentally retarded students. Plaintiffs claimed that children were denied a public-supported education. Court ruled in favor of plaintiffs.

Legislation. Public laws or statutes passed by Congress.

Levels of Reinforcers. Hierarchically arranged sequences of reinforcers from least intrusive (praise) to most intrusive (edibles).

Litigation. Refers to the act or process of bringing a court suit against another party for the purpose of redressing an alleged injustice.

Mainstreaming. A colloquial term used to describe educational settings where handicapped and nonhandicapped are integrated.

Mastery. Tasks which are completed above ninety-nine percent correct.

Mediator. An individual who has access to and influence over the target individual of the consultation and who could be considered a liaison between the consultant and the target subject or group.

Mills v. Board of Education (1972). Class action suit in which parents of handicapped students claimed that their children were denied a public education. Court ruled in favor of parents.

Mirror Model of Parental Involvement. Describes the potential role and function of parents and professionals in a comprehensive parenting program.

Modeling. A process whereby a set of instructions, skills, or behaviors are demonstrated (modeled) for an individual to imitate (see also Covert Modeling).

Multi-Modal Data. Data collected from a variety of sources and under a variety of conditions, but addressing a common question.

Narrative Recording. Written description of behavior used to generate questions for further observation or research—an anecdotal record.

Needs Assessment. Process whereby student, teacher, or parent is assessed for the purpose of determining strengths and weaknesses.

Negative Reinforcement. Removal of an aversive stimulus, contingent upon a response, which increases the future probability of the response.

Negative Reinforcer. The stimulus or event which is removed.

Nondiscriminatory Evaluation. An assessment which takes into account a student's psychological, sociological, and personal background.

Occupational Guidance and Preparation Skills. A wide range of skills related to obtaining employment.

Occupational Therapist. A professional who provides direct service to handicapped students to increase self-help, balance, and coordination skills.

Opportunity to Respond. The number of times a student has a chance to interact directly with the teacher or be engaged in the learning assignment.

Parent Conference. A regularly scheduled meeting between teachers and parents for the purpose of discussing a student's program.

Parent Training Program. General term used to describe a myriad of approaches to help parents fulfill their responsibilities more effectively.

Parent Tutoring Program. Refers to programs which help parents serve as aides or paraprofessionals in schools.

Peer Tutoring. Instructional approach in which students of the same age teach one another. See also Cross-Age Tutoring.

Percentage. An index of accuracy based on number of correct responses or behaviors divided by 100. Contrast with Rate.

Permanent Product Measure. Any class of observations that can be viewed repeatedly (e.g., written tests, tape recordings).

Personal-Social Skills. A wide range of skills related to personal and social behavior and interaction.

Pennsylvania Association for Retarded Children v. Commonwealth of Pennsylvania (1972). Class action suit brought by parents of mentally retarded children. Case settled by consent decree, which in effect redefined educational opportunity.

Physical Therapist. A professional who works in concert with physician to develop an individual physical therapy plan and the means to evaluate it.

P.L. 93–380. Forerunner to P.L. 94–142. Established a national policy of equal educational opportunity by declaring that every citizen is entitled to an education at public expense designed to achieve the individual's full potential.

P.L. 94–142. The Education of All Handicapped Children Act of 1975. Termed the "Bill of Rights for the handicapped." It extends equal educational opportunities to handicapped populations.

Positive Reductive Procedures. A class of tolerant, convenient procedures that systematically reinforce lower levels of inappropriate behavior.

Positive Reinforcement. The procedure that involves the presentation of a positive consequence immediately after the performance of an appropriate behavior and increases the likelihood that the same behavior will reoccur in the future.

Positive Reinforcer. A stimulus or event that follows a behavior and is used to reward the behavior.

Preferred Reinforcers. Reinforcers that students esteem over other reinforcers.

Premack Principle. A behavioral technique in which access to a high probability behavior is contingent upon the performance of a low probability behavior.

Problem-Centered Consultation. A form of consultation that is limited to solving specific and immediate problems. Long-term involvement is not anticipated. See also Consultation Process and Developmental Consultation.

Procedural Due Process. Refers to standards specifying how due process is to be applied.

Programmed Instruction. An arrangement of academic material into small steps that provides information to the student, sets the occasion for a response, and provides feedback.

Proportional Interaction. Each student receives the teacher's attention for appropriate behavior on a consistent enough basis to maintain performance.

Psychometric Approach. A research methodology that enables an observer to obtain numerical data suitable for statistical or graphical analysis.

Psychological Context. Includes teacher's theories, beliefs, and values about teaching and learning.

Punishment. The presentation of an aversive stimulus following a behavior, which has the effect of reducing the future probability of that behavior.

Rate. An index of proficiency. Contrast with Percentage.

Rating Scale. The frequency with which a behavior is observed along a basic continuum.

Related-Service Personnel. Includes a variety of therapists (e.g., physical, occupational, speech), counselors, and the school bus driver. The term also includes professionals who provide school health services and social work services (see Support Personnel).

Reliability Check. Observation conducted by independent person to reduce risk of observer bias.

Remedial Model. Designed to teach student skills directly in basic subjects.

Remedial Teaching Model. A system based on a series of instructional decisions that enables a teacher to meet long-range goals.

Response Cost. The removal of a specific amount of positive reinforcement contingent on a response.

Response Generalization. Occurs when the change in one class of behavior spreads to other classes of behavior as well.

Right to Education. Principle which states that all children are entitled to a free, public education.

Rules and Regulations. Standards that accompany federal legislation indicating how law would be implemented and interpreted.

School Bus Driver. A related-service individual responsible for transporting students to and from school each day.

School Psychologist. A professional primarily responsible for formal assessment of student intellectual or behavioral functioning. Serves as a resource for teachers on matters related to curriculum, management, and parenting.

School Social Worker. A professional who serves as the major link between the school and family. The social worker provides counseling and referral services for parents.

Secondary Effects. Results that coincide with the main effects of an intervention. May or may not be planned.

Section 504 of the Rehabilitation Act of 1973. First federal civil rights law that specifically protects the rights of the handicapped against discrimination on the basis of physical or mental handicap.

Self-Contained Classroom. Refers to a special education setting where students are homogeneously grouped for instruction.

Shaping. The reinforcement of successive approximations to a terminal objective.

Short-Term Objective. Measurable intermediate step between current performance level and annual goal.

Situational Generalization. Occurs when a behavior learned in one setting is demonstrated in a different setting.

Small Group Instruction. Instruction delivered to a portion of the class.

Social Relationships. The verbal and nonverbal interactions between students.

Sociogram. A schematic representation of student's responses on a sociometric questionnaire.

Sociometric Analysis. Procedure where social status is ascertained by analyzing student choices on questionnaires.

Specific Level. Factors contributing to the student's problems are assessed and analyzed.

Speech Clinician. A professional who works with handicapped students to improve communication ability. Focus might be on speech, language, voice, fluency, or articulation.

Substantive Due Process. Degree of protection under a given set of circumstances before a decision is rendered.

Summative Evaluation. Conducted at the end of an intervention to determine overall effects of the intervention.

Support Staff. Usually considered to be related-service staff, for example, therapists, psychologists, counselors (see Related-Service Personnel).

Survey Level. First step in assessment. Attempt is made to diagnose a given problem.

Systems Model. A five-phase, closed-loop approach for providing school consultation. The five phases: assessment, specification of objectives, planning, treatment, and evaluation are an extrapolation of a directive teaching model.

Target. A person or group for whom the consultation is ultimately designed. Depending on the nature of the consultation, targets can include students, teachers, administrators, or parents.

Teacher-Student Interaction. Any verbal or nonverbal encounter between a teacher and a student or group of students.

Temporal Integration. The total amount of time a handicapped student spends with nonhandicapped peers expressed in periods per day or academic subject areas.

Time-out. Removal of the access to earn reinforcement or the physical removal from the reinforcing environment. A form of punishment.

Time Sampling. Observation technique in which an observer records the occurrence of a behavior at every *n*th interval.

Token Reinforcer. A physical object or symbol (chip or check mark) that can be exchanged for back-up reinforcers.

Triadic Model. A linearly arranged consultation sequence that portrays the relationship between the consultant, the mediator, and the target. The model describes a functional sequence of consultation.

Tutorial Model. At the secondary level, the tutorial model emphasizes content acquisition rather than basic skill learning.

Unconditioned Reinforcer. Refers to a biologically determined reinforcer which satisfies a basic human need.

Vermont Consulting Teacher Program. A statewide collaborative effort between local school districts, the state department of education, and university personnel aimed at training educators to provide consultation services to regular education teachers who teach handicapped students.

Vocational Counselor. This professional is responsible for assisting high school students in identifying work interests, aptitudes, and abilities.

Vocational Education. Training program designed to teach students a marketable skill.

Work Coordinator. A teacher responsible for coordinating academic and work experiences.

Work-Study Model. Program whereby secondary-level students spend a portion of their day (or week) in class; the rest of the day (or week) is spent on a job.

References for the Consultant

Consultants and supervisors working in applied settings often need to check reference texts to help with a question or problem. The references that follow are intended to provide the starting point for the consultant's professional library. Texts and media are included that the consultant can use in a wide variety of situations (e.g., clarification and interpretation of P.L. 94–142, suggestions for improving academic and social performance in the classroom, working with parents of handicapped children, etc.).

The list of references is not intended to be exhaustive. Rather, we feel that these texts and media are representative of the topics which should be a part of the consultant's personal library.

TEXTS

ALLEY, G., & DESHLER, D. *Teaching the learning disabled adolescent: Strategies and methods.* Denver: Love, 1979.

> The focus of this text is the learning disabled adolescent. Ideas for assessing and remediating academic and social behaviors are provided.

AXELROD, S. *Behavior modification for the classroom teacher.* New York: McGraw-Hill, 1977.

> Provides a description of applied behavior analysis principles. Case studies and graphs are included, which illustrate how principles were applied in classroom settings.

BROLIN, D. E., & KOKASKA, C. J. *Career education for handicapped children and youth.* Columbus, Ohio: Charles E. Merrill, 1979.

> The major focus of this text is on procedures and competencies related to career education. Strategies for implementing career education programs are included.

BROWN, D., WYNE, M. D., BLACKBURN, J. E., & POWELL, W. C. *Consultation: Strategy for improving education.* Boston: Allyn & Bacon, 1979.

> This text provides a comprehensive overview of various forms of consultation (e.g., teacher curriculum, student, parental, organizational, and community). A discussion of P.L. 94–142 and the consultant's role with exceptional students is included.

COOPER, J. O. *Measuring behavior* (2nd ed.). Columbus, Ohio: Charles E. Merrill, 1981.

> Provides a description of techniques for measuring, graphing, and interpreting data. Numerous classroom-related examples show how data can be recorded. Single-subject designs and self-evaluation tests are also included.

COOPER, J. O., & EDGE, D. *Parenting: Strategies and educational methods.* Louisville, Kentucky: Eston Corporation, 1981.

Provides guidelines for helping parents manage a wide range of social behaviors at home. Numerous case studies illustrate how behavior change procedures can be implemented and evaluated.

DARDIG, J., & HEWARD, W. L. *Sign here: A contracting book for children and their parents.* Bridgewater, New Jersey: F. Fournies and Associates, 1976.

This text provides information for the consultant planning to work with families to solve home-based problems. Sample forms and contracts are provided in the text.

HAMMILL, D. D., & BARTEL, N. R. *Teaching children with learning and behavior problems* (3rd ed.). Boston: Allyn and Bacon, 1982.

This text contains practical suggestions and guidelines for diagnosing, assessing, and remediating learning problems in the skills areas. Classroom management strategies are included as well as techniques for evaluating commercially produced educational materials.

HEWARD, W. L., DARDIG, J. C., & ROSSETT, A. *Working with parents of handicapped children.* Columbus, Ohio: Charles E. Merrill, 1978.

Provides information on such topics as principles of behavior change, behavior management systems for the home, opportunities for parenting, and parent education. A resource directory on parenting is included.

HEWARD, W. L., & ORLANSKY, M. D. *Exceptional children.* Columbus, Ohio: Charles E. Merrill, 1980.

An introductory text on exceptionality that contains basic information for all areas of handicap.

HOLLAND, R. P. *Clarification of P.L. 94–142 for the paraprofessional and support staff. Clarification of P.L. 94–142 for the special educator. Clarification of P.L. 94–142 for the administrator. Clarification of P.L. 94–142 for the teacher.* Philadelphia, Pa.: Research for Better Schools, Inc., 1980.

This series of four booklets is designed to help professionals and support personnel better understand P.L. 94–142 and how the law relates to their duties. Annotated references for additional hardware and software are included.

MARKS, J. R., STOOPS, E., & KING-STOOPS, J. *Handbook of educational supervision: A guide for the practitioner* (2nd ed.). Boston: Allyn & Bacon, 1978.

This handbook integrates principles of supervision and research to provide practical assistance to beginning and experienced field-based supervisory personnel.

MEYERS, J., MARTIN, R., & HYMAN, I. *School consultation: Readings about preventive techniques for pupil personnel workers.* Springfield, Illinois: Charles C Thomas, 1977.

This collection of twenty-seven articles relates to techniques that consultants use with pupil personnel workers. The articles are excerpted from professional journals.

PARKER, C. A. *Psychological consultation: Helping teachers meet special needs.* Minneapolis, Minnesota: Leadership Training Institute/Special Education, 1975.

A collection of articles on the theory and practice of school consultation. Comments, questions, and a discussion of points covered within each article are included in the text.

STEPHENS, T. M. *Teaching skills to children with learning and behavior disorders.* Columbus, Ohio: Charles E. Merrill, 1977.

Introductory text designed for the practitioner working with learning and behavior-disordered children. Text contains an overview of directive teaching and management strategies for these populations.

STEPHENS, T. M. *Social skills in the classroom.* Columbus, Ohio: Cedars Press, 1978.

Provides over 700 recommendations for assessing and teaching social skills in the classroom. Teaching procedures are explicitly described.

SULZER-AZAROFF, B., & MAYER, R. *Applying behavior analysis procedures with children and youth.* New York: Holt, Rinehart & Winston, 1977.

This text provides a comprehensive description of applied behavior analysis techniques. Information is presented on procedures to increase, decrease, maintain, and generalize a wide range of academic and social behaviors.

TURNBULL, A. P., & SCHULZ, J. B. *Mainstreaming handicapped students: A guide for the classroom teacher.* Boston: Allyn and Bacon, 1979.

A comprehensive text that presents information for the practitioner on issues related to mainstreaming. Included in the text are specific suggestions for classroom teachers in several academic subject areas (e.g., reading, math, spelling).

TURNBULL, H. R., & TURNBULL, A. P. *Free appropriate public education: Law and implementation.* Denver: Love, 1978.

Provides information and techniques for testing, classification, least restrictive placements, increasing parent participation, procedural due process, and the right to education. Answers to common objections to P.L. 94–142 are included.

WALLACE, G., & LARSEN, S. C. *Educational assessment of learning problems: Testing for teaching.* Boston: Allyn and Bacon, 1978.

Provides information on the purpose and principles of educational assessment. Guidelines for conducting a wide range of assessments in academic areas are provided. Text also includes suggested activities.

WEINTRAUB, F. J., ABESON, A., BALLARD, J., & LAVOR, M. L. *Public policy and the education of exceptional children.* Reston, Virginia: The Council for Exceptional Children, 1976.

A comprehensive edited text on public policy and education. Included within the text are presentations on major legislative and litigative milestones, as well as alternatives for funding special education programs.

WIEDERHOLT, J. L., HAMMILL, D. D., & BROWN, V. *The resource teacher: A guide to effective practices.* Boston: Allyn and Bacon, 1978.

Provides information for establishing and maintaining a functional resource room program. Suggestions are offered for assessing and remediating a variety of academic skill deficits.

FILMS AND OTHER MEDIA

Who Did What to Whom. (16mm/color/17 min.) Film provides opportunity to practice behavior analysis in everyday interactions. Each of the forty short scenes is followed by five seconds of blank leader so that the projector may be stopped and the scene discussed. The behavior principles of positive and negative reinforcement, punishment and extinction are shown in scenes in home, school, and office. Research Press Co., Box 31772, Champaign, Illinois 61820.

Peer Conduct Behavior Modification. (16mm/color/20 min.) A child's parents are taught to use behavior management procedures in modifying maladaptive behaviors. Illustration of use of the child's classmates in influencing problem areas is provided. Emphasis is given to the effects of both positive and negative reinforcement. Neuropsychiatric Institute MRCPP Media Unit, 760 Westwood Plaza, Los Angeles, California 90024.

CEC/BEH Filmstrip on Public Law 94–142. This media package, which contains three filmstrips accompanied by an audio cassette and printed script, a copy of the law, and a ten-page question and answer summary, is designed to explain the provisions of P.L. 94–142. An introductory booklet is included, which illustrates how the materials might be used with various groups. Materials are not copyrighted. To purchase or borrow this media package contact: The Council for Exceptional Children, 1920 Association Drive, Reston, Virginia 22091 or your state director of special education.

Workshop Media and Materials: Creating Instructional Materials for Handicapped Learners. Three audio cassettes, two color filmstrips, and a 117 page coordinator's guide for workshop leader are included in the package. Price: $34.25. Order from National Audiovisual Center, Sales Order Desk (GSA), Washington, D.C. 20409. NAC Order No.: 009688.

This in-service media and materials package shows teachers how to generate instructional materials for handicapped learners, and to adapt, select, and evaluate existing commercial materials.

Author Index

Subject Index

Biosketches

Timothy E. Heron received his B.A., M.Ed., and Ed.D. at Temple University. He is an Associate Professor in the Faculty for Exceptional Children at The Ohio State University. Prior to his present appointment, Dr. Heron served as a developmental and day care supervisor for cerebral-palsied students, taught learning disabled students, and supervised a training program for resource room teachers in an inner-city school. He has published several articles, presented numerous papers at regional, national, and international conferences, and has served as a consultant to teachers, parents, and administrators on issues related to the mainstreaming process.

Kathleen C. Harris is an Assistant Professor at California State University, Los Angeles. Prior to this appointment, she completed her doctorate in the Department of Special Education at Temple University. Dr. Harris taught mildly and moderately handicapped adolescents for several years in public schools and residential settings. Additionally, Dr. Harris has served as a learning consultant at a child diagnostic clinic. She holds certifications as a special education teacher and a learning disability teacher-consultant.